An OPUS book

A History of Western Philosophy: II

MEDIEVAL THOUGHT

David Luscombe is Leverhulme Personal Research Professor of Medieval History in the University of Sheffield. He has written extensively on the history of medieval thought. His books include *The School of Peter Abelard* (Cambridge, 1969) and an edition of *Peter Abelard's Ethics* (Oxford, 1971). He has contributed to the *Cambridge History of Later Medieval Philosophy* (1982), the *Cambridge History of Medieval Political Thought* (1988), and to Peter Dronke (ed.), *A History of Twelfth-Century Western Philosophy* (Cambridge, 1988). He has also (with C. N. L. Brooke) published the second edition of David Knowles, *The Evolution of Medieval Thought* (Longman, 1988). He is currently engaged in the preparation of an edition of *The Letters of Peter Abelard and Heloise*. He is a Fellow of the British Academy.

D0166795

OPUS General Editors

Christopher Butler

Robert Evans

John Skorupski

OPUS books provide concise, original, and authoritative introductions to a wide range of subjects in the humanities and sciences. They are written by experts for the general reader as well as for students.

A History of Western Philosophy

This series of OPUS books offers a comprehensive and up-to-date survey of the history of philosophical ideas from earliest times. Its aim is not only to set those ideas in their immediate cultural context, but also to focus on their value and relevance to twentieth-century thinking.

Classical Thought
Terence Irwin

Medieval Philosophy
David Luscombe

Renaissance Philosophy
C. B. Schmitt and Brian Copenhaver

The Rationalists
John Cottingham

The Empiricists
R. S. Woolhouse

English-Language Philosophy 1750–1945
R. S. Woolhouse

Continental Philosophy since 1750
Robert C. Solomon

English-Language Philosophy since 1945
Thomas Baldwin (forthcoming)

A History of Western Philosophy: II

Medieval Thought

DAVID LUSCOMBE
The University of Sheffield

Oxford   New York

OXFORD UNIVERSITY PRESS

Oxford University Press, Great Clarendon Street, Oxford OX2 6DP
Oxford New York
Athens Auckland Bangkok Bogotá Buenos Aires Calcutta
Cape Town Chennai Dar es Salaam Delhi Florence Hong Kong Istanbul
Karachi Kuala Lumpur Madrid Melbourne Mexico City Mumbai
Nairobi Paris São Paulo Singapore Taipei Tokyo Toronto Warsaw
and associated companies in
Berlin Ibadan

Oxford is a registered trade mark of Oxford University Press

First published as an Oxford University Press
paperback 1997

British Library Cataloguing in Publication Data
Data available

Library of Congress Cataloging in Publication Data
Luscombe, D. E. (David Edward)
Medieval thought / David Luscombe.
(A history of Western philosophy ; 2)
"An OPUS book"—Ser. t.p.
Includes bibliographical references (p.) and index.
1. Philosophy, Medieval. I. Title. II. Series.
B721.L87 1997 189—dc21 96-29604
ISBN 0-19-289179-0

3 5 7 9 10 8 6 4 2

Typeset by Best-set Typesetter Ltd., Hong Kong

Printed in Great Britain by
Mackays of Chatham,
Chatham, Kent

For
Nicholas, Mark, Philip,
and Amanda

Contents

Introduction

I should not begin with the word obviously, but obviously, even though we can scarcely avoid using the term, there is no such thing as 'medieval thought'. There were thinkers in the Middle Ages. They sometimes formed or followed schools and traditions—the Porretans, for example, in the twelfth century or the Thomists or Scotists later on. There were questions pursued over long periods, in varying ways, with a common core or foundation or upon the basis of different written sources. There was much continuity of thought in the Middle Ages, and many affinities were created among thinkers. But there were also many different philosophies, and many 'sea changes' over time, as well as breaks, revivals, and rediscoveries. For some historians one great change during the medieval period has appeared to be a move away from a predominantly Platonic to a predominantly Aristotelian outlook. This view, which is disputed, is reflected in *The Cambridge History of Later Greek and Early Medieval Philosophy* and in *The Cambridge History of Later Medieval Philosophy*. In the former volume, although there is an explicit repudiation of the generalization which opposes the Aristotelianism of the thirteenth century to the Platonism of earlier Christian thinkers, and a clear recognition of the importance of the interaction of Platonism and Aristotelianism in the early Middle Ages, Platonism receives the greater amount of attention.[1] In the latter volume, which has the great merit of reaching to the end of the sixteenth century, the editors set out, as part of their aim, to present the medieval Aristotelian tradition, but they state that they must for this reason reach back to consider philosophers who were left out in the earlier volume.[2] To fill what was, none the less, still seen as a gap between the two volumes, and as a brilliant period which has tended in other surveys to be overlooked by comparison with later centuries, there has appeared *A History of Twelfth-Century Western Philosophy*, edited by Peter Dronke.[3] There were, amid all this, elusive currents, even undercurrents, of Stoic ideas, which surface when Cicero and Seneca are studied and cited, and which impinged especially on cosmology, ethical theory, and logic.[4] There were also deep, ongoing divisions, such as those between nominalists and realists, that erupted into fierce conflicts from time to time, although it is a simplification to see these as constituting the central feature of medieval thought.

The Middle Ages—to adopt a conventional view among Western historians—run from the conversion of the Roman emperor Constantine to Christianity in 312 to the 1520s and 1530s when Martin Luther, John Calvin, and King Henry VIII broke with papal Rome, a period of well over a millennium. There are continuities that override these chronological boundaries and make them fictitious, even obstructive. Pagans continued to develop ancient thought after the 330s, with the help of Christian thinkers also, and, however mighty the Protestant reformation was in the sixteenth century, it by no means killed off, either then or for centuries to come, all the traditions of thought in the Middle Ages, even in the countries where the reformed religion took firm root. An example in the sixteenth century is Aberdeen, where New College was founded to provide education for Protestant youths who were not in sympathy with the continuing Catholic traditions upheld in King's College. A further example is the initiative by, among others, William Laud (1573–1645), fellow, later President, of St John's College, Oxford, and finally archbishop of Canterbury, to restore to the shelves of the college library the medieval works that had been thrown out in the previous century but which had none the less been pouring off the presses in continental Europe throughout the sixteenth century.[5] By and large over Western Europe as a whole, and surprising as it may seem, during and after the Reformation, the new did not only displace but also sat alongside the old. The writings of medieval thinkers continued to be read.

In 1879, in the encyclical letter *Aeterni patris*, Pope Leo XIII appealed to Roman Catholics to uphold as their model of Christian philosophy the traditions of enquiry laid down by St Thomas Aquinas. In doing so, he selected for special attention one of several stars that shone brightly in the late medieval intellectual firmament. As a result and as seen in retrospect, Leo XIII may have led many subsequent scholars in the late nineteenth and in the twentieth centuries to see the history of medieval thought, not to mention the history of Christian philosophy and theology at large, through lenses that were too favourable to the synthesis of Thomas Aquinas. They were thus encouraged to view the thirteenth century as the golden age of medieval scholasticism and Aquinas as the central point of a story for which earlier chapters were a preparation and later ones a postscript, possibly also an anticlimax, even a decline.[6]

What, then, is medieval thought? Philosophy in the Middle Ages is widely regarded as having a theological and a religious orientation. Philosophers in the Middle Ages were usually employed by the church and wrote and taught in an ecclesiastical setting. They often set out to use reason in order to understand faith. Reason stood between faith and vision. But it was still reason, and reason was used in many different ways. Medieval thought was, for example, largely the activity of studying texts written outside Christendom both before and after the end of the ancient world. Within medieval Christendom this activity was largely undertaken in order to enrich Christian experience: human reason had been debilitated by the fall of Adam, and the medieval philosopher took into account differing states of reason and knowledge—the knowledge possessed by God, by angels, by human beings enjoying the beatific vision, face to face with God, as well as by fallen man. Specifically theological or religious considerations, such as those of sin and redemption and divine foreknowledge, while they did considerably influence the ways in which such subjects as ethics and psychology were taken up, did not, however, eliminate the need to use the techniques of enquiry provided by, for example, logic and the study of language. The thinker had before him a range of problems that included theological ones—the Trinity, the Incarnation, God's omnipotence, future contingents, predestination, grace, infinity, and so on—but all these problems invited philosophical analysis, and some would say that the best analyses came in the fourteenth century in the light of the work of John Duns Scotus and of William Ockham.

These thoughts come close to those expressed by R. W. Southern in the first volume of what is designed as a trilogy on *Scholastic Humanism and the Unification of Europe.* Southern contrasts the popular use of the word 'humanism' to indicate merely human interests and human knowledge with the humanism he discerns in medieval thinkers, especially during the eleventh, twelfth, and thirteenth centuries. Of the former type of humanism he writes:

> most of those who practise [it] look back on the medieval period with their emphasis on the supernatural end of man, with their assumption of the primacy of theology among the sciences, with their source in a predominantly clerical culture and hierarchical organization under a universal papal authority, as an embodiment of all that they oppose.

But 'nothing could be further from the truth', because (and Southern has in mind especially the twelfth and thirteenth centuries)

> the great intellectual achievement . . . was vastly to extend the area of rational investigation into every branch of human life and cosmic being. The scholastic programme did not indeed seek to include the supernatural. Quite the opposite: it *required* the supernatural as a necessary completion of the natural world. But this extension did not diminish the area of rational investigation: it simply added a further dimension to the complexity and richness of the scene of human life.[7]

With that view I concur.

Étienne Gilson in *The Spirit of Medieval Philosophy*[8] found Christian philosophy in the medieval period. Gilson's Middle Ages have never been everyone else's and it has been objected that Gilson, who was a very profound scholar, created for medieval thought an impression of harmony, success, and unity that underemphasized, although it did not ignore, the reality of division, failure and diversity, and, moreover, gave too much attention to systems of thought, and too little to modes of thinking.[9] His single volume *History of Christian Philosophy in the Middle Ages*[10] remains an immensely impressive and usable achievement. Since it appeared, new approaches have been developed, although it may be more correct to say that older ones have been reasserted.[11] To some extent more recent approaches have reflected the publication of new editions of previously unprinted medieval texts as well as of critical editions of texts printed many centuries ago; this work continues vigorously and has a considerable effect in altering the interests of scholars and, as it were, the shape of the landscape. For example, the editions of the *Logica modernorum*,[12] and those (in progress) of the works of German thinkers such as Ulrich of Strassburg, Dietrich of Freiberg, and Berthold of Moosburg in the *Corpus philosophorum teutonicorum medii aevi*,[13] have enriched knowledge of the study of logic in the twelfth century and of the world of thought in the thirteenth and fourteenth centuries. The influence of both modern analytic and continental philosophy has also been brought to bear upon the subject. As well as studying medieval philosophy as the handmaid of Christian theology, a more focused attention has been given to the study of logic, language, and philosophy of science. Instead of regarding the condemnations of 1277 as the end of the finest period of Christian philosophy, many scholars do regard the condemnations as an opening of the door to another 'spirit of medieval philosophy' and a new appreciation of the 'status' of medieval philosophy. The fourteenth century, often presented in terms of a decline from the pinnacle of a thirteenth-century synthesis, is also viewed by many as a no less seminal period—for example, in the history of natural philosophy. In the fourteenth century the concerns of thinkers to some extent moved away from the concerns of their thirteenth-century predecessors—some would say from synthesis to analysis. We need, therefore, to try to be sensitive to the changing opportunities and ambitions of different thinkers in different periods and contexts during the Middle Ages. The Middle Ages need to be broken up into a number of periods—Patristic,

Carolingian, early universities, Early Renaissance, and so on. More important still is the need to keep in mind the fact that, alongside the prevalent tradition of studying and teaching philosophy in the Middle Ages in the Latin language and in Christian monasteries, schools, and universities, there were flourishing Arab and Jewish cultures which contributed to the Latin traditions increasingly and repeatedly. Much in the history of medieval thought reflects the work of translators: from Greek into Latin, from Greek into Syriac and Arabic, from Arabic into Latin, from Arabic into Hebrew, from Hebrew into Latin, from Latin into Old or Middle English or into medieval French. The story involves repeated crossings of cultural boundaries—and so it remains today: the written sources for the study of medieval thought—mainly written in, or once translated into, Latin—now need to be, and are vigorously being, translated into our languages—English, French, German, Italian, Japanese, Spanish—in order to cross what are only the latest, but not the last, in a succession of many linguistic and cultural frontiers.[14]

This is a short book. It is not written for specialists. I hope that it will lead readers without previous knowledge of the subject to take an interest in it.

I should like to thank Pat Holland and Hilary Walford for their help in the preparation of this book, and especially my wife, Megan.

I

Three Authorities

When did medieval philosophy begin?

This question immediately raises other questions about the transformation of the intellectual world of classical antiquity to the intellectual world of the Christian Middle Ages, a transformation that occurred unevenly in different parts of the Roman Empire, including the Greek eastern provinces and the Latin barbarian kingdoms. It is temptingly easy in a brief general history to pass from Plotinus to Augustine and then to Boethius and into the Middle Ages, after drawing attention to the decline of Rome, the rise of Christianity, and the closure of the philosophical schools of Athens by the Emperor Justinian in AD 529. But to do this would be to undervalue the influential work of less-well-known pagan, Christian, and Jewish thinkers in the Hellenistic world, particularly in the period between AD 200 and 600. Here Aristotle and Plato continued to be studied and interpreted by commentators, most of whom wrote in Greek, some of whom, such as John Philoponus in the sixth century, were to become known in the Latin West only very much later, in the twelfth and thirteenth centuries, and many of whom were to become known to Arab scholars in the Muslim world created in the seventh century in the Middle East, in North Africa, and in Spain. The thought of Plato and Aristotle on such fundamental issues as God, creation, and the immortality of the soul was subjected repeatedly in late antiquity to reinterpretations which, when Arab and Greek texts were translated into Latin from the twelfth century onwards, had a considerable influence upon the perception by medieval Latin Christian scholars of what ancient thought amounted to.[1] Many of the writings of ancient, classical thinkers were not available before the rise of Islam outside the greatest libraries of the Hellenistic world of the eastern Mediterranean, and knowledge of the Greek language, in which such texts were largely written, was not widespread, even in educated circles, in the western provinces in the late Roman Empire. So part of an answer to the question 'When did medieval philosophy begin?' is to point not only to the western Dark Ages and to figures such as Isidore of Seville (*c*.560–636) or Alcuin of York (*c*.735–804) —influential though both were—but to the east and to the Arab transmitters of Hellenistic learning whose achievements largely began to be known in the west only later, in the twelfth century.

But between the late fourth century and the early sixth century there are three figures whose writings were in time to acquire the status of authorities among philosophers who are on any definition truly medieval, whose works were largely available in the West by the ninth or tenth century and did not have to travel the Islamic route via North Africa and Spain. These are Augustine, Boethius, and Pseudo-Denis. To seize upon just these three is still to be unjust to the richness and the variety of intellectual effort that characterizes the Roman and Hellenistic world in late antiquity. In the Greek or Byzantine east, until the days of the Emperor Justinian I (483–565) and also thereafter, a succession of thinkers, as has been observed, wrestled with the Greek texts of Aristotle and Plato. But the works of some of these commentators were not to be known in the medieval Western world, where Latin language and culture were dominant, until translations were made in (especially) the twelfth century. We shall look at our three thinkers less for how much they represent and convey of the thought, learning, and beliefs of the fourth, fifth, and sixth centuries, and more for what they gave to their medieval Western successors who regarded them as authorities of the greatest importance. Their later significance is so great that some account of the contributions they made is indispensable.

Augustine of Hippo

Augustine of Hippo (345–430) appears to be both an heir to ancient culture and the precursor of medieval culture.[2] His education in North Africa introduced him to the Latin culture of Rome; Augustine always had some difficulty in studying Greek thought. He was 'converted' to philosophy at the age of 18 through reading a now lost work by Cicero called *Hortensius*. This reading enabled him to see beyond the largely literary and rhetorical education he had hitherto received, and he embarked upon a quest for wisdom. For a while he thought that this was to be found in the teachings of the Manichees, the followers of Manes (or Mani, *c.*216–76) who postulated the existence of two separately created worlds in perpetual conflict with each other, a world of goodness and light, in which Augustine longed to be, and, secondly, a world which is evil and dark in which he was held. According to the Manichees, Zarathustra, Buddha, and the Prophets of the Old Testament as well as Jesus were helpers in the task of deliverance from darkness, while Manes himself had claimed to be the Paraclete promised in the Gospels.

Later, in or after 383, and after a period as a teacher at Thagaste and at Carthage, Augustine rejected Manicheism. He went to Rome in 383 and then to Milan in 384, still teaching rhetoric. Manicheism now appeared too materialistic, especially as light and darkness were both matter. He found in contemporary versions of Platonism a more balanced evaluation of the union of body and soul in man: the human body enables the human mind to cultivate reason and virtue. Augustine distinguished, in the light of Platonism, an intelligible world where truth lies (beyond matter) and a sensible or physical world which is the world of sense perception. In 386 Augustine became a Christian and he was baptized in 387. He describes in his *Confessions* (VIII.20.26) how his study of Platonism came to lead him towards Christianity, for the Platonists, unlike (and better than) other schools of thought, saw true reality as spiritual or intelligible, not physical, and offered a view of God—as incorporeal,

immutable, infinite reason—that accorded with the God of
the Old and New Testaments. He also came into contact
with Ambrose, the bishop of Milan, and with other Christians
who helped him to draw nearer to, and finally to embrace,
Christianity, after an agonizing crisis which he describes in his
Confessions, books VI–VIII. His Christian friends were also
followers of Plato; like them Augustine found close similarities
between Platonism and Christian teaching on God as the light
shining in darkness, and on philosophy and the love of God.
His most important debts in these respects were to the
Neoplatonist philosophers Plotinus (*c*.205–70) and Porphyry
(*c*.232–303), as well as to Marius Victorinus (*fl.* 360s), who
had translated part of the *Enneads* of Plotinus, and finally to
St Paul, as he describes in his *Confessions* (VIII.8.19) in
the famous scene which took place in the garden of his house in
Milan. This is the beginning of the most philosophical
period in Augustine's life. He began in 386 to write *Dialogues*
which embody his vision of Christian Neoplatonism and also
provide his refutation of Manicheism. Through the writings of
the Platonists, through his own experiences, and also by drawing
fully on the resources of Christian revelation, Augustine came
to write pre-eminently about God and about the other great
immaterial reality, the human soul. These are, for Augustine,
the two most important themes of philosophy (*De ordine*,
II.18.47). He was explicit on this in his *Soliloquies*: 'I desire',
he says (I.2, n. 7), 'to have knowledge of God and the soul.
Of nothing else? No, of nothing else whatsoever.' And
again (II.1, n. 1): 'O God, always one and the same, if I know
myself, I shall know Thee [*noverim me, noverim te*].' For
a philosophy of science or the created universe one would
look in vain in the writings of Augustine, because he
focused on the highest levels of being. Much that he read
in 'the books of the Platonists'—for example, about reincarna-
tion—he discarded, but he adapted the Platonic teaching
about Ideas or Forms (which the human mind can contemplate)
to the Christian doctrine of the Word of God—that is,
Christ who brought light into the world. Augustine wrote a

work *On the Ideas* (*De ideis*) in which he presented Plato's theory:

The reasons for everything that will be, and for everything that has been, created are contained in the mind of God. Nothing except what is eternal and unchangeable can be in the mind of God, and Plato calls these principal reasons for things the ideas. They are not only ideas; they are also true because they are eternal and unchangeable. It is through their participation that whatever is is whatever it is.[3]

The human soul can find the ideas of things, for they are reflected within and illuminate the human mind, and they are as real as the things themselves of which they are the ideas (or forms or species or reasons[4]) which are in the mind of God. This is the gist of the medieval, Augustinian doctrine of the divine illumination of the human mind. Our knowledge arises within our soul. Of course our bodies are acted upon in physical ways, and through our senses we perceive physical reality. But this is sensory perception. Knowledge of true reality arises in the soul accordingly as it is enlightened by God. In part Augustine rested his case upon St John's Gospel: God sent the Word into the world and this was the true light that enlighteneth every man (John 1: 9). But he had a developed doctrine of the mind and understanding. Understanding is for the mind what seeing is for the senses; it is intellectual sight. Truth, especially the truths of ethics and logic, can be perceived independently of the bodily senses because an intellectual light is present in the mind. The understanding or sight of truth, or of wisdom itself, is made possible by an 'irradiation' into the human intellect of some of the first principles of knowledge which are in the mind of God. This doctrine of illumination is especially central to Augustine's thought about ethics. Just as the light of truth is present in the mind, so too the law of God is inwardly written in the human heart or conscience.

Augustine never devoted as much thought to nature as he did to God and the human soul. But he was especially interested in the problem of creation, the problem that includes the problem of an absolute beginning not of all things but certainly of time

which Augustine sees both as a relation between those things
that are created and as the measurement of their changes by
the human mind.[5] In accounting for the continuing emergence
of creatures since the original divine act of the creation of
things, Augustine employed the analogy of a seed: the processes
of nature are a developing germination and growth following on
from the divine implantation of 'seminal reasons' into creation.
This is what is accounted for in the Book of Genesis.

While in Milan in 386, Augustine wrote *De ordine* (*On Order*). Philosophy, or the love of wisdom, meant to Augustine and
to the other Platonists of the day the comprehension that 'higher
things' (the Ideas of the Platonists) are better than 'lower things'
but that all creation is good and harmonious and the work of a
perfect God. Seeking God, the author of all creation, required,
as it had for Plotinus, *ascesis*, a certain withdrawal from the
ordinary life of the world and the cultivation of an inner, ultra-
worldly life, a new life or a conversion. Philosophy, therefore,
was the search for the highest good, and Christianity was the
true philosophy. *De ordine* sets forth the new cultural programme that this life requires: it is based on the search for God
and contemplation of him, through the understanding of the
order given to this world. Divine reason has implanted an order
which can be discovered by the use of the disciplines of human
language and of mathematics, by the use of poetry and music,
geometry and astronomy. The ancient study of these liberal arts
was thus given ethical and religious value as part of the search in
which philosophy consists. For example, the study of grammar
constitutes the first stage in the passage from material things to
immaterial things, as the intrinsic rationality of words is grasped
and as speech is built up following the laying-down of rules.
Dialectic is recommended to those who would study Scripture.
The arts therefore are routes to truth.

In 388 Augustine left Italy to return to Africa as a monk, but
in 391 he was made bishop in Hippo. He now embarked on
writing his greatest works, including fifteen books on *The Trinity*
and twelve books *On Genesis*. He was also drawn into the
struggle against the Donatists and against the Pelagians. The

Donatist Christians in North Africa had split the church since 312 and also threatened a radical social revolt against Catholicism until forcibly repressed by imperial power.[6] The teachings of Pelagius (d. 418), a Briton who had successfully settled in Rome and into Roman intellectual life, insisted on the capacity of human free will to procure spiritual and moral progress in obedience to God's command, but in ways that seemed to Augustine to place too much weight on fallen human nature and too little on the role of divine action, grace, and predestination. For Augustine, man was as utterly dependent on God as a baby on its mother's breast; for Pelagius, man was a son whom his father had emancipated. A story is recorded in Augustine's book on *The Gift of Perseverance* (chapter 53) of a fellow bishop who met Pelagius and who quoted to him a prayer from Augustine's *Confessions* (X.29): 'Grant, Lord, what you command and command what you will.' Pelagius, however, took exception to a preceding sentence: 'All my hope, Lord, is set on your very great mercy.' This seemed to Pelagius to be a permit for personal moral inactivity or indifference, for Pelagius maintained, as Augustine wrote, that 'the grace of God is given according to our merits'. Pelagius won highly cultivated supporters, such as Julian (*c.*386–454), bishop of Eclanum in southern Italy from *c.*416 until 417 when he was dismissed, who vigorously challenged Augustine on his view of original sin:

You ask me [Julian wrote] why I would not consent to the idea that there is a sin that is part of human nature. I answer: it is improbable, it is untrue; it is unjust and impious; it makes it seem as if the Devil were the maker of men. It violates and destroys the freedom of the will. . . . You imagine so great a power in such a sin, that not only can it blot out the new-born innocence of nature, but, forever afterwards, will force a man throughout his life into every form of viciousness.[7]

Pelagius' supporters were very skilful in uncovering inconsistencies and inadequacies in Augustine's earlier writings and behaviour: as one perceptive and also sympathetic scholar has written, 'seldom in the history of ideas has a man as great as Augustine or as very human, ended his life so much at the mercy of his own blind-spots'.[8]

Because of these great controversies in Augustine's last years, he has come to be seen by much of posterity as the victor over Pelagius, as the theologian of original sin and grace, and also as the 'Doctor of Predestination'—of eternal election or reprobation—who exaggerated human concupiscence and wretchedness as well as the optimism of Pelagius. Augustine's stand was broadly ratified by the second council of Orange in 529; Pelagius' writings completely disappeared until this century. By Augustine medieval readers were alerted to the large questions about the relationship between God and man which involve faith, grace, and human action. Augustine's anti-Pelagianism had been an evolving process and his influence for many centuries to come was many-sided.

One of Augustine's most important debts was to Cicero, and this is especially evident in all that he wrote about love and friendship. Augustine always lived within circles of friends and he used Cicero's writings on friendship to describe, sometimes passionately, his experiences of love, companionship, and grief. On one occasion—at Milan before his conversion to Christianity—he described how he lived with two of his friends 'making one common household for all of us, so that in the clear trust of friendship things should not belong to this or that individual, but one thing should be made of all our possessions, and belong wholly to each one of us, and everybody own everything'.[9] At the heart of this ideal of shared trust, at least from the time of his conversion to Christianity, was the conviction that friendship and charity are the work of God: 'no friends are true friends unless you, my God, bind them fast through charity.'[10] He gave Cicero's ideal of friendship a Christian focus both in his vision of the church and in his own later monastic life; the classical ideal of friendship, as portrayed for example in Cicero's *De amicitia*, helped to mould the ethos of Christian monasticism during many centuries to come. There was always a practical, existential aspect to Augustine's thought on God and the soul.

Towards the end of his life he completed a large, new work on Christian culture and education, *De doctrina christiana*, in which he surveys the ancient programme of the liberal arts as a means towards the understanding of Holy Scripture which contains what the pagans do not believe but what man needs to know if he is to be saved—that is, to attain to wisdom. Augustine was fond of writing *intellige ut credas*: you must understand in order to believe. He was also fond of writing the antithesis *crede ut intelligas*: you must believe if you are to understand. Faith seeks, understanding finds (*fides quaerit, intellectus invenit* (*De Trinitate* XV.2.2)). On this Augustine based a broad cultural programme. Without the mediating support of the liberal arts, Scripture cannot be properly read and understood. Each art is a means to understanding religious values, the truths that are immaterial and transcendental. Logic and arithmetic are particularly valuable to an understanding of Scripture, logic because it discovers true arguments, solves problems, and is the opposite of sophistry; arithmetic because it explains the numbers used in Scriptural allegories. Augustine did not distinguish philosophy from theology: philosophy has become the process of enquiry into, and of understanding, the Christian faith. In his *Retractations* I.6 he declared that he had intended to write seven textbooks, one on each of the arts (*libri disciplinarum*) in order to show how the mind may be brought from material things to immaterial ones (*per corporalia ad incorporalia*). The seven books were to be on grammar, music, dialectic, rhetoric, geometry, arithmetic, and philosophy.[11] He did write the *Dialectic* and it was frequently copied among collections of works on logic during the Middle Ages.[12]

In 410 the city of Rome, the capital of the empire, was sacked by the Visigoths under their king Alaric. Augustine's *City of God* (413–27) gave an answer to those pagan critics who accused Christians of being responsible for the decline of the Roman Empire. Augustine drew a picture of two 'cities' or allegorical societies which were defined by the wills or loves of the individuals within each. Those who love themselves and hold God in contempt are members of an earthly 'city'; those who love God and hold themselves in contempt belong to the heavenly. Neither 'city' is identifiable with any actual society past or present;

perfect justice can be found only in the city of God, not in the city of Rome or in any other actual state. So Augustine argued that the passing-away of ancient Rome would not entail the destruction of perfect justice or of true peace which is eternal, however great the disturbances consequent upon invasions and war. The state exists to provide for man's necessities in this world, but man is also a pilgrim travelling towards (or away from) a heavenly city.

Boethius

Our second authority, Boethius (*c.*480–*c.*525), has been described as both the last Roman thinker and the first medieval schoolman.[13] Boethius was born *c.*480 into a prominent senatorial family in Italy, which was then under the rule of the Goths. He became a consul in 510 and was executed *c.*525. Realizing that the Roman world was possibly nearing its end, he attempted to revive and to sum up the philosophical learning of antiquity. His medieval successors were deeply influenced by his partial achievement. Medieval thinkers owed to Boethius nearly all the knowledge that they possessed of ancient logic as well as some of their knowledge of ancient mathematics and musical theory. They knew too of his efforts to apply philosophical concepts to problems of Christian theology and they found in his book on *The Consolation of Philosophy* a masterpiece of reflection.

Boethius was a Christian. He was deeply learned and knew no less about the philosophical and literary achievements of Greece and Rome than he did about the writings of Christian theologians, including, it deserves to be emphasized, those of Augustine, which much influenced him. Earlier Christian thinkers had tended to avoid Aristotle's philosophy; when they turned to Greek thought it was likely to be to Plato or to the Stoics—and in this Boethius was no exception. Aristotle, who was deemed to have taught that the world was eternal and to have denied divine providence as well as the immortality of the soul, seemed too much of a pagan. But among non-Christian thinkers Aristotle was studied and taught, by Plotinus, for example, in the mid-third century, and by his pupil Porphyry, who wrote some ten commentaries on Aristotle's works. The works of Aristotle were read and expounded in the schools of Athens and Alexandria. And this tradition Boethius followed also. Indeed, he lamented the decline of classical culture in the Roman world and was fearful that the Greek legacy of thought might be lost for ever.

Among his greatest achievements were his translations of Aristotle's books of logic into Latin—the *Categories*, *De interpretatione*, *Topics*, *De sophisticis elenchis* (or *Sophistical Refutations*), the *Prior Analytics*, and the *Posterior Analytics*.[14] He also provided commentaries in Latin on the *Categories*, the *De interpretatione* (twice), the *Topics* of Aristotle (probably), and the *Topics* of Cicero. The *Categories* presents the ten categories into which things are classified: first, substance, then nine accidents (quantity, quality, relation, active, passive, when, where, having, position). Boethius, like other commentators before him,[15] saw that there was a problem in knowing whether to treat the categories as the kinds of being or simply as concepts representing them. *On Interpretation* is the study of propositions and of modal sentences which are sentences which state possibility and necessity. Statements of facts include such statements as 'fire heats' and 'mankind possesses rationality'. Statements of possibilities sometimes refer to future contingent events of the kind that are as likely to happen as not to happen. The examination of future contingent events leads Boethius into some discussion of determinism and free will: a proposition predicting the future, e.g. 'there will be a sea battle tomorrow', is either true or false, even though we may reflect that there is not enough evidence to be certain now whether it is true or false. But if it is true now, is the sea battle a necessity? Aristotle thought not; Boethius added that God knows this and other future contingent events, although, being outside time, he does not *fore*know them.

In addition, Boethius translated and twice commented on

Porphyry's introduction to Aristotle's logical works, the *Isagoge*.[16] Porphyry's introduction deals with the five predicables—that is, the five kinds of object which can be predicated of a subject in a proposition such as '*x* is *y*', when *x* is the subject and *y* the predicate. The predicables are: genus, species, specific difference, *proprium*, and accident. In a sentence such as 'the ass is an animal', the predicable chosen is a genus; in a sentence such as 'the ass is small', the predicable is an accident. Porphyry, in this introduction, states but does not seek to pursue the question whether these predicables exist in human understanding only or also in reality, whether also they are incorporeal or corporeal, and whether they exist apart from sensible objects or only with them.[17] Boethius, in his two commentaries, inclines to an Aristotelian rather than a Platonic view, although he does not reach a final decision: concepts cannot be substances; what is common to many (e.g. the genus of the species which belong to it) cannot be individual. On the other hand, these general concepts (or universals) are not simply in the mind because they are thoughts of things, and they correspond to physical realities. The human mind can extract universal ideas from things and think of these ideas separately, although they do not exist separately. In his commentaries Boethius provided his readers in later centuries with the opportunity to face large and fundamental questions without, however, having access to the works of Plato and Aristotle on which Boethius based his own discussion. Boethius also examined the question whether logic was (as the Stoics considered it to be, along with ethics and physics) part of philosophy or whether it was an instrument for analysing arguments in whatever field of study they occur. He maintained that logic was both, just as a hand is part of the human body and an instrument of the whole body.

Boethius also wrote some works of his own—*On Division* (which deals with procedures in logic such as how to divide a genus into species and a whole into its parts), *On Topical Differences*, two works on *Categorical Syllogisms*, and one on *Hypothetical Syllogisms*. These two last titles assemble different types of unconditional and conditional syllogism. However, all this was merely the fragment of a vaster design to translate into Latin and to comment upon all the works of Aristotle—the ethical and the scientific as well as the logical ones—and all the dialogues of Plato. The rest of this plan was not carried out, but Boethius explained in the course of the second of his two commentaries on *Interpretation* that he wished to undertake this task in order to demonstrate the fundamental agreement between Plato and Aristotle. Not all of Boethius' partial achievement survived into later centuries; his translation of the *Posterior Analytics* and his commentary on Aristotle's *Topics* did not survive, and some other works were scarcely anywhere to be found for several centuries to come. His translation of the *Categories* did not begin to circulate until the late ninth century; until then another translation, that had been formed out of quotations contained in Boethius' commentary on the *Categories*, held the field.[18] Apart from a few fragments, his translation of the *Topics* was not known until the twelfth century;[19] before then Cicero's *Topics* was known, as well as Boethius' commentary upon it and Boethius' treatise *De differentiis topicis*.[20] But, until at least the twelfth century, what was known in the West about Aristotle and about logic was in large part due to Boethius and formed a corpus that was called in the later Middle Ages the 'old logic' (*logica vetus*). Furthermore, in these centuries the tradition of training thinkers—indeed all students—in logic became established; and throughout the Middle Ages the principal method used in the study of philosophy was Aristotelian logic, which was also applied to other disciplines as well, notably theology. In general the Latin terminology was provided by Boethius. He was the principal transmitter of Aristotelian thought, at least until the thirteenth century, and was himself in time to be treated as an authority whose writings were to be the subject of further commentaries.[21] Hundreds of surviving manuscripts attest the fundamental place occupied by Boethian texts on logic during the Middle Ages. A further part of Boethius' design to save the liberal arts from destruction in a world that was about to collapse comprises his writings on *Arithmetic* and

Music, and perhaps also on *Geometry* and *Astronomy*. These were all seen to be mathematical arts, and ones that by and large were not well served by the available books written in Latin. There is in Boethius' writings on these subjects an overriding sense of cosmic harmony which is assured by numbers and which is perceived through the study of them.

A part of Boethius' plan that was not fulfilled was that of showing the agreement in thought of Aristotle and Plato, their concordance rather than their dissensions, 'at least on many matters, especially the chief ones in philosophy'.[22] In the study of logic Boethius was unquestionably the disciple above all of Aristotle. But, in the study of being, Boethius was also the disciple of Proclus (412–85), of Ammonius of Alexandria (435/45–517/26), and, ultimately, of Plato himself. For Boethius the One is supreme and God is pure form; other beings are a compound of form (*quo est*: that by which being is what it is) and subject (*quod est*: what being actually is). Created being is composite, divine being is simple.

Boethius took an unusual step, one which was to have great effect upon the development of medieval thought, of applying the logic of Aristotle to pure being. His efforts to apply philosophical concepts to theology are largely contained in five treatises known as the *Opuscula sacra* which survived into the Middle Ages.[23] They deal largely with Christian doctrinal disputes which were current in Boethius' time and which concerned, for example, the definition of and the distinction between person and nature—God and man—in Christ, or the differing ways in which terms such as 'good' and 'just', Father and Son, substance and relation, may be applied to the divine Trinity. His definition of person—the individual substance of a rational nature—was formulated in order to embrace all rational nature, human beings, angels, and also the divine persons of the Trinity. Boethius aimed to resolve disagreements between Christian schools of thought by the application of philosophical clarity. In his first treatise, *On The Trinity*, Boethius examined the relationship between God and other things such as forms and matter. In the third treatise, the *Hebdomads* (groups of seven), Boethius deals with being, and particularly with being good. Everything is good in that it is; it also gains its goodness from the Good (which is God). Is everything therefore identical with God? God—pure being—does not participate in any other thing; everything participates in being. Boethius rests his solution of the problem on his distinction between being (*esse*) and existence (*id quod est*): existence is derived from being, and what makes beings what they are (a man, a horse, a stone) is distinguishable from being. These speculations, which derive from the traditions of Platonic thought, and other discussions too concerning terms such as providence, eternity, nature, and person, were to become familiar to medieval thinkers, especially from the ninth century when they first aroused great interest. Through the *Opuscula sacra* comes a large part of the philosophical vocabulary and orientation of the Middle Ages.

Finally, Boethius bequeathed to the Middle Ages his *Consolation of Philosophy*.[24] This dialogue, a mixture of poetry and prose, was written while its author, who had been disgraced for alleged treason by the Gothic ruler, Theodoric, awaited execution. The scene is Boethius' prison, in which he is visited by Philosophy. Philosophy is personified as an old and beautiful lady, the same lady who had appeared to Socrates in Plato's *Crito* and who had also helped other martyrs to philosophy, such as Anaxagoras and Seneca. Boethius protests his innocence to her and pours forth his anguish. Philosophy urges Boethius to turn his thoughts to the world that lies beyond the senses and matter. They enquire together into the relationship between Fate or Fortune and Providence. Was consolation to be found by recognizing, as the Stoics did, that the world was ruled by necessity and by a fickle fortune? Philosophy urges Boethius not to blame Fortune for taking away from him the gifts he had formerly enjoyed of honour and power and pleasure, for a wise man will not value these highly. These are, as the Stoics taught, only imperfect or relative goods; they cannot last. What is unchangeable is the highest Good, which is God. Fate is subject to providence, a providence that rules the universe through love than which nothing is better, that rules the world *fortiter ac suaviter*, strongly and sweetly, as is affirmed in the Old Testament (Wisd. 8), that foreknows everything—or rather, being outside time, knows everything at once—without destroying human free will. Philosophy prays to God for the power to understand God's mysteries. Much of Boethius' earlier writing provides the foundations for the *Consolation*: the principle (for example) that the first principle of all things is good, his ideas about necessity and God's foreknowledge, the theme that the harmony of the universe is based on number. These and other reflections inspired by Plato and by Proclus, as well as much of the lore of classical mythology, are explored in the work, and in particular in the poem *O qui perpetua*, in which Boethius petitions his Creator:

> O Thou who dost by everlasting reason rule,
> Creator of the planets and the sky, who time
> From timelessness didst bring, unchanging Mover,
> No cause drove Thee to mould unstable matter, but
> The form benign of highest good within Thee set.
> All things Thou bringest forth from Thy high archetype:
> Thou height of beauty, in Thy mind the beauteous world
> Dost bear, and in that ideal likeness shaping it,
> Dost order perfect parts a perfect whole to frame.
> The elements by harmony Thou dost constrain,
> That hot to cold and wet to dry are equal made,
> That fire grow not too light, or earth too fraught with weight.
> . . . .
> Grant, Father, that our minds Thy august seat may scan,
> Grant us the sight of true good's source, and grant us light
> That we may fix on Thee our mind's unblinded eye . . .[25]

Much of medieval philosophy was concerned with the problems pursued in the *Consolation*—those of fate and free will, of providence, chance, and evil—as well as with those that Boethius had written about when at liberty. Boethius' *Consolation* was acknowledged throughout the Middle Ages to be a masterly handling of (and a rich source of material from) the various ancient schools of thought, especially Stoicism and

Platonism.[26] There was, from the ninth century onwards, a very rich and varied tradition of commentary upon the text and the problems with which it deals.[27] King Alfred translated it into Old English in the ninth century, as did Chaucer in the fourteenth; Thomas More, another tragic prisoner, found comfort in reading it. The work survives in around 400 medieval manuscripts and, like the *Confessions* of St Augustine, continues to be reprinted often in our day.

Denis the pseudo-Areopagite

Both Augustine and Boethius wrote in Latin and lived in the West, in North Africa and in Italy. In the eastern parts of the Roman Empire, where Greek was more often read and spoken, pagan philosophy also had a deep and widespread influence upon both Christians and non-Christians. In the schools of Athens and Alexandria students were able to appreciate a mixture of Christian and gentile thought and learning. But the works of the pagan philosophers of late antiquity—for example, of Plotinus (*c*.205–70), Porphyry (*c*.232–*c*.303), Iamblichus (d. 326), and Proclus (*c*.410–85)—were (with rare exceptions) not translated into Latin. Even the Greek Christian writers who drew upon them—such as Gregory of Nyssa (*c*.330–94) and John Chrysostom (*c*.347–407)—were to be imperfectly known in the medieval West. As for Plato himself, Calcidius in the fourth century made an incomplete translation of about half of his *Timaeus* (stopping at 53b); for most of the Middle Ages that was all that was available of Plato's work. Plato came across, therefore, not so much as the author of the *Republic* (to which the *Timaeus* is the sequel) or of his other dialogues, but rather as the enquirer into the origins of the universe. Another important source of Greek thought for readers of Latin was Ambrosius Theodosius Macrobius, who, in the early fifth century, wrote *Commentaries* on Cicero's *Dream of Scipio*.[28] *Scipio's Dream* was the closing portion of Cicero's *De re publica*, where Cicero, partly in imitation of Plato's *Republic*, discusses the ideal republic and the development of Rome. Macrobius' *Commentaries* are an encyclopaedic exposition of Neoplatonist thought. He presents, for example, a classification of the virtues, including political virtues, based on Plotinus and Porphyry, and he expressed Platonic thought about the origin and the immortality of souls. Following Plotinus, he depicts a golden chain of being hung from heaven to earth and linking the very lowest things to the One via the Soul, which gives life to all things, and via the Mind, from which the Soul is derived. His work was to be the most widely read Latin survey of Neoplatonic thought in the Middle Ages; the range of learning it transmits also includes mathematics, geography, and astronomy.

However, one Greek Christian writer did come to exert a profound influence upon medieval Latin thinkers. This was Denis or Dionysius the Areopagite (*fl. c.*500), who wrote in Greek shortly before or after 500 and who presented his writings as the work of the man converted by St Paul on the Areopagus in Athens in the mid-first century (Acts 17: 16–34). That the name of Dionysius Areopagita was the writer's pseudonym was scarcely ever suspected before the fifteenth century.

Denis owed most of his inspiration as a speculative thinker to earlier Christian Platonists, especially Gregory of Nyssa, and also to Proclus, whose concept of emanation Denis largely adapted to a Christian context. Proclus was one of a number of Neoplatonist thinkers who exploited Plotinus' vision of the differing levels of reality and being in the universe—the One, the Intellect or the Ideas, and the sensible world (the world of the senses). According to Plotinus, the One is, both ontologically and causally, anterior to all other being, and intelligible being is a causal principle of material being. Proclus, in explaining how beings descend from the One, presented a procession of grades or hierarchies arranged into triads which participate in the level of being both above and below themselves. All reality, therefore both emanates from and returns to the One, which is itself beyond being. But, whereas Proclus hereby explained the role of the pagan gods, Denis used Proclus' ideas to explain the orders of angels in a Christian universe and also the orders and grades in the church on earth, which is an extension of the chain of beings which fill the invisible spiritual world. None of Denis' angelology would have seemed unfamiliar to many contemporary or earlier Greek Christian writers. Already in the time of Origen (c.184/5–254) speculation on the role of angels was well advanced. But in the fourth century Christian thought about angelic beings and Neoplatonist thought drew closer together in the work of Marius Victorinus (d. c.363) and Gregory of Nyssa. Denis was more systematic in his classification of being, and he was to become known in the medieval West.

Denis's writings were translated into Latin in France in the ninth century; their influence was at first restricted, then from the twelfth century onwards highly pervasive. His ideas on hierarchy are contained in the two treatises on *Celestial* and on *Ecclesiastical Hierarchy*.[29] Hierarchy today has a multitude of connotations in social organizations, in the natural sciences, and in computing science. It was probably Denis who invented the word, and for him, as well as for his readers over the course of more than a millennium, it did not have the extended range of meanings we are now used to, although from the twelfth century onwards in the Latin West it was applied to ecclesiastical and secular structures in an increasing variety of ways. Denis defined the term in his *Celestial Hierarchy* III.1: 'Hierarchy, for me, is sacred order, knowledge and activity assimilating itself, as far as it can, to the likeness of God (deiformity) and raising itself to its utmost, by means of the illuminations granted by God, to the imitation of Him.' Hierarchy is, then, an order in which creatures are divided into ranks; it is also a science, for it imparts knowledge of God to souls which are like mirrors receiving light from God and enlightening in their turn those creatures who are below them; and, thirdly, it is an activity providing for the union of creatures with God.

The object of hierarchy is, then, as far as is possible, assimilation and union with God, for it is God Himself whom hierarchy takes as the master of all holy knowledge and activity. Hierarchy never turns away from contemplating His very divine beauty and it receives as far as it can the mark of His imprint. It turns its followers into finished images of God, perfectly clear and unstained mirrors, ready to receive the primordially luminous beam of the Thearchy and . . . illuminating in their turn, in all generosity, the beings who come after them, according to the prescriptions of the Thearchy. (*Celestial Hierarchy*, III.2)

Thus, there is a universal concord and a spiritual ordering of intelligences or spirits, a 'great chain of being',[30] and its foundation in Plato's theory of forms is marked, although in some key ways Denis breaks with earlier Neoplatonism.

In broad terms the Platonic background to this double universe is the distinction between the intelligible and the sensible world, the world of Ideas and the world of shadows. But present also are the biblical ideas of divine providence and of redemption. An infinite gap separates God from dependent beings, but these all have being, life, and intelligence by participating in God in varying degrees of purity, illumination, and perfection according to their place—higher or lower—in the hierarchy of things. Each order in the hierarchy (except the last) purifies, enlightens, and perfects, although it does not cause, the order beneath it. This activity is graduated: Denis uses the image of the Sun, which warms and lightens objects nearer to itself more powerfully and easily than it does more distant objects, which frequently do not receive light and heat from the Sun directly but via intermediate objects. But the diffusion of light and warmth throughout the whole world gives it unity. So too with the angels and then with human spirits, which are all arranged into triads, each placed in a position above and below the others.[31]

Each order or degree of angels and of members of the church on earth receives, according to its proximity or remoteness from God, more or less purification, illumination, and perfection from him. But each order mediates this activity to the next, forming a continuous, connected chain. Hierarchic activity is not only a descending theme; the divinizing of spirits or intelligences leads them to return and cleave to God by corresponding ascending mediations. The hierarchies thus form an immense procession of divine light which attracts and unites all intelligences to itself, although the brightness of each and the perfection of the divine image which it presents is proportionate to its spiritual proximity to the Thearchy, the source of illumination. Every divine intervention in human history—the gift of the Law to Moses, the purification of the lips of Isaiah, the Annunciation to Mary of the birth of Christ, to name some—has been mediated to man through the hierarchies. These bring God out of His darkness and silence and by imparting knowledge lead its recipients towards him. This double movement is conjoint: Denis compares it to the experience we might have of tugging on a chain which hangs from the sky, feeling that we are pulling the chain down when in fact we lift ourselves upwards, or of a man in a boat tugging on a rope attached to a rock, feeling that he is drawing the rock closer when in fact it is the boat which moves closer to the rock.

In two other works, *Divine Names* and *Mystical Theology*, Denis wrote about God. To the Christian, God was transcendent; and to the Neoplatonist, he was even beyond being and wholly indescribable. In the *Divine Names* Denis presents two ways of speaking about God, the negative and the positive. The first arises from God's unknowability; the second arises from God's self-revelation to creation. The distinction reflects God's double movement towards himself and towards the multiplicity of creatures. Negative theology emancipates God from anthropomorphism—that is, from the imposition of human characteristics to God; it ends in silence. Positive or affirmative theology uses names such as light or beauty but only as metaphors or symbols of God. Negative theology does not eliminate affirmative theology but purifies the concepts and symbols which human beings imperfectly apply to God. Denis brings together, therefore, the God of the Scriptures and the Forms of Plato. God is the source of all perfections, Wisdom, Intelligence, Reason, Truth, and so on. Creatures can participate in these perfections, which are communicated to them. But God is himself beyond all that can be known, and is even beyond being, and thus is ultimately inaccessible. The idea that he can be approached more through ignorance than through knowledge, by going beyond every intelligible object, and by abandoning everything through purification of self, underlies the very short but influential treatise on *Mystical Theology*, in which Denis describes how one who seeks God must abandon all knowledge if he is to achieve an ineffable union with God in darkness.

2

The Beginnings of Medieval Philosophy

The liberal arts in Carolingian Europe

The sixth and seventh centuries in Western Europe—unlike those same centuries in the world of Byzantium—were in general not conducive to advanced study. For this to develop, an educational revival was needed such as happened in the age of Charlemagne. King of the Franks from 754 to 814, Charles legislated for the establishment of schools for the clergy in every cathedral. One of Charlemagne's advisers was Alcuin of York, who encountered Charlemagne at Pavia in 781. Charlemagne asked Alcuin to enter his court. Thereafter Alcuin promoted cultural and educational reform on behalf of the Frankish king. He became abbot of St Martin's at Tours, and through his writings and letters he encouraged the adoption by the Carolingian Franks of a programme of education in the liberal arts.

These were the seven liberal arts derived from the educational programmes of antiquity. The seven arts consist of the trivium of grammar, dialectic, and rhetoric, and of the quadrivium of arithmetic, geometry, astronomy, and music, and they were to be studied using ancient textbooks. These were chiefly the works of Cassiodorus, Isidore, Augustine, and Boethius. Cassiodorus (490–*c*.580), who had founded a monastery at Vivarium in Calabria in 555, had provided in his *Institutiones* an encyclopaedic summary of the contents of both divine and human learning.[1] He sanctified the liberal arts as human aids to divine learning. Isidore of Seville (560–636), in his *Etymologies* or *Origins*, also surveyed the seven arts and provided a fundamental work of reference, an encyclopaedia no less, that was widely available throughout the Middle Ages.[2] New summaries of the arts were now also produced by such educationists as Alcuin himself and by his followers such as Theodulf of Orleans and Raban Maur. An education in the arts, and therefore some knowledge of the legacy of antiquity, was to be part of the common culture of educated men, mostly monks and clerics, from Carolingian times onwards.

Alcuin laid very modest yet very enduring foundations for a tradition of study which served as the cradle in which philosophical thought was nurtured. He wrote introductory textbooks and dialogues on grammar, rhetoric, and dialectic in which he summarized classical sources. In his treatise on *Dialectic* he used the *Isagoge* and the *De interpretatione*. He used too the *Categoriae decem*, a work which provided a paraphrase of Aristotle's *Categories*, the categories being substance and the nine accidents. In reality the *Categoriae decem* was written by Themistius (who lived between c.317 and c.388), but in Alcuin's day it was believed to be a work of St Augustine, and it is Alcuin himself who was responsible for increasing its readership and circulation, with the result that interest in the Aristotelian categories grew.[3] There is no clear evidence of the use of Boethius' translation of Aristotle's *Categories* before the end of the ninth century,[4] but there is much evidence from Alcuin's day of interest in its subject matter as provided in the *Categoriae decem*. Alcuin also read Boethius' *Consolation of Philosophy*. He composed treatises *On the Reason in the Soul* and *On the Trinity*; in these he followed Augustine and Boethius, showed an interest in the power of reason to make Christian doctrine understandable, and in particular applied the Aristotelian categories to discussion of God and of the human soul, its capacity to know, and the nature of existence. Alcuin and his followers made the first attempts in the West since the time of Boethius to assimilate the techniques of logic. In pursuit of the aim of reviving education and of basing this on the study of the ancient Roman arts, Alcuin helped to put dialectic before the schoolboys of his own generation, and they in turn perpetuated the tradition. Moreover, by following the example of Augustine and Boethius in presenting the arts as a way forward to the acquisition of wisdom, Alcuin and his contemporaries developed the practice of applying the tools of logic to the discussion of Christian doctrine. Alcuin described the arts as seven columns which hold up the temple of Christian wisdom.

Wrestling with the categories (substance and the nine accidents) and with the predicables (genus, species, difference, property, and accident), and wrestling too with Latin grammar and the definitions of the parts of speech given by Priscian, was now the task of a growing number of teachers, and this activity led into discussions of the relationship between logic and reality, including theological reality, and also between logic and language, including theological language. It is clear that in the ninth century the ancient textbooks of the arts were read and expounded in schools, and surviving manuscripts not infrequently contain glosses added by ninth-century scholars and teachers. Sometimes these glosses show an interest in philosophical issues. Thus, copies of the *De nuptiis Mercurii et Philologiae*, the work in which Martianus Capella, an African pagan and rhetorician of the fourth century, surveyed the arts (under the guise of allegory), sometimes contain discussions or at least allusions to ancient ideas on such matters as space, time, and the soul.[5] Glossators of Boethius' *Consolation of Philosophy* made references to Neoplatonic ideas about the universal soul and the Ideas. The *Categoriae decem*, which, as has been noted, was ascribed to St Augustine, provided ample encouragement for readers to make notes about the rudiments of logic and sometimes about more advanced technicalities as well. The notion of substance attracted particular attention in various Carolingian centres of study, and discussions often led into theology and into study of the relationship between God and the other categories.

For the most part these studies were very brief and in many cases have not been traced to known masters or scholars. But some scholars do stand out, especially Remigius of Auxerre, who advanced from intermittent glossing to the writing of some rather more sustained commentaries and who dominated scholarship in the later ninth and early tenth century at Rheims and

then at Paris. The importance of these activities lies in the fact
that a tradition of discussion was being formed, based on the
trivium, which coupled the study of logic with that of language
and grammar as well as rhetoric, based too on the writings of
Boethius and Augustine and paying particular attention to concepts that were central in Aristotelian and Platonic thought. In
trying also to bring these concepts together with the teachings of
Christianity, scholars of the Carolingian age were largely renew-
ing the efforts of Augustine to study the categories and the soul
and also divine foreknowledge and the human will. So, when
theological disputes broke out in the ninth century, philosophical ideas were brought into play.[6] One set of discussions concerned the human soul and its relationship to space. Alcuin's
interests in this were shared by Hincmar, Ratramnus of Corbie,
and Gottschalk of Orbais (*c*.800–*c*.870). The soul was spiritual in
nature, but attention centred on questions regarding its form,
location, and circumscription, its origin and its immortal destiny,
and its resemblance to God the creator. The body was seen as
either a prison or a temple in which the soul was placed.

Connected with this were discussions on the universal soul.
Augustine, in a passage in his *De quantitate animae*,[7] raised the
problem whether there is one soul or many. A ninth-century
Celtic monk called Macarius argued that individual souls are
emanations from a universal soul. Ratramnus, arguing dialectic-
ally with the aid of the *Isagoge* of Porphyry, in his (second) *Liber
de anima* written in the 860s, viewed the universal soul not as a
real object but as a general or abstract concept of soul; individual human souls do not derive from it but are individually
made by God.[8] There were also disputes over predestination and
human free will. There were thinkers such as Gottschalk, who
seemed to lay so much emphasis on divine foreknowledge and
predestination that decisions taken by a human individual
seemed to lack merit. Salvation or damnation is therefore the
absolutely gratuitous act of God. On the other hand, John the
Scot (Eriugena), in his work *On Predestination* (851),[9] defended
human freedom against the views of Gottschalk: there would be
no point in God prohibiting sin if man did not have the freedom

to commit it. The notion of grace implies that of a freedom on the part of man to accept it, otherwise grace would not be a free gift. John the Scot was aware, however, that human language was inadequate for such discussion because it inevitably tended to place God within the framework of man's finite understanding. Terms such as foreknowledge or predestination are not literally applicable to God, who is above and beyond time. But it was with the tools of dialectic that John set about proving where Gottschalk had gone wrong; he blamed Gottschalk's errors upon his defective knowledge of the liberal arts.

John the Scot (Eriugena)

Like Alcuin, John the Scot (Eriugena, *c.*810–*c.*877) helped to mould the agenda for much of the later development of medieval thought. His exceptional position arises from the fact that, almost for the first time in the West he used, cited, and also translated the writings of some of the Greek Christian thinkers, including Gregory of Nyssa, Maximus the Confessor, and Denis. They, even more than Latin writers such as Boethius and Augustine, were thoroughly imbued with the concerns of the Neoplatonists of late Antiquity, and with their aid John the Scot—an Irishman, as his other name of Eriugena indicates—gave a fresh expression to the problem of the relationship between God and created nature.

To translate the writings of Denis, John the Scot used the manuscript copy given by the Byzantine emperor to the Carolingian emperor Louis the Pious in 827. The manuscript was then deposited at the abbey of Saint-Denis near Paris. The abbot, Hilduin, translated the works into Latin and wrote a life of their author in which he identified the patron of his monastery with Denis, the disciple of St Paul as well as the author of these works. Hilduin's translation was successfully supplanted by a new one made by John the Scot, who in addition wrote a commentary on Denis' *Celestial Hierarchy*.[10] When translating the

Ambigua of Maximus the Confessor, John the Scot also encountered, as he did when translating the writings of Denis, the two ways—affirmative and negative—of signifying divinity: affirmative when one says what God is (for example, being, goodness, wisdom, or truth), negative when one calls God (for example) invisible, infinite, or incomprehensible. The negative way, according to Denis, was preferable to the affirmative way, because God transcends and is beyond being and beyond goodness, wisdom, and truth.

John the Scot's masterpiece is the *Periphyseon*, a work of striking originality which he completed by 866. The title means 'On Nature'; the Latin title which was attached to the work was more explicit, *De divisione naturae* or *On the Division of Nature*. Here John the Scot employs Denis and Maximus frequently to explore the parts of nature in terms of their procession from and their return to God. The universe is thus dynamic, but it is also created and comes to an end. God himself, the principal origin of all, is *anarchos*—that is, without beginning, creating but not created. He is also, however, not the end and yet everything tends towards him. He is the means by which everything subsists. Beyond all human understanding and reason, beyond the ten categories, God even seems to be beyond being. This is the negative way of describing God. Yet, remote and inaccessible as God is, there is also a positive way of describing him through his creation. The Old and the New Testaments are full of accounts of divine apparitions to men and women. To account for these, John the Scot employs the notion of theophany which he derives from Denis and Maximus, theophanies being appearances, albeit indirect, of God to his creatures—created manifestations, that is, of uncreated nature. One theophany occurred when the Word of God—Christ—became known to angelic and to human nature by assuming a human nature and thereby joining the sensible world to the Godhead. Theophanies happen when divine wisdom descends into angelic and human natures and when these intelligences ascend to wisdom. Moreover, all creatures, both visible and invisible, are theophanies or apparitions of divinity because each order or division of nature is a manifestation of the order of nature which is above it. The closer theophanies are to the invisible cause of all, the obscurer they are to human minds, and conversely the further theophanies are removed from their cause, the more evident they are. Hence all creation is a graduated revelation of God, yet no creature can fully perceive God, who is in himself unknowable. Theophanies have the dual role of both revealing and hiding the divinity; they are the images of the eternal causes, but the causes themselves are unseen and subsist in God.

Division, which is mentioned in the Latin title of John the Scot's work, and on which Boethius had provided a monograph, is one of four logical procedures, the other three being resolution, definition, and demonstration. John the Scot uses resolution as well as division to explain the double movement of creatures, descent and ascent or emanation and return. The division of nature, which provides John with a detailed framework for his enquiries, is fourfold. The first division is that which creates and is not created, the second that which creates and is created, the third that which does not create and is created, the fourth that which is not created and does not create. He also uses the hierarchy of genus and species, with species unfolding from genera and individuals unfolding from species, just as effects unfold from primordial causes and, conversely, are enveloped in species and genera as all things return to their higher natures and these all return to God. The first division of nature is God. The second is the intelligible world, the world of Ideas or of primordial causes which is created and creates. The third is the world of things perceptible by the senses and created from the intelligible world but not itself creating. Just as man is created in God's mind and is a notion in the mind of God, so too the human body or nature is a manifestation of the soul. The fourth division, as well as the first, is God—God, that is, as the point to which all things (both good and evil) return, the final cause which is not created and does not create.

Many themes are interwoven in John the Scot's grand design. One of these is eternity and time: God is anterior to creation, not according to time but according to reason. Another is matter:

this derives from God and is made by him; Adam's fall was a fall from an ideal world into a material world where the human struggle is experienced in time and space.

John the Scot, celebrated as he is for his translation of Greek religious writings and above all for his masterpiece, the *Periphyseon*, also promoted the arts. Like Alcuin, John was a teacher of the arts. Like Alcuin, John attracted to the Carolingian royal court and chapel, and inspired, a circle of thinkers who gave his work sustained and enthusiastic attention. But, whereas Alcuin had used the seven liberal arts as introductions to philosophy and as instruments for the study and understanding of Scripture, John the Scot emphasized their intrinsically philosophical character. Still more than Alcuin, he found in logic a pointer to metaphysics.

John the Scot defines each of the arts in his *Periphyseon*.[11] He often reflects on them[12] and shows his esteem for them. He praises dialectic especially as the 'mother of the arts',[13] as a technique invented not by man but by God. God engraved dialectic into the very heart of created things.[14] Dialectic teaches us how to divide genera into species and species into individuals. It also teaches us how to combine individuals into species and species into genera. Likewise the multiplicity of reality flows down from its source in the uncreated nature. And multiplicity also returns and climbs back into unity. So logic and ontology coincide. The two processes are one. Dialectic lies in the nature of things. Reality was created by God, who also created all the arts.[15] Reason is part of divine creation, an inseparable constituent of its procession from God and its return to God. John the Scot wrote that no one can enter heaven except by philosophy. True religion is true philosophy.

So, like his predecessors in the Carolingian royal court but with a far greater depth of understanding, John the Scot found the arts essential as a means towards the understanding of Scripture. The arts converge on Christ, the Word, the source of all wisdom. The arts are more than pedagogic aids. They are more than guides to wisdom. They are more than instruments of philosophy. They are an intrinsic element in the division of natures and in their return to the unity from which they begin. Human language, the vehicle of rational communication between creatures, is important here: the first word of John the Scot's *Homily* on the Gospel of St John is *vox*. *Vox* is a sound which is heard one moment and gone the next. But *vox* conveys *verbum*, the Word, and the Word is the eternal essence which *vox* conveys.[16] John the Scot also commented on the work of Martianus. He was perhaps not the first in the Carolingian age to do so and he performed the task in 859–60.[17] His *Annotationes* made an impact on later commentators such as Remigius of Auxerre.[18] In his commentary John the Scot brought together rhetoric and dialectic. In antiquity there had been tensions between rhetorical culture and philosophy. Alcuin had written dialogues on both rhetoric and dialectic and knew that Cicero had written in *De inventione* 1.1 that wisdom without eloquence does too little for the good of states but eloquence without wisdom is never helpful. John the Scot interpreted the first two books of Martianus as a rhetorical preface to the study of the liberal arts.

The fact that education in and after the Carolingian age was rooted in the study of the trivium—grammar, logic, and rhetoric—does much to explain why many medieval philosophers were also excellent writers. John the Scot and his circle were never far from poetry. Martin of Laon, who read the *Periphyseon*, was also a poet. So was Heiric of Auxerre, John's disciple in the teaching of the liberal arts. Heiric's long poem on the Life of Saint Germanus of Auxerre is accompanied by glosses which are often extracts from John's *Periphyseon*. These glosses—whether or not they were arranged by Heiric himself—illustrate the close links between poetry and philosophy in Eriugenian circles at the end of the ninth century. The liberal arts, then, are given by John and his followers a more decisive place in philosophy than had been characteristic even of Alcuin and his followers, who had used them as introductions and as aids to philosophy. With John the arts are fully a part of man's innate cognitive and communicative powers, not merely artificial techniques useful to understanding the Scriptures. With the arts man may uncover his origins by coming to an understanding of his resemblance to his creator, a resemblance that comprises the freedom, dignity, and rationality that man had enjoyed fully before the fall. For a generation or two John the Scot strongly influenced other Carolingian scholars working, for example, at the schools of Laon and Auxerre and believing like him that faith and reason are not separable and that the Scriptures are enriched when approached with knowledge of profane learning.

3

The Revival of the Eleventh and Twelfth Centuries

The challenge of logic

Boethius' writings are the foundation on which a revival of logic took place in the eleventh century. As he had written, the verb 'to be' can either signify existence (as in 'Socrates is') or it can function as a link in a sentence (as in 'Socrates is a man' or 'this man is Socrates'). Questions arise when we ask in which circumstances the use of the verb 'to be', as in the case of 'x is y', posits an identity between x and y or proffers a definition. To say 'this man is Socrates' is to forge an identity; to say 'Socrates is a man' is to define him and to attach him to a class or group which includes other objects which are not identical with Socrates. To say 'Socrates is white'—to attach an adjective to a noun—is to qualify him and to indicate a quality in or about him. The grammarian Priscian had in fact defined noun as a word which indicates both substance and quality. Nouns are either individual or universal. An individual or proper noun can be readily understood to relate to an existing object, as when we say 'this man is Socrates'. But when we use general nouns like 'man' as in 'Socrates is a man' and 'man is an animal', it is more difficult to determine what is referred to and in what way the reference is made. To some, 'man' may seem a label of convenience we use to collect together a number of individuals possessing characteristics in common that distinguish them from other objects such as—say—horses. To others, in addition to particular men, 'man' may seem to be a nature which is universal to all men, a single object with its own existence. Some may arrive at an understanding which enables us to use and resort to the word 'man' from the presence of species and genera and of other forms in the world. Others may do so on the basis of the experience of observing some selected similarities between individual things.

Roscelin of Compiegne was one master who opted for an out-and-out nominalist viewpoint: the universal noun was just a word, indeed just a sound when spoken. For Roscelin, logic and syllogistic argument dealt not with reality but with language and with the putting of terms and arguments into a correct linguistic form, a science of discourse that is formal and that does not pretend to discover or prove facts about the real world. This emphasis on language, on terms and speech, brought logic and grammar close together. It was not an entirely new emphasis: commentaries on the *logica vetus* that are attributed to Heiric of Auxerre (d. *c.*876) show an emphasis on the role of the subject in attaching names such as genus or species to objects. Priscian in his *Institutiones grammaticae* had raised problems about the nature of nouns and verbs and adjectives that were close to the problems discussed in Boethius' commentaries on Aristotle's logical writings. Such problems included the use of the verb 'to be' and the question of what is referred to by a noun or an adjective. Boethius, likewise, had raised, although he did not pursue, the question whether the predicables are things (*res*) or are words (*voces*). But now, in the eleventh century, this question was taken up in vigorous debate.

The legitimacy of the study of logic seldom went without challenge for long at any period in the Middle Ages. Peter Damian (1007–72) was one of the most influential of those in the eleventh century who re-examined the relationship between Christian faith and profane culture. After starting a career as a teacher of grammar and dialectic, from about 1035 he lived the life of a hermit at Fonte Avellana and became a leading champion of the eremitical way of life and of the need to break away from all forms of worldly attachments. He also became a cardinal and vigorously championed church and especially papal reform. His treatise *On Giving Priority to Holy Simplicity over*

Vainglorious Learning addressed the question of the usefulness of literary and philosophical culture and levelled criticisms at the exaggerated value put upon the liberal arts. Damian himself was an accomplished grammarian and rhetorician, thoroughly versed in pagan culture. None the less, he insisted that God, in choosing simple fishermen to be his apostles, had no need of philosophers or orators: all true understanding comes from God as a reward for renunciation of the world. Damian did not particularly recognize in the order of nature a world of reality which was open for free and independent human enquiry with the aid of the trivium and quadrivium. The world of nature was the effect of the will of God and will not be understood by means of philosophy: reality is in the last analysis the will of God. In his treatise on *The Omnipotence of God* (1067) Damian forcefully expressed his view of the limitation of human reasoning.[1] Possibility and reality, as they appear to human understanding, are different from possibility and reality as they are in the perfection and eternity of God. Whereas human beings might say that omnipotence consists in doing whatever one may will to do, Damian saw in this a limitation on divine omnipotence, because divine omnipotence is not limited by will or by human ways of speaking about reality. Logic lacked scope when applied to theology. The key issue was the relationship between God's power and human freedom. Both Boethius (in his *Consolation of Philosophy*, bk. V) and Augustine had explored the question of the compatibility of divine providence and omnipotence with human free will. In part this compatibility rested upon the view that God was outside time; therefore the past, the present, and the future as they are understood by those who live in time are everpresent to God. So the question whether God can, for example, bring it about that what has happened did not happen or can alter the past, for example, by restoring virginity to a girl who has lost it or by undoing the foundation of the city of Rome—and such possibilities might be granted on the premiss that God is almighty—is dealt with by Damian, first by removing the dimension of time, and secondly by invoking God's justice. God can do what he wishes and there is nothing he cannot do;

but he only does what he wishes and what he wishes is what he judges to be just. So to say that God cannot do evil is not to deny his omnipotence but to affirm his goodness. Likewise for time past, present, and future: human beings might agree that what has happened is past or that what is happening now is happening now, and that there is no way of altering the fact. There is, in human terms, a necessity attaching to the past and also to the present whilst it is present, but Damian argues that this necessity lies in the statements we make. So to say 'if it happened, it cannot not have happened' or 'if it is, it is' and (about future events) 'if it is going to be, it is going to be' is not to say that 'God must necessarily do whatever happens and cannot not do it'. Rather it is to say that certain types of statements produce necessary consequences as statements. This necessity about statements is a necessity on the level of logic and language, not on the level of reality or of God. Clearly Damian is attempting to provide a better understanding about God, but he is also setting forth a trenchant view of the function of reason and logic: the art of dialectic deals with the way in which we make statements and arrange words so as to make sense for ourselves. Logic is a tool to be applied to language; it is not an indicator of realities beyond language. There are no theological implications to be drawn from the conclusions of the logicians. Logic and theology cannot be mingled any more than water and oil.

The controversy that developed from the mid-eleventh century over the doctrine of the eucharist, and especially over the reality of the presence of the Body and Blood of Christ in the form of bread and wine after their consecration during Mass, also provoked thought about the role of reason and dialectic, and about the Aristotelian categories. Berengar of Tours (c.1010–88) argued that Aristotle's doctrine of substance and accidents, available through the writings of Boethius, permitted a clearer explanation of the eucharist. When the priest pronounces the words of consecration he says—as Christ had said during the Last Supper, and with reference to the bread and wine about to be consumed by those present—'This is my Body' and 'This is my Blood'. But what is the status of the pronoun 'this'? If, as Berengar believed, it directly represented the bread and the wine, the reality of what is physically present, the substance of the bread and the wine would remain present.

Lanfranc (1005–89) defended the doctrine of the real presence of Christ's Body and Blood in the form of bread and wine against the criticisms of Berengar and with the aid of dialectic.[2] As he wrote in his *Commentary* on St Paul's Epistle to the Romans: 'dialectic is not an enemy of the mysteries of God, rather it confirms them if it is rightly used when the matter demands it'. Since Berengar had used dialectic to challenge the traditions and the accepted presentation of Christian doctrine, Lanfranc must also use it to refute him. Whereas Berengar thought that the accidents of bread and wine—e.g. their colour—could not survive a change of substance, Lanfranc argued that such accidental qualities could continue to exist after a new substance has replaced an original substance.

Anselm of Bec and Canterbury

The most famous of Lanfranc's pupils from 1060 at the abbey of Bec is Anselm (1033–109). Anselm, an Italian from Aosta, became a monk and later prior and abbot of Bec in Normandy before becoming archbishop of Canterbury in 1093 and Lanfranc's successor in this position. His writings arose from conversations and discussions in the monastic cloister as well as from prayer and reading.[3] They are principally concerned with the central doctrines of the Christian faith on which Anselm meditates but to which he also brings the tools of logic and grammar as well as an extremely sharp mind. Their inspiration is again and again the work of Augustine, like whom Anselm sought understanding of faith: 'I desire', Anselm wrote in his *Proslogion*—a work which is an address to God written at Bec around 1077–8—'I desire to understand in some measure thy truth, which my heart already believes. . . . And indeed I do believe it, for unless I believe, I shall not understand.' Anselm did not seek to prove what is believed in the sense of establishing its truth or credibility by the test of reason. He sought to explore his existing beliefs with the instrument of reason—and not with this alone for prayer was used as well—and with the aim of bringing out and elucidating the meaning, the implications, and also the truth and the plausibility of Scripture and of revealed truth. This means that the premisses to Anselm's arguments are provided by faith but the arguments proceed logically. 'I do not seek to understand in order to believe, but I believe in order that I might understand.'[4] So, in his *Monologion*—a soliloquy written in 1076—and in his *Proslogion* Anselm starts from the premiss that there is a God and then proceeds to demonstrate that God cannot not exist and what his attributes are, as well as to meditate upon this. The original title of Anselm's *Monologion* was: 'an example of meditation on the reason for faith' (*exemplum meditandi de ratione fidei*); the original title of the *Proslogion* was: 'faith seeking understanding' (*fides quaerens intellectum*). Anselm was also concerned with problems of language and with the concepts that Boethius had presented. In his *De grammatico* (*On the Grammarian*) he dealt with a series of paradoxes arising from the use of nouns and adjectives. For example, according to Priscian every noun indicates both a substance and a quality, but the Latin word *grammaticus* can be both a noun (grammarian) and an adjective (grammatical). An adjective (as in 'a grammatical man') can signify 'having skill in grammar' but it can also indicate or call a particular individual, i.e. this or that grammatical man. Anselm shows a recurrent interest in technical questions relating to logic and grammar in his other treatises; he was in this respect like other students of dialectic of his time. He considers the meaning of necessity in the course of considering the divine will and human freedom in the light of Boethius' own discussions. For example, to say that God will do what he wills to do is to impute some sort of necessity to God, whose will is, however, entirely unconstrained. But, when, in saying that 'God will do what he wills to do', we imply that 'this is a necessity', the sort of necessity that is here at issue is purely logical or conditional: the statement is true because the fact is correctly described and God will do it—the necessity lies in the statement only, not in any constraint upon the divine will.

Necessity is one of Anselm's favourite concepts, the necessity in particular that leads from one reasoning step in an argument to another (*necessitas rationis*, *rationes necessariae*), but also the necessity attaching to God's existence and the difference between this necessary being and the ways in which other contingent beings exist. Anselm's celebrated argument for the existence of God appears in chapters 2 and 3 of his *Proslogion*. He had earlier in his *Monologion* given four arguments in favour of the existence of God. They include the argument that there must exist a single nature which is the highest goodness and the highest greatness and the highest being since less than perfect goodness and less than absolute greatness and less than absolute being can be seen in the world, and likewise that there must be an absolute or ultimate single cause and an ultimate perfection beyond relative degrees of perfection. But Anselm wanted to go beyond these arguments, beyond showing what God is, to show that God exists necessarily, and to discover a single 'self-sufficient and all-sufficient' argument in favour of this. In the *Proslogion* he uses a definition of God which is: 'we believe that you are something than which nothing greater can be thought' (*credimus te esse aliquid, quo nihil maius cogitari possit*), and he argues that 'that than which nothing greater can be thought' necessarily also exists outside the thinker's mind. God cannot exist as a thought in the human mind alone because 'that than which nothing greater can be thought' exists in reality as well as in the mind. Anselm's definition was not new—it is found in Cicero, Seneca, Augustine, and Boethius—but his argument is, and Anselm was enthusiastically convinced that his argument was true; others from his day to ours have been divided in their reactions, and clearly no consensus has been found unless it be that the argument is extraordinarily stimulating. We should note especially the emphasis attached by Anselm to the greater degree of existence enjoyed by something which exists in reality and is not just a thought, and his confidence both that the greatest thing that can be thought must exist in reality and that 'the greatest thing' (God) can be grasped by human thought. Platonism underlines this view, for to the Platonist the most real things are ideas (the Forms) that exist and are more than mental constructions. Anselm certainly did not intend to mean that any concept in the mind must exist in reality. His earliest known critic, Gaunilo, who was a contemporary monk in northern France, questioned what was meant by 'that than which nothing greater can be thought'—what sort of a 'thing' it must be and what our mind makes of such a concept. Gaunilo proposed that, according to Anselm's argument, the most beautiful island imaginable in the middle of a remote and lost ocean must also exist outside the mind as well as in it because otherwise a more beautiful one could be conceived. But Anselm replied to this that such a perfection as is presented by the most beautiful island that can be thought did not have to exist outside the mind. Anselm admits that 'that than which *nothing* greater can be thought' is not a clear concept, but it is understandable. Moreover, it is necessary: 'that than which nothing greater can be thought' cannot even be thought not to exist because there must be something than which nothing greater can be thought. Gaunilo noted too that Anselm had proceeded to prove existence on the basis of only a definition. And he noticed a problem arising from the phrase 'exists in the mind'—for it is not God who exists in the human mind but an idea or an image of God. To this some have replied that to a deeply religious mind God is present, and what is intuitive in such a mind can be analysed and its existence understood rationally. But this is probably not what Anselm intended: he entered the argument on the basis of religious experience but wanted to find dialectical proof as well. Others have been persuaded by the way Anselm proceeds from a concept to proof of the object being outside the mind, because it is an external being which is the cause of the concept and an external being which is necessarily existent.

Peter Abelard

Peter Abelard (1079–142) first sprang to fame during the course
of his attacks on the realist positions of his teacher in Paris,
William of Champeaux. The controversy was over the nature of
the universals. As a controversy it sprang into new life with
Abelard, but few would deny, in changing conditions and contexts, its long life from the time of Plato to the end of the Middle
Ages, and then again into modern times. It may no longer tend
to be seen as the only principal issue in medieval philosophy,
and it was never exactly based on the same set of questions, but
the issues raised remain, none the less, central in the study of
philosophy in the Middle Ages.[5] Abelard gives an account of his
own disputes in his autobiography, the *History of My Troubles*.
Here he describes how in 1108 his teacher William moved from
the canonry he held in the cathedral of Notre Dame to the newly
founded abbey of Saint-Victor nearby on the left bank of the
River Seine:

This change in his way of life did not oblige him either to leave Paris or
to give up his study of philosophy, and he soon resumed his public
teaching in his usual manner in the very monastery to which he had
retired to follow the religious life. I returned to him to hear his lectures
on rhetoric, and in the course of our philosophical disputes I produced
a sequence of clear logical arguments to make him amend, or rather
abandon, his previous attitude to universals. He had maintained that in
the common existence of universals, the whole species was essentially
the same in each of its individuals, and among these there was no
essential difference, but only variety due to multiplicity of accidents.
Now he modified his view in order to say that it was the same not in
essence but through non-difference. This has always been the dialectician's chief problem concerning universals, so much so that even Porphyry did not venture to settle it when he dealt with universals in his
Isagoge, but only mentioned it as a 'very serious difficulty'. Con-
sequently, when William had modified or rather been forced to give up
his original position, his lectures fell into such contempt that he was
scarcely accepted on any other points of dialectic, as if the whole subject
rested solely on the question of universals.[6]

Abelard's writings on logic arose from the need to expound and comment upon seven basic textbooks: the *Isagoge* of Porphyry, the *Categories*, the *De Interpretatione* of Aristotle, and Boethius' works on the *Categorical Syllogism*, the *Hypothetical Syllogism*, *De differentiis topicis*, and *On Division*. Over many years he was to explore again and again the problems arising from these texts for the construction of arguments and propositions. The content of an argument, its matter or *res*, was of secondary concern to him as a logician. He referred the study of things to the domain of physics. He was concerned pre-eminently with the art of judging and finding valid and invalid arguments and propositions. Dialectic is the means of telling the difference between truth and falsehood. One may characterize Abelard's method, whatever the subject on which he reflected, as the practice of methodical doubt: 'he who inquires', he wrote in his *Dialectic*, 'expresses doubt in order to do pursue and obtain certainty'.[7] So his teaching of logic was very much concerned with the truth or falsehood of propositions and with establishing whether what is expressed by a proposition is in fact the case. Such study entails, on the one hand, the study of grammar and syntax as well as of the rules and forms of syllogisms, and, on the other hand, the study of Porphyry's five predicables (genus, species, difference, property, and accident), and of Aristotle's categories (substance and the nine accidents). Reasoning involves the formulation of inferences but it is also about things.

A basic element in language and in human communication is the word: words generate ideas (*intellectus*) in the mind of the listener or of the reader, and at the same time they refer to something (*res*). But, before a thing (*res*) can be expressed in language and given a name, there must first be some idea of what it is. The same goes for propositions: they deal with things (*res*) and they generate ideas (*intellectus*) about these things. So between language and reality there lies an idea—an understanding and a meaning. To produce meaning—significance—propositions must include a predicate; that is, there must be a subject–predicate relationship as in 'Socrates is a man'. However, when we say 'Socrates is a man', although the proposition is grammatically correct and although the proposition seems true, the function of the word 'is' leads Abelard into protracted enquiry. One theory—we may call it the identity theory—would lead to the view that the sentence indicates an identity of essence between the subject and the predicate; another theory, which we may call the inherence theory, is that 'man' stands for a universal nature which inheres in the individual 'Socrates' (as well as in other persons).

This brings us back to William of Champeaux and to the main issue in Abelard's dispute with him. Is the universal noun 'man' just a word or is there a universal nature or thing which is 'man'? In using the word 'man' as a predicate we invoke a species which includes any number of individual members that share common similarities, even though as individuals they are also divided by any number of differences. Socrates and all other individual men share undeniable resemblances (*convenientia*) in being men and in exhibiting a common state or nature. But what is this 'being man' and what is this 'nature'? Abelard denied that it is a thing (*res*), because a thing is always individual. But 'man' is not just a word because it is a name which indicates a state of likeness that the human mind has perceived from reflecting on the evidence presented to it. It is a name that has a basis in things. It names no thing yet it means something. Abelard called this something that is meant: 'a common and confused image of a large number of beings'.

By these steps Abelard undermined realist positions such as those he associated with William of Champeaux. In other words, he refuted efforts made by others to attach the word 'essence' or 'substance' to the likenesses between individuals in a species— that is, to species themselves or to genera. He believed that the view that a substance (e.g. man) exists in each and every man wholly and simultaneously is contradicted by physics: nothing can be wholly and simultaneously in more than one place. Another view of realism that was more immune and less vulnerable to this line of criticism was that the resemblances between individual men (or between the individual members of any species of being) may be defined negatively—that is, as the sum of the non-differences between different individuals. This appears to be the second position attributed to William of Champeaux in the passage quoted above from the *Historia calamitatum*. But this still meant that what men shared in common was the status of 'being man'. A universal noun designates 'a common form'. We conceive such a form when we use a universal noun. But what is a common form? The answer that Abelard gave is that it is not a thing nor is it a concept (*intellectus*) but it is a significa-tion. A name that signifies stands between reality and under-standing. A universal noun generates a concept but it is not itself a concept. This still left Abelard with the problem of the concept or *intellectus* that is generated by the production of a noun that has significance. And in the last analysis Abelard was fully pre-pared to say that, although the human mind may never know the true nature of things, in the mind of God states of nature, genera and species, are not confused.

Abelard's interest in exploring the relationship between real-ity, understanding, and language was not limited to the realm of formal logic. Although in matters of Christian belief dialectic was always held to be subordinate to divinely revealed truth, Abelard (like Lanfranc and Anselm) insisted that dialectic can play a role in evaluating objections to what has been revealed about God and to what is held by faith. In his *Theologia* he makes considerable effort to summarize and to refute objections that may be put to belief in God and the Trinity; he does this in the conviction that rational arguments can refute those who object to Christian faith on the basis, allegedly, of logic. For support Abelard turned to Augustine: dialectic, the opposite of sophistry, solves problems, including the problems presented by (or from) Scripture. In one of his letters, Abelard defends dia-lectic against criticism of its inappropriateness for use in matters of religious belief.[8] He does so by equating God with Truth and truth with what can be tested by a dialectician. The second Person of the Trinity (God the Son) is also the Word of God, in Greek the *Logos* which Abelard defines as the wisdom or the reason of God. The word *logica* is derived from the word *Logos*.

In Greek the wisdom of God—God the Father—is also called *sophia*. Philosophers are lovers of *sophia* (*philo:sophia*). A Christian philosopher is therefore a true philosopher, being a seeker after the wisdom of God.

In respect of theology—by which Abelard meant chiefly the study of God and the Trinity—he was constantly at pains to draw attention to the proper role and the limitations of language; words used of God are imperfect and lose their normal meaning. Language, when used of divine realities, undergoes an alteration (*translatio*) of meaning. God transcends the rules of Aristotelian logic. The most we can do is to draw terms from the realm of created being and to note resemblances between creatures and God. This we do when we speak of God as (for example) 'lord' or 'immense' or when we speak of the Trinity as three 'persons' or when we speak of God as 'Father'. Created things bear the traces of the image of their Creator, so some reference back from creatures to God makes a good starting-point for enquiry into God. But we have to remind ourselves that, when used of God, words that are normally used of creatures and the creation lose their customary meaning. We may *call* God a substance but Aristotle, Boethius, and Porphyry have taught that substance is susceptible of accidents, which God is not. Words which are used of creatures come to have a metaphoric and enigmatic meaning when applied to God, although there are limited similarities between the creator and creation.[9]

The relationship between three persons in one God provided Abelard with an opportunity to examine the nature of oneness and plurality, identity and difference, and the forms of propositions in which the names of persons and the divine essence are used as subjects and predicates. He argues that God is *essentially* identical but *numerically* plural in the divine persons, and that the Father, Son, and Spirit are one in essence but different in their properties. In 1140 many of Abelard's speculations were formally condemned by Pope Innocent II as heretical.

Abelard wrote two works which deal with moral philosophy.

One of these is the *Ethics* or, as he also called it, *Know Thyself*, after the celebrated oracle of Delphi; the other is the (so-called) *Dialogue of the Philosopher with the Jew and the Christian*—in reality two consecutive dialogues. As far as I am aware, no other work entitled *Ethics* was written in the Middle Ages before Abelard wrote his own.[10] Ethics was well known to be one of the branches of philosophy but it had no place as such in the actual teaching of philosophy in the schools of the twelfth century. The study of ethics was then—for practical purposes—part of the study of grammar and rhetoric—that is, part of the reason for reading the literary classics of ancient Rome. Ovid, Vergil, and Horace, among other Roman poets, provided much moral advice, and this was an important reason, along with their value as examples of good Latin style, that justified their place within schools attended by Christian monks and clerics.[11] Abelard himself greatly valued the moral ideals supported in Latin literature. But in his *Ethics* he provided an original and independent philosophical analysis of ethical terms and concepts, and thereby revealed, albeit implicitly, the lack of contemporary or recent philosophical enquiry into the assumptions that underlie moral judgement. He explored the relationship between human actions, intentions, and the moral law. It is easy to see in this a parallel with the way in which, in studying logic, he fastened upon the relationship between things, understanding, and language.

The thrust of Abelard's arguments in his *Ethics* is in the direction of demolishing the kind of speech which attributes goodness or wrongness to the sphere of deeds or events. For example, if we say that 'killing people is wrong', we not only make the mistake of including in the observation cases of killing in a just war and in self-defence, and cases of accidental killing and of judicial punishment, but we also make the mistake of associating the moral judgement with a purely physical event (*res*) instead of with a decision taken by an agent who, before proceeding to kill, consents in his mind to a course of action either for a good or for a bad reason—that is, either out of love of God or out of contempt for God. Sticking a sword into another human body may be done rightly or wrongly but the act itself is neither right nor wrong. When someone kills he is acting either well or badly, rightly or wrongly, but not doing something which is itself right or wrong, good or bad. The physical act from the moral point of view is indifferent, neither right nor wrong in itself. But the decision taken by its perpetrator, his intention and what he consents to, is either in accordance with God's law or it is not, and deserves respectively either praise or blame from God, because the decision he takes has to be judged (and only God can make this judgement certainly) in the light of other factors such as the degree of knowledge of the moral law possessed by him. Only the intention to conform to the will of God can win merit for man—and only a knowing consent to committing a deliberate contempt of God incurs guilt. What matters in morality is not what we do but why we do it. However, one of the reasons why Abelard was condemned for heresy in 1140 was that he chose to pursue his reasoning with the help of the provocative example of the crucifixion of Christ by men who, if they believed that they were fulfilling orders and doing their legal duty, did not, according to Abelard, act wrongly. In the view of Abelard's critics, who used plain words, doing wrong was wrongdoing, especially when murdering the Son of God.

Abelard's *Ethics* also put into circulation a philosophical definition of virtue derived from Boethius' *De differentiis topicis*: virtue is the habit of the well composed mind.[12] To Boethius habit (*habitus*) was one of the categories, and in later years in the twelfth century there developed a greater interest in the philosophical discussion of natural as distinct from theological or catholic virtue, the latter being supernatural virtue or a gift of God.

Abelard's other work of moral philosophy is the *Dialogue of the Philosopher with the Jew and the Christian*. The goal of the debates between these three figures is an understanding of the nature of the supreme good and the supreme evil. The work takes the form of a confrontation between spokesmen for the three main types of moral thought, one based on the natural law which men know through reason, the second based on the written law given by Moses to the Jews, and the third being the life according to grace that comes to Christians through Christ. Comparisons are made between the doctrines of good and evil that were advanced by the pagan philosophers of ancient Greece and Rome and those advanced by Christian writers, between doctrines which locate supreme goōdness and supreme evil in this life on earth and doctrines which locate them in a future life in the world to come. To an extent Abelard took up themes that had been explored more fully by Augustine of Hippo in his *City of God*. But the *Dialogue* also gives Abelard an occasion to pursue the resemblances between the teachings of the Prophets and the teachings of the Philosophers—a pursuit which is a familiar one in several of his other writings. The debate proceeds by means of eliminating inadequate notions of good and evil, such as those of virtue and vice, pleasure and misery, rewards and punishments. Eventually the Philosopher and the Christian agree that supreme happiness and supreme wretchedness for human beings have to be defined in terms of what gains for man his final reward—namely, supreme love of God or its opposite. As for the supreme good itself, all right philosophers agree that this is God;[13] supreme happiness for human beings consists of the vision of God. The Philosopher and the Christian find that there is a large measure of agreement on this in Christian thought and pagan philosophy: God has revealed himself both through the Bible and through nature and reason. Moreover, the Christian asks the Philosopher to define for him the virtues and the vices which are the ways to goodness or to evil. The Philosopher's elucidations are accepted by the Christian: virtue is, he says, the very best habit of mind and vice the worst; habits are not naturally situated in the mind but are acquired by deliberate effort.[14] We may say that someone is, for example, naturally chaste, but such chastity is in reality natural frigidity; only when a battle has been firmly and decisively won against concupiscence is there virtue and merit, and a habit which is difficult to remove. Likewise, to judge justly once does not make a person just nor does an isolated act of adultery make a person a confirmed adulterer. Virtue and vice require a lasting commitment of the mind and will to be properly virtue or vice. According to Socrates, virtue has four species: prudence, justice, fortitude, and temperance, although the Philosopher has some reservation over calling prudence a virtue, as it is the ability to distinguish between right and wrong, an ability that may as well be found in bad as in good people.[15] Justice may be divided into two types—natural and positive. Natural justice and natural law are naturally understood by all people through their reason, which persuades them to worship God, love their parents, and punish wrongdoers. Positive justice, on the other hand, consists of the rules created by people to ensure that justice is effectively promoted—by means of, for example, procedures for examining those suspected of wrongdoing, procedures that include in some societies trial by battle and the ordeal of hot iron, but in other societies trial on the basis of oaths and the discussion of the testimony of witnesses.[16] Abelard was not alone in his time in wishing to explore pagan teaching concerning virtue and vice; we find a similar enthusiasm in the writings of one of his admirers, John of Salisbury, especially in his *Policraticus*.[17] This activity, however, antedates knowledge in the West of Aristotle's *Nicomachean Ethics*, and its scope was limited by ignorance of this work, for Aristotle's own contributions include the doctrine of virtue as the mean between two extremes, criticism of the division of virtue into four cardinal virtues, and a distinction between moral and intellectual virtues. None the less, as Abelard's *Dialogus* and also his *Ethics* show, even without the help of Aristotle's *Nicomachean Ethics*, there were thinkers who were fully prepared to go beyond the practice of moralizing with the aid of examples taken from Roman literature and to absorb—not merely to survey—ancient ideas concerning natural, as distinct from theological, virtue.

Both in ethics and in theology Abelard liked to underline the convergences between ancient pagan philosophy and Christian teaching. He found that in antiquity the pagans had developed a notion of the natural law which led philosophers to lead good lives and to practise abstinence and continence, and he reproduced stories of some of these lives from Jerome's work *Against*

Jovinian and from Augustine's *City of God*. He noted that ancient philosophers had a knowledge of God and that much in Plato's *Timaeus* does, when carefully interpreted, even accord with the Christian doctrine of the Trinity. Ancient philosophers also arrived at a belief in the immortality of the soul and in eternal rewards and punishments. In his autobiography, the *History of My Troubles*, several pages are filled by a report of the arguments which Heloise put against Abelard's proposal to marry her. She was represented as having argued that marriage would be inconsistent with the pursuit of the life of a philosopher which, like that of a Christian monk, should consist in detachment from secular life for the sake of contemplation and study. And later in the same account the reader finds Abelard justifying his life in an isolated oratory with examples, also taken from Jerome's *Against Jovinian*, of ancient philosophers who had given up earthly comforts which impede thought about God. Socrates and Diogenes were numbered amongst these, but Abelard emphasized the universality of this instinct: the ideal of the wise man, the lover of wisdom, the philosopher, was shared by the Jewish Prophets, by the gentile Job, by John the Baptist, by the Essenes, by the Christian Desert Fathers, and by Christian monks. On a number of occasions in his works Abelard equates philosophy with love of Christ, who is the wisdom or *sophia* of God, and who was himself the true philosopher.

Gilbert of Poitiers

Peter Abelard commented in detail on Boethius' translations of Aristotle's logical books, but not on Boethius' *Opuscula sacra*, which he none the less knew well and used much. These five short treatises use logic to discuss questions of theology. There is much in them about the notion of, for example, person, nature, and substance, terms with an obvious relevance to discussion of God and the Trinity of three divine persons. And there is much too about form, matter, and being.

Gilbert of Poitiers (also known as Gilbert Porreta or de la

Porrée, 1085/90–1154), who taught in Paris and who was Chancellor of the cathedral of Chartres until 1137, is the most eminent of those who during the first half of the twelfth century studied the *Opuscula sacra* and offered close commentary upon them.[18] There is no longer any need to try to associate exclusively with the cathedral school at Chartres a number of celebrated commentators in Gilbert's time and earlier, including William of Conches and Thierry of Chartres.[19] Their writings were largely completed elsewhere, and 'demand for teaching in the Arts and Theology was rising to its flood' not at Chartres but at Paris.[20] None the less, those who did work at Chartres for some of their time included original thinkers. One of the cornerstones of Boethius' thought about being, and it is thoroughly Neoplatonist, is that what exists (*id quod est*) must share both being and whatever else is needed to make it what it is. Being itself comes from the Good which is the source of all being. There is a distinction to be made between *quod est* and *quo est*—between what is and that by which it is. This is in accordance with Priscian's definition of a noun as both a substance and a quality. Thus (for example) man is man by his humanity. Humanity in a man such as Socrates is different from humanity in another man such as Plato; the qualities of Plato and Socrates are partly similar and also partly dissimilar. The relationship between *quod est* and *quo est* is also a mathematical one, mathematics here meaning what Boethius called the study of the forms of bodies without matter. In reality, humanity is found only in man and not separately from him, but mathematically (in Boethius' sense) a distinction can be made between form and matter. Another word for *quo est* (e.g. humanity in the case of man) is subsistence (*subsistentia*) or what underlies man. Gilbert somewhat avoided the question of universals—the question, that is, whether subsistences exist and what they are. The concept of subsistence is a piece of mathematical speculation.

The abstract character of Gilbert's speculations is also to the fore when he passes from mathematical speculation to another branch of Boethian thought, theological speculation. Theological speculation is concerned with God, and also with the Ideas from which all beings come and the matter (which is primordial) in which they are created. The four elements of matter (fire, air, water, and earth) derive from Ideas. Primordial matter (*yle*) has no properties but exists. In speculating theologically upon the origin of things, Gilbert attempts to show that they derive from *yle* and from the Ideas of the elements. The only being which does not derive from another being is God. Whereas man is man by his humanity, God is not God by his divinity. Rather God is— full stop. God's being is the being of all other beings, not in the sense that all other beings are identical with God, but in the sense that without God they would not be there at all. Whereas mathematical speculation can surround created being, it cannot be applied to God, as no distinctions can be made of him, except in a formal way. And Gilbert did make a formal distinction in God between *quod est* and *quo est*, and he was able to write that in God is God by his divinity, but he also maintained that in God these two coincide. For this he was made to answer accusations of heresy at an ecclesiastical council held in Rheims in 1148 in the presence of Pope Eugenius III. He was not condemned, as Abelard had been, although he was no less fiercely criticized by Bernard, abbot of Clairvaux. When a few years later Peter Lombard wrote his *Four Books of Sentences*, he displayed the reverberations of these discussions: for Peter Lombard, who had attended the trial, even a technical distinction between *quod est* and *quo est* is not admissible in the case of God who is absolutely simple; whatever is in God is God and whatever God has is what God is.[21]

William of Conches

Cosmology and cosmogony—the study of (and speculation concerning), respectively, the physical structure and the origin of the universe—is a prominent and important aspect of medieval thought, one that owed much to Platonic theories and myth, to antique scientific reasonings, to astronomical lore and also to the book of Genesis. Among the most thorough investigators of this

physical branch of philosophy, in this still early period of medieval thought, must be numbered William of Conches (*c.*1085–
after 1154). A Norman by origin, William was a student of
Bernard, an influential master in the cathedral school of Chartres, in about the second decade of the twelfth century. Later
William became tutor to Henry, son of count Geoffrey of Anjou.
Henry, after Geoffrey annexed Normandy, also became king of
England in 1154. William's writings, which range over the period
from about 1120 to 1150, include glosses on Boethius' *Consolation of Philosophy*,[22] on Macrobius' *Commentary on the Dream
of Scipio*, and on Plato's *Timaeus.* (in the Latin translation of
Calcidius),[23] as well as two treatises, one on the *Philosophy of
the World* (*Philosophia mundi*)[24] and the other a revision of this
undertaken at Geoffrey's court, in the form of a dialogue between a philosopher and a duke, and under the title of
Dragmaticon or *Dialogue about Physical Substances* (1147–9).[25]
William may also be the author of the *Moralium dogma
philosophorum* or *Doctrines of the Moral Philosophers*, an an-
thology of quotations from ancient writers such as Cicero and
Seneca which illustrate ethical teachings in a manner which
reflects the Ciceronian distinction between what is honourable
and what is advantageous (*honestum/utile*), a manner which is
found also in other works of the time which are collectively
known as *florilegia*, or pluckings of flowers, the flowers being
edifying in their nature as well as literary.[26] In approaching the
Timaeus William was aware that he confronted a powerful interpretation of the formation of the world, and one that differed
markedly from the account given in Genesis. He studied the
theory of the elements contained in the *Timaeus* and attempted
to explain with its aid the formation of the stars and the emergence of animal life. All this William examines scientifically,
although William accounts for the creation of human souls by
reference directly to the creative work of God. William's account is not designed to counter the teaching of Genesis that
God made the world and all the living creatures that inhabit it.
Rather he shows how, with the aid of the natural forces which
God created, certain effects are the natural result of those

forces. For example, William explained that the account given in Genesis of the creation of Adam's body from the mud does not indicate God's work alone, because there were natural forces and causes created by God which enabled the human body to be formed from the four elements. Likewise with the creation of Eve, William does not believe that Scripture should be read as signifying literally that she was made from Adam's rib, but rather that the body of woman is not different from that of man nor the same. William enlarged the area of enquiry into how created nature works and into the reasons that regulate it. The cosmologists of the twelfth century, including William, did much to widen the scope of rational and scientific enquiry.

However, the *Timaeus* teems with problems of interpretation, especially concerning the concept of a universal or world soul. It was tempting to draw parallels between Plato's concept of the world soul and the Christian doctrine of the Holy Ghost who broods over the waters, the Comforter or Spirit who gives life and warmth to creation. William held back increasingly from emphasizing the parallels between the two, but he did believe that underlying Plato's actual text there was a deeper meaning which, while not identical with Christian teaching, enriched understanding of it. William was attacked by his contemporaries for what was felt to be a departure from Christian teaching on the Trinity, but he avoided an official condemnation, perhaps because he shifted his positions in his later works.

4

The Twelfth and Thirteenth Centuries: New Sources—New Problems

Translations

Until about the middle of the twelfth century only a limited amount of Aristotle's contributions to the study of logic was available. The books on which this 'old logic' (*logica vetus*) was based included Boethius' translations of Aristotle's *Categories* and *On Interpretation*. These were the only two of Aristotle's works that were yet available in a Latin translation. For the most part the *logica vetus*, as we have already seen, was supported by Boethius' own commentaries on these two texts, by his translation of Porphyry's *Introduction* (*Isagoge*), by his commentaries upon this work and upon Cicero's *Topics*, and by his own treatises on *Categorical Syllogisms*, *Hypothetical Syllogisms*, *Topical Differences*, and *Division*. From about the mid-twelfth century, however, four more books of Aristotle's corpus of logic (the *Organon*) made their first appearance in Latin translations: *Prior Analytics*, *Posterior Analytics*, *Topics*, and *Sophistical Refutations*. These became known as the *logica nova* or new logic. That this recovery was possible may have been due (in general terms) to the growth of activity, opportunity, and demand in the schools, such as those of Paris and elsewhere. A precise explanation of when and how these works became available has not so far been found, although we do know that, sometime before 1159, when John of Salisbury completed his *Metalogicon*, the *Posterior Analytics* was translated by James of Venice out of Greek.

The new sources were not limited to logic. Aristotle's

Nicomachean Ethics was first translated into Latin in the late twelfth century, although the translation covered only books two and three and evidence of their study is not available from before the early thirteenth century. In the early thirteenth century a new translation was made of these two books and also of book one,[1] and in 1215 the *Ethics* is listed among the books for study in the Paris Faculty of Arts.[2] A complete translation of the work appears to have been made in the early thirteenth century, possibly by Michael Scot.[3] An anonymous translation (known as the *Media*) was made of most of Aristotle's *Metaphysics*. In the thirteenth century William of Moerbeke—the most important of Aristotle's Latin translators[4]—partly revised this and partly made a new translation, including the first translation to be made of book K. A much copied translation was made of Aristotle's *Physics* in the first half of the twelfth century, perhaps by James of Venice and out of Greek. This too was to be revised by William of Moerbeke, *c.*1260–70, and was also frequently copied. Three translations were made of Aristotle's *On Generation and Corruption*, two in the twelfth century—one out of Arabic by Gerard of Cremona (d. 1187), the other (the *translatio vetus*) anonymously[5]—while a third (the *translatio nova*) was made out of Greek in the second half of the thirteenth century, probably by William of Moerbeke. Aristotle's *De anima* (*On the Soul*) was translated out of Greek before 1150 by James of Venice and revised by William of Moerbeke, perhaps before 1268. The translations mentioned so far were largely translations of Aristotle's work made out of Greek. Also important, however, are the translations of works which were (wrongly) supposed to be by Aristotle. Nearly 100 such pseudonymous works are known to have circulated in the Middle Ages, and, although most of them dealt with astrology and alchemy, they distorted Aristotle's philosophical profile.[6] One such work, the *Secretum secretorum*, which contained pseudo-scientific material derived from Arabic sources, survives in over 600 manuscripts, and was arguably more popular and more widely read during the Middle Ages than any genuine work of Aristotle.[7] Another, called *De pomo*, purports to describe the death of Aristotle in the manner of the *Phaedo* of Plato. This work originated in the Arab world in the tenth century and was first translated into Latin out of a Hebrew version in Sicily around 1255; it survives in more than 100 manuscripts. Also, around the year 1280 a work called *Economics*, which was thought to be by Aristotle, was translated into Latin and was henceforth studied and commented on alongside his *Ethics* and *Politics*.[8]

Muslim thinkers

The Muslim world stretched from the Middle East and beyond over North Africa and into Spain. Within it there had developed distinguished traditions of philosophical, religious, and scientific thought, but these had remained, until the twelfth century, almost completely inaccessible to Latin scholars in the West as well as to Greek scholars in the world of Byzantium.[9] From the eleventh century onwards, the growth in contacts between Christians and Muslims in the Mediterranean world—for example, through the Latin 'reconquest' of the Iberian Peninsula—underlies the increase in the number of translations from Arabic into Latin of the writings of many thinkers and scholars, Jews as well as Muslims, who lived in the Arab world. Arab philosophy–*Falsafa*—was largely inspired by Greece; its great names—al-Kindi (*c*.870), al-Farabi (d. 950), al-Ghazali,[10] Ibn Gabirol (known to Christians as Avicebron and as Avicebrol),[11] Avicenna (980–1037), and Averroes (1126–98)—were soon to become great names in the Latin West also, the last two of these especially so, and these thinkers knew far more about the thought and the writings of the ancient Greeks than any of their Latin contemporaries.[12] But the Arabs wrote and thought within the culture and civilization of Islam.

The range of thought of Avicenna or Ibn Sina was encyclopaedic. His *Shifa* (*Healing*) in particular offers a synthesis of the various disciplines of philosophy—logic, physics, and metaphysics—and was written *c*.1000.[13] Avicenna's interpretations of Aristotle's metaphysics were especially influential, including his reflections on the distinction between existence and essence, and between necessary being and contingent being. For Avicenna, essence does not explain existence: the essence of what may exist does not explain what does exist; existence requires some other explanation. Essence, moreover, is neither universal nor particular; it must be considered without regard to existence. Only one being is necessary; this has no essence, only existence, which is what is necessary about (and what characterizes) this being which is also a unity. Every other being is only possible being, not necessary, and it may or it may not exist. Such being is composite through having both essence and the factor that causes this essence to exist. Note that Avicenna transcends the distinction between substance and accidents and does not regard existence as an accident of substance. Among other main topics on which Avicenna's views were most often invoked and debated in the Latin West was Aristotle's doctrine of matter and form. All physical beings, acording to Aristotle, are constituted by matter which has form. All physical beings have bodily form, but Avicenna went on to argue that, in addition, they have other layers of form, such as (in the case of animals or men) animality or humanity. This became the basis of a debate in the thirteenth-century Latin West over the 'plurality of forms'. On God and intelligence Avicenna was largely Plotinian: from God comes the First Intelligence and from this descends a hierarchy of beings through the heavenly spheres. God therefore governs the universe through their mediation. Man therefore is under the influence of the spheres and not of God's personal providence. On epistemology Avicenna divided the human intellect into two aspects: a receptive aspect, by which it takes in sense impressions and remembers experiences, and an intuitive aspect, by which it grasps principles. But to achieve intellectual knowledge of universal forms the human mind also needs illumination. Human intellects are possible intellects; they may be enlightened by an active intellect which is external to them. This active or agent intellect is unique, single, and universal.

Averroes or Ibn Rushd (1126–98) may have been an even stronger influence on medieval Western thought than

Avicenna[14]. He was an exceptionally thorough commentator of the works of Aristotle, and when his commentaries were translated into Latin, they offered a very detailed guide to the interpretation of Aristotle's thought. The most important translator of Averroes' works—Michael Scot (d. *c.*1236), who translated Aristotelian works in Toledo from *c.*1215, and in Sicily, in the service of King Frederick II, from *c.*1227—translated Averroes' great commentaries on Aristotle's *De caelo*, *De anima*, *Metaphysics*, and *Physics*. On the *Nicomachean Ethics* Averroes wrote his Middle Commentary or Paraphrase in 1177. This was translated into Latin in Toledo in 1240 by Hermann the German and into Hebrew by Samuel of Marseilles. Among many contributions, Averroes' literal interpretations of Aristotle's *Physics* proved to be the starting-point for innumerable medieval debates about the nature of movement, the extra-mental reality of time and of number, and the definition of place.

The most influential single work translated out of Arabic was an anonymous *Liber de causis* or *Book of Causes*. The translation was made by Gerard of Cremona before 1187. It served to complete the discussion of the universe and of transcendent deity found in book Λ of Aristotle's *Metaphysics*. It presented a monotheistic view of God who is One and Infinite, pure Being and pure Goodness. But the *De causis* was also largely based on ideas found in the *Elements of Theology* by Proclus, who was a Platonist, as well as on a work called the *Theology of Aristotle*, which had been compiled by Arab authors in the ninth century. As a result, Platonist teachings circulated in the thirteenth century under the guise of Aristotelian authority. It was Thomas Aquinas who first recognized the Proclean foundation of the *Liber*, because he obtained a copy of the Latin translation of the *Elementatio theologica* made by William of Moerbeke in 1268. There were to be numerous commentaries made of it in various ways by, among others, Roger Bacon, Albert the Great, Aquinas, Siger of Brabant, and Giles of Rome. The *Liber de causis* was officially accepted into the curriculum of the Arts Faculty in Paris on 19 March 1255.[15] One of the principal contributions the *Liber de causis* provided to thirteenth-century

Western thinkers was the idea of the participation of all beings in the One, who is also called the first being (*ens primum*). This first being is the measure (*mensura*) of all other beings; they participate in the One but by degrees. Their powers and operations are more intense, and their goodness is greater, the closer they are to the source of perfections and the higher the grade which they occupy in the scale of beings. Moreover, the higher a being is, the less quantity it has (*quantitas*), while, conversely, the lower it is, the greater is its quantity. Higher beings receive more universal intelligible forms than lower ones.

From the mid-eleventh century and into the early thirteenth century translations were made into Latin of many other writings by Arabic and (to a lesser extent) Jewish scholars. The new translations slowly but surely found a largely willing readership in centres of scholarship throughout the Latin world for centuries to come. Broadly put, in the earlier part of this period opening in the eleventh century, translations of Arabic scientific works predominated; philosophical and religious texts become more prominent in and from the second half of the twelfth century. The translations of Arabic works of philosophy were largely undertaken in Spain, and among the most important were translations of sections of the great encyclopaedia, called the *Shifa*, of Avicenna, and then in the early thirteenth century came translations of the works of Averroes.

Translations of works of science enabled Latin thinkers both to improve their understanding of the natural world, and to develop a philosophy of nature.[16] Some medical writings were translated in the eleventh century by Constantine the African. Texts on the science of the stars came via Spain and Sicily between the second and the fifth decades of the twelfth century, and accompanied the works of such scholars as Adelard of Bath and Hermann of Carinthia. Adelard presented the science of the abacus, and also translated astronomical tables from Arabic, *c*.1126.[17] Works on mathematics, including algebra, appeared, as well as works on optics and alchemy. One consequence was that the old framework of the seven liberal arts no longer sufficed to keep together and in balance all the subjects that could now be studied in some detail. The seven arts retained their pre-eminent authority; Adelard of Bath, for example, wrote an introduction to them which he called *De eodem et diverso* (*On Identity and Difference*) and dedicated to a bishop in Sicily, William, bishop of Syracuse c.1112. But one of Adelard's contacts, Petrus Alphonsi, who also translated Arabic astronomical tables and who shared Adelard's particular interests, wrote to the 'Peripatetics and others nourished on philosophical milk everywhere in France' to say that, while the arts of grammar and logic are useful tools for understanding other subjects, the arts of the quadrivium are useful both in themselves and for the support they give to other subjects—for example, astronomy to medicine. The widening range of interest in science (in our sense of the word) is further illustrated by the activity of Hermann of Carinthia, who, in 1143, dedicated his translation of Ptolemy's *Planisphere* to Thierry of Chartres. Hermann's *De essentiis* (an account of cosmology inspired by Plato's *Timaeus*), was also complete in 1143.[18] Dominic Gundissalinus, another of the translators of the twelfth century, provided a new *Division of Philosophy* in which the quadrivium was replaced by an enlarged list of sciences, including not only (and as before) arithmetic, geometry, music, and astronomy, but also perspective, astrology, the science of weights, and the science of technical processes. The old quadrivium was based on the study of numbers; it was never wholly abstract, but the newly available knowledge concerning the movements of stars and planets and concerning medicine and mechanics encouraged an interest in natural science and practical knowledge.

In respect of astronomy, Ptolemy's universe now became better known: a universe of which the centre was the spherical (not flat) Earth, surrounded by a series of seven globes or spheres, in each of which is fixed a luminous body, the nearest being the Moon, the furthest Saturn. Beyond Saturn's sphere lies the *Stellatum* which contains the stars; and beyond this is a further sphere called the *Primum Mobile* or First Movable. But beyond this? Aristotle's answer to this question in *De caelo* (279[a]) was: 'Outside the heaven there is neither place nor void nor time.'

Christian writers such as the poet Dante answered: pure intellectual light from which descends the power to cause the *Primum
Mobile* to rotate and for the *Primum Mobile* to cause the
Stellatum to rotate, and then for this to cause the Spheres themselves to rotate. How movement was itself caused was another
question. In the *Metaphysics* Aristotle presents an utterly un-
moving Mover who moves by love (1072^b)—that is, as an object
of desire moves those who desire it. The *Primum Mobile*, and
the rest of the universe moved by it, is moved by its love for God.
This implies that each sphere is a conscious being moved by love
of God, there being an Intelligence in each sphere, as there is a
soul in each living body. The planets themselves are animate
bodies. There was dissension on this point: Christian thinkers
did not readily accept that there were souls in the heavenly
spheres.

Unlike many of the works of science, the works of philosophy
did not enter a pure vacuum, since the Arabs themselves, like
their Latin Christian counterparts, owed much (and much more)
to the intellectual achievements of the ancient Greeks. But Arabic thought had to be fitted into Western traditions. There were
implications for vocabulary. To a large extent the vocabulary of
thought in the earlier Middle Ages in the West had been provided in the writings of Augustine and Boethius, and it was a
Latin vocabulary. Translators from the Arabic were faced with
Arabic terms and concepts which had also been derived largely
from Greek philosophy, but had been juxtaposed with terms and
concepts used in Muslim theology. Sometimes, translators were
faced by a whole variety of Arabic terms for which no such
equivalent multiplicity existed in Latin. Dominic Gundissalinus
when translating Avicenna's *Metaphysics* (*De metaphysica*) used
the Latin word *esse* (being) to translate thirty-four different
Arabic expressions which between them gave a wide variety of
nuances of 'being'.

In the particular case of the study of the intellect there was
much to be found in Arabic texts that was hitherto unknown.
One of the foremost problems presented was the question of
what it is that makes us think: either a higher power external to

us—that is, an agent intellect (*intelligentia agens*) which might be God or an angel and which might also have the power to move the spheres in the universe—or a power within us, an internal human intellect (*intellectus*), or some combination of the two. The problem is found already in the writings of Aristotle, especially Aristotle's *De anima*.[19] On the one hand, the mind of man is his greatest possession and activity (*nus*). On the other hand, the higher animals resemble man in also having a soul or an internal vital source of life (*psyche*). Yet man differs from animals in possessing reason and intelligence. The soul is, along with the body, a component of both man and animals, and the soul has the role of guiding and coordinating the faculties of the living being whether man or animal. Such a soul does not survive the death of its subject. But the mind (*nus*) of man, which distinguishes him from the animals, is wholly spiritual and immaterial, being the intellective and reasoning faculty. It receives concepts and expresses them as definitions rather like the bodily organs receive sense impressions, except that the action of understanding includes both a receptive aspect and an active or abstractive one. The active side of the intellect is the agent intellect. This intellect is pure intellect and can survive separation from the body. It is a substance, but its relationship to the soul or *psyche* was not made altogether clear nor was its relationship to the receptive intellect. In book 3 of *De anima* Aristotle says of the intellect that it is 'that with which the soul knows and thinks' and, being 'immortal and eternal' (430^a17–23), 'separate'. With this problem later interpreters of Aristotle were to wrestle.

As we have seen, Avicenna held that the agent or active intellect was unique and universal. It was an external substance or power which acted upon the human soul. Augustine had written of a divine light which lit up the human mind and enabled it to rise to a higher kind of knowledge. Avicenna's teaching offered tempting attractions to a follower of Augustine, for Avicenna presented the intellect as a separate substance which transmitted the intellectual light of forms to the human soul.

Arab debates over Aristotle's *De anima* had their roots in divisions between Aristotle's commentators in late antiquity. Alexander of Aphrodisias (*fl. c.*200), whose own *De anima* became well known in the Middle Ages, interpreted Aristotle's teaching in such a way that the soul of a human being, the form of his body, is mortal and his mind is material and purely receptive. Mind only becomes activated when struck by light from the agent intellect and it then becomes capable of understanding. So the agent intellect is an external mind and is itself divinity. There was a second view, however, that of Themistius (*c.*317–*c.*388), who held that the material mind was a correlative of the active intellect, and both are within the soul and both survive bodily death.[20] Among the Arabs it was Alexander's view which was predominant, although not without considerable adaptation. Al-Kindi did not identify the agent intellect with God but with a separate non-divine external intelligence which acted singly upon all human beings. Al-Farabi placed the external agent intellect at the bottom of a hierarchy of intelligences which radiate upon the material world and enable the receptive intellect to know the intelligible forms of material things. Avicenna allowed that the soul is an intellect or a reasoning faculty which can acquire knowledge, but to acquire the highest kind of knowledge—which is knowledge of pure form abstracted from individual things—it needs to receive light from the separate agent intellect. Averroes, on the other hand, saw the human soul as a purely sensitive form of the body, united with it in life and disappearing at death. The intellective soul, which is immortal, is external to the human being, an active intellect which enters into contact with human souls when it successfully makes them receptive of intelligible truth, just as physical objects are lit up when the sun's rays strike them. When the Arabs first made an impression in the Latin world, it was Avicenna who held the field: the agent intellect accompanies or replaces Augustine's teaching on divine illumination. But when Averroes became known, problems appeared because he destroyed the individual human intelligence and replaced it by a single common intellect, one and the same for all human beings, and separate.

Arab discussions of separated intelligences or separated sub-stances also drove Latin thinkers to review their ideas about angels. Christian tradition had upheld their existence and their intermediate position between God and human beings, and the writings of Denis the pseudo-Areopagite had provided a deep and elaborate understanding of their ranks and of their spiritual functions. Anselm of Canterbury had examined concepts of just-ice and will by reference to the angels. But the Arabs brought a wider tradition of thought about knowledge and understanding among created but non-corporeal, intellectual substances. This could be broadened into a noetic applicable to created intelli-gences generally. There was, however, some caution in the Latin West about this. As Aquinas wrote, we can develop views about a separated immaterial intellect only on the basis of our experi-ence of thinking as human beings.[21]

Jewish thinkers

Jewish works written in Islam, and in Arabic, were also sought out by Latin translators.[22] Jewish thinkers living among Muslims followed the development of Muslim thought and writing, and were also, like the Arabs, the beneficiaries of the legacy of both classical and Jewish antiquity. From the twelfth century onwards those Jewish scholars who lived in 'reconquered' Spain particip-ated more easily in the intellectual life of the Latin West. There were many interests and aims that were common to medieval Jewish as well as Muslim and Christian thinkers, including the concern to relate the Bible to philosophy. From the thirteenth century onwards there were tensions between Jewish philo-sophers and Jewish kabbalists, the kabbal being a tradition of Jewish mystical thought about God and the world which was opposed to philosophy.[23] Whereas philosophers investigated the world and found in metaphysics the summit of knowledge, the kabbalists turned to contemplation of the hidden, unknowable God and the study of his chosen people of Israel. Philosophers were the inheritors of Greek learning (as in Islam), the kabba-lists were the heirs of the Prophets.

Very few of the many thirteenth- and fourteenth-century Jewish commentaries on the works of Aristotle have been printed; many discoveries remain to be made, and the study of Jewish medieval thought still needs to be brought closer to the study of Western Christian thought. The best-known medieval Jewish thinker was (and remains) Moses Maimonides (1135–204) of whom Colette Sirat has observed:

The whole history of Jewish medieval thought revolves about the personality of Maimonides; with him one period comes to an end and another begins; he is its term of reference as Thomas Aquinas is for scholasticism, and it is no accident but rather the mark of a profound affinity that the latter so often cites Rabbi Moses. Both followers of Aristotle, each constructed a *summa* of religion and philosophy, a summation constantly opposed, but still remaining a source of inspiration for the faithful of the two religions.[24]

Born in Cordoba in 1135, his family moved to Fez in 1160, then to Acre, and finally to Egypt. Maimonides himself become famous throughout the Jewish world, above all as a writer on law. His most popular work is his *Mishneh Torah*, which is an account of the Jewish legal code in which Maimonides lays especial emphasis on the worship of God, the search for perfection and the life of the world to come.[25] Maimonides is anything but dry or simple: he unravels the Story of the Chariot—which is an allusion to the visions of the prophets Isaiah (ch. 6), Ezekiel (ch. 1), and Zechariah (ch. 3) of the heavens and the divine throne—as an account of metaphysics; and he presents the Story of Creation—as provided in the beginning of the Book of Genesis—as an account of physics. For these the study of the divine law is a preparation. His *Guide of the Perplexed* is a work of philosophy but one that is set within the context of the Old Testament and of the study of Prophecy and of the Talmud (the Jewish oral law). In the work Maimonides expresses his fidelity to Aristotle—'the summit of human intelligence'—and also, among Arab philosophers, his admiration for Averroes. He was esoteric in the sense that he believed that it is given to only a few men to understand truth, on account of its subtlety and of the learning required to reach it. For most people truth is difficult, dangerous, and liable to result in doubt, largely because there is much in the Bible and the Talmud that should not be interpreted in a literal sense, as it is divine allegory. Only those with philosophical aptitude can discover the secrets of true knowledge of the Law. In particular, in book one Maimonides entered into debate on the attributes of God. Since God is one, how (Maimonides asked) can he have the attributes which are mentioned in the Bible—attributes such as intelligence, existence, goodness, wisdom, justice, mercy, and power? If a distinction is drawn between God and his attributes, God ceases to be one. Maimonides' answer consists in a reformulation of these attributes so as to convert what seems a positive affirmation into a negative one. Thus, to call God wise means: God is not foolish *and* being 'not foolish' means that God does not have the attribute of being foolish. In this way we can say that attributes are not truly predicable of God. But to know this is to know that we do not know what God is. Maimonides acknowledged that there are practical benefits to be gained from describing God with the aid of anthropomorphic terms such as justice and mercy; these help ordinary people to know and to obey God. Such terms when predicated of God lack the sense they have when predicated of creatures—but perhaps not completely, for there are both similarities and dissimilarities between God and creatures. Provided that we recognize that terms predicated of the creator do not have the same meaning as they do when they are predicated of creatures, there is a legitimate role for their use.[26] There lay ahead in the Latin West a considerable debate over the names of God. At least one Western thinker—Nicholas of Cusa—was to acknowledge his indebtedness to Maimonides in reflecting on what were known as the two ways—the affirmative way and the negative. Maimonides' work in this respect complements that of Denis the pseudo-Areopagite.

5

The Thirteenth Century: Until 1277

The assimilation of new knowledge

The growing flood of translations of Arabic and Jewish works marks a watershed in the history of medieval speculation and learning. It splits the history of medieval thought into two periods, with the break coming most dramatically in the early thirteenth century. We now move away from a period of thought nurtured by what will seem a very narrow range of sources and enter into a period of increased activity and turbulence created by an explosion of knowledge. A far wider range of ancient Greek thought was now available, and the range continued to grow, but no less important than this was the arrival of Arabic and Jewish work that was largely based upon that of the Greeks. Henceforward the study of translations of works of Plato, Aristotle, and others was associated with the commentaries on them written by or available to Arabic scholars. Finally, we need to underline the substantial growth of study and writing in the new universities in the Latin West in the thirteenth century.

One of the earliest Latin writers to try to wrestle with the influx of new ideas about intelligence was John Blund, who died in 1248 and who had written earlier a *Treatise on the Soul* in which Avicenna's own *De anima* was much invoked.[1] Avicenna's work presents the Intelligences as separate substances that produce and move the heavens. Souls enter or are infused into bodies by the 'First Giver of forms'. Blund equates this with God and represents God as the imprinter in the soul of the formal intellect. However, Blund notes that the texts he is faced with ascribe this activity to an Intelligence acting under the guidance of the 'First Giver of forms' or to an angel who is at the service of the human soul. Thus, man's rational soul is in communication with the angels and other Intelligences.

David of Dinant (d. *c*.1214), is another key figure in interpreting and translating the new Aristotle. He lectured upon Aristotle's writings in Paris, and in particular, in his *Tractatus naturalis*, he tackled the problems of the soul and the mind in the light of Aristotle's teaching. He asked the question whether any part of the soul is separable from the body, and what is the relationship between mind, matter, and God. As he writes in the *Tractatus naturalis*, there are three things in the soul: knowledge, intellect, and will. Each of these is passible—that is, receptive or on the receiving end of things. Passible knowledge comes from the bodily senses. Passible intellect is the imagination which is formed from a prior sense of perception. Passible will is desire or affection which arises in the heart. All these three things occur in the body and only in it. But is there anything in the soul which is separable from the body? Yes, there is a mind which is impassible. The mind also consists of knowledge, intellect, and will, but in the mind these three are impassible. However, there is only one mind, not as many minds as there are souls, just as there is only one matter and yet many bodies. Are mind and matter identical? Do they form one single entity? Yes, because mind is God and the world of matter is what comes forth from God. The form that comes to matter is God making himself perceptible—by converting into quantity, motion, corporeality, etc. So there is only one substance of all bodies and all souls and this is God, the substance being the matter of bodies as well as the mind of souls. David's teaching was formally condemned in Paris in 1210.

In general, the early progress of the reception of the recently translated materials by Latin scholars was rather slow.[2] There was, in particular, opposition to the arrival in Paris of the writings of Aristotle on natural philosophy. Lecturing upon these texts within the University of Paris was banned by an ecclesiastical synod there in 1210; their possession was prohibited and copies were to be burnt. But although the assimilation of the new Aristotle and of other new material was a long-drawn-out process, it was to be completed in the thirteenth century. The prohibition in Paris, which was not binding elsewhere, was supplanted in 1255 by the requirement that all Aristotle's works— on logic, natural philosophy, metaphysics, and ethics—should be taught in the Faculty of Arts within a programme of study lasting—for the student—six years.[3]

The new Aristotelian learning was brought into works of philosophy and theology, although in varying degrees, in the course of the first half of the thirteenth century, especially in the newly founded universities such as those of Paris and Oxford.[4] This was the work of the (also) newly founded Orders of Dominican and Franciscan friars no less than of their established counterparts among the secular clergy. Among the Dominicans in Paris these masters included Roland of Cremona (1229–36) and Hugh of St Cher (1230–5); among the Franciscans there were also Alexander of Hales (d. 1245),[5] John of La Rochelle (1238–45), and Odo Rigaud (1245–8). In Oxford there were the Dominican Richard Fishacre and the Franciscans Thomas of York and Richard Rufus of Cornwall (d. after 1259).[6] Richard Rufus appears to be the first in the period to have commented on Aristotle's *Physics*.[7] An important figure among the secular masters in the newly founded University of Paris who made extensive use of the newly available Aristotelian material as well as of the writings of Avicenna was William of Auvergne, who was bishop of Paris from 1228 and who died in 1249. He, like Avicenna, wrote on an encyclopaedic scale and produced a vast study of *The Universe* (*De universo*).[8] He dissented from Avicenna's doctrines of the eternity of the world, of the separate active intelligence, and of determinism. In place of the agent intellect, William returns to Augustine's teaching on the illumination of the soul by God, who acts (so to say) as a mirror in which the human mind can see the ideas of things. William is evidence of the rich 'cocktail' of ideas that faced scholars who confronted the new Arabic and Jewish material and tried to find their way through Aristotle and Augustine as well.

Logic

One benefit gained from the new material for the study of logic was the study of fallacy, which is laid out in Aristotle's *Sophistical Refutations*.[9] The study of fallacies or sophisms—puzzles—now developed, and scholars have shown that medieval logicians after the time of Abelard, but even before the assimilation of the new material, were developing freshly independent interests. This observation also holds true for the period which opens with the arrival of the *logica nova*. Professor L. M. de Rijk has shown, through many editions of texts and published papers, that, although much activity still remains invisible to modern scholarship, the *logica modernorum*—which had such a pervasive influence on medieval thought from the thirteenth century onwards—was brought into being in the twelfth century—say, between *c.*1130 and *c.*1220—especially in Paris but after Abelard. In part this arose from a concentration on the study of fallacies; in part the roots also lie in the study of grammatical theory, which fed into theory of language. The latter study, of grammar, focused upon the study of supposition (*sub-positio*) of terms, including the study of appellation and copulation, as well as the study of the properties of terms and their link with signification.[10] One of the first men who can both be named and be seen to make a powerful contribution to the study of the *logica nova* is William of Sherwood, an Englishman from Nottinghamshire who was probably born before 1210 and who had a great influence in mid-century on other logicians, often called the summulists, and including Peter of Spain and Lambert of Auxerre, who both taught, like William himself, in Paris. By 1252, however, William had moved to Oxford; he subsequently became treasurer of Lincoln cathedral. Peter of Spain (1210/20–77; Pope John XXI 1276–7) produced a textbook that remained in use for centuries, but his work (the *Summulae logicales*[11]) owes much to the work of William of Sherwood. William's *Introduction to Logic*, by contrast, survives in only one manuscript, and his *Syncategoremata* did little better by surviving in two.[12] Syncategoremata are, as William explains, consignificative words which are determinations of a subject. Examples which he studies include: all, none, each, only, necessarily, neither, besides, and not. All these words have a special effect on the subject to which they may be attached, and William seems to mark the opening of a period in which an enormous investment of effort was put into the study of these small but important parts of language. William's *Introduction to Logic* is important because it covers both the old and the new logic and represents the first successful attempt to assimilate and to synthesize both. It has six parts: Propositions (based on *On Interpretation*), Predicables (based on the *Categories*), Syllogisms (based on the *Prior Analytics*), Dialectical Topics (*Topics*), Properties of Terms, and Fallacies (*Sophistical Refutations*). It is possible that, in the part on syllogism, William invented mnemonic verses which summarize the moods and figures of syllogisms and which were to be used by learners and those who taught them for centuries to come; and even if William did not invent them, he made them popular, at least through Peter of Spain. Syllogisms can be arranged in differing ways called figures, and the figures can combine or conjugate terms and propositions in what are called moods. For example, in the first figure the first mood consists of two universal affirmatives leading to a universal affirmative conclusion (every man is an animal, and every animal is mortal, so every man is mortal), and the second mood consists of a universal negative major premiss and a universal affirmative minor premiss leading to a universal negative conclusion (no animal is a stone, every man is an animal, therefore no man is a stone). The verses came about by giving each type of proposition a letter—*a* for a universal affirmative proposition, *e* for a universal negative, *i* for a particular affirmative, *o* for a particular negative, and so on:

> *Barbara celarent darii ferio baralipton*
> *Celantes dabitis fapesmo frisesomorum*
> *Cesare camestres festino baroco*
> *Darapti felapton disamis datisi bocardo ferison.*[13]

In the vowels in the first word of the first line—*barbara*—the first mood of the first figure is recorded, in the second word—*celarent*—the second mood, and so on.

The most original part of the *Introduction* is the fifth (on the Properties of Terms), where William considers the subtleties of the meaning of terms in often quite ordinary contexts unexplored by Aristotle. He presents four properties: signification, supposition, copulation, and appellation. Most attention is given to making divisions in supposition and in appellation. Supposition (*sub-positio*) is the placing of one understanding under another—for example, when we say: man is (under) a species. William analyses the various ways in which a word may supposit for another and the various kinds of descent that can be traced. At one point he distinguishes three modes of simple supposition using three examples. 'Man is a species': in this first mode—manerial supposition—man supposits for his specific characteristic, the *maneries* of the species. 'Man is the noblest of creatures': in this second mode the predicate is not abstract but refers to all the admirable things which belong to the species. 'Pepper is sold here and in Rome': this third mode is unlike the first because the species itself is not sold and unlike the second because pepper does not mean everything that belongs to the species. Instead pepper here relates in a loose, unfixed way to the things that belong to it, not a particular consignment of pepper, but simply pepper.[14] He goes on to explore whether statements such as 'this plant grows here and in my garden' can be true. William defines appellation as being in a term in so far as it is predicable of the things subordinate to it. A term appellates when it serves as a predicate (e.g. 'man' in the statement 'Socrates is a man'); it supposits when it serves as a subject (e.g. 'man is an animal'). He formulates rules for appellation. For example, if only two men exist (these are *appellata*), and not three, there are insufficient *appellata* to say with truth that 'every man exists'.[15] In William's own century the study of the properties of terms (subjects and predicates) as well as the study of the syncategoremata (other kinds of terms) became known as modern logic (*logica moderna*) and all other logic, both *nova* and *vetus*, came to be classed together as ancient logic (*logica antiqua*). The moderns—*moderni*—were also called *terministae* because of interest in terms.[16]

The thirteenth-century summulists, led by William of Sherwood, did not develop much interest in Aristotle's *Posterior Analytics*. In this work Aristotle explored the idea of scientific knowledge and of scientific demonstration, and the task of exploring it for the first time in an influential way was taken up, as we shall see shortly, by an Englishman with an interest in the empirical sciences—namely, Robert Grosseteste.[17]

Metaphysics

Aristotle's *Metaphysics* gained a new lease of life in the thirteenth-century Latin West. Readers of the *Categories* in previous centuries had studied Aristotle's doctrine of substance and accidents. Now they received a full science of being, one moreover that was now escorted by Avicenna's idea of what the primary intelligibles are. Avicenna called them: things, being, and what is necessary (*res, ens, necesse*).[18] Other escorts for Aristotle's *Metaphysics*, on its entry into the Latin West, included Averroes' commentary, the *Liber de causis*, the writings of Denis the pseudo-Areopagite and of Boethius, and also, in the second half of the thirteenth century, the newly translated *Elements of Theology* by Proclus. One of the most important issues that was debated was that of the nature of the dependence upon God of every creature which participates in being and in goodness. A theological current flowed into a philosophical one. It came, via Augustine, from the Bible, and especially from the definition God gives of Himself in Exodus 3:14: 'I am who am.' With Greek metaphysics brought alongside the Bible, many efforts were to be made to explore Being as the source of contingent things.

What was looked for by many was a fundamental philosophical concept which expresses the universal features of being and which went beyond the categories. What was developed was a notion of *transcendentia*, or transcendentals which surround all the categories.[19] There is one determinate category—being—but this has concomitants: one, true, good. Aristotle in his *Metaphysics* book Γ, ch. 2 (1003^b) had acknowledged the convertibility of being and one: being is one and one is being (and to this one adds the notion that it is indivisible). However, the *Metaphysics* does not develop a doctrine of transcendentals. The first Latin thinker to do so in an influential way is Philip the Chancellor in his *Summa de bono* (*c.*1225–8).[20] He set out his idea of the *communissima*—the realities that are the most common to all being: one, true, and good. Alexander of Hales, Bonaventure, and Albert the Great were all influenced by this, as was Aquinas when he came to write *De veritate* (q. 1, art. 1).

A further influence on the development of this original theory in the thirteenth century was the growth of interest in Denis's treatise on *The Divine Names* which attracted commentators such as Albert and Aquinas. Here the names affirmed of God are similar ones to those discussed by the metaphysicians— goodness (ch. 4) and being (ch. 5), for example, as well as other names such as love, life, and wisdom. These names of the transcendent God belong also to all other beings; in fact they are the names of being, of what being is, and they transcend the categorical types of being such as accidents.

From an Aristotelian viewpoint the first of the *transcendentia* must be being; other *transcendentia* can then be presented as types of being—Alexander of Hales called them *determinationes*, Bonaventure *condiciones*, Albert *modi essendi*. But not everyone in the thirteenth century or later was content to place being in the centre of the *transcendentia* or in first place. Ulrich of Strassburg, for example, in his *De summo bono*,[21] put goodness first and then included light, beauty, and love.[22] In addition to debates over the ordering of the *transcendentia* there were variations between thinkers over their extent. Aquinas, for example included both thing and something (*res* and *aliquid*) among them.[23]

Psychology

In Aristotle's *De anima* was found a rational account of the soul as the essential principle of any living thing and as the formal principle determining a living thing to be the kind of thing that it is. For Aristotle every formal principle required its correlative material principle, which in the case of a living being is its body. Put in other terms, the soul must be the quiddity of something— namely, the body. Many, particularly Dominican, thinkers in the thirteenth century saw the soul standing in relation to the body in the same way as form to matter.[24] Aristotle's teaching is that the soul is the 'first entelechy' or perfection of the body. Another tradition, the Neoplatonic, held that the soul was the active principle in man and intimately united with his passive body. The soul exists as a separate immaterial substance created directly by God even when it is united with the body. All man's faculties or functions are only accidents of the substantial soul. Throughout the thirteenth century thinkers disputed the distinction between the soul and its faculties, the plurality of souls in man, the active and passive intellect, free will, intellectual and moral virtue, good and evil within the soul, and whether there existed an active faculty of sensation within the soul.

Aristotle had characterized the soul's faculty of sensation as the perception through the five senses of the body of the qualities of objects. The qualities include size, shape, number, colour, and motion, and they are perceived through the senses of touch, taste, smell, hearing, and sight. But, in addition to perceiving these sensibles, the soul apprehends the substance in which such qualities inhere. In other words, the sensation is not just of the whiteness, movement, or coldness of the particular object—for example, a snowball—but of whiteness, movement, or coldness.[25] Sensation of these objects was elicited by the presence of their sensible forms in the sensitive soul stimulating the ensouled body into an immediate interaction with the sensible forms. So the soul was passive in the act of sensation. However, in Averroes' commentaries on the *De anima* there was an interpretation of Aristotle that seemed to support the position that the soul was active in the process of sensation. Averroes argued that there had to be a moving principle in the soul's faculty of sensation which brought immaterial, sensible forms into act.

So, in the thirteenth century the problem of the metaphysical structure of the human being was situated in the context of the body/soul distinction, of debate over the intellective and sensible functions of the soul, and of debate over the question of forms, in particular the question whether there is one substantial form in man or a plurality of forms. Man is a union of body and soul, and the latter is the vital principle, the natural principle of human activity, both intellectual and physical or sensible. That a distinction may be drawn between human intellectual activity and human sensible activity caused no difficulty. The problem was whether this distinction required the soul itself to be divided into more than one substantial form—such as an intellective or reasoning soul and a sensible or vegetable soul—or required the soul to be regarded as a single substance having different functions or activities. An example may highlight the problem: when we are tired our body may tell us to sink into a comfortable chair, yet at the same time our brain may tell us that we ought to continue to read and write until a task is done. In other words, two vital principles are making calls upon ourselves, one sensible, the other intellective, and both require the human body for their activity in this mortal life. The question was put, therefore, whether the variety of activities of the soul was to be explained in terms of the soul having a variety of substantial forms, or whether one substantial form could account for the various sorts of activities. On the whole, theologians, among them Aquinas and his followers, tended to say that the soul is a unique substance and form, and cannot consist of a plurality of substantial forms; the soul, none the less, has a number of powers. Masters in the faculties of arts, on the other hand, found little difficulty in admitting within the soul a plurality of forms (or substances or essences), some higher and some lower. Franciscan theologians also, unlike Aquinas, supported the plurality of forms in the soul. Linked to this was the question of how these forms were generated: were they of material origin? Does matter have a generative function in relation to the soul or is it purely passive? Is the soul mortal and corruptible, like the human body, or can it separate from the body?

Ethics

Aristotle's *Nicomachean Ethics* for a time occupied only a lowly position among the books of his that began to be studied in the Latin West; Aristotle's logic continued to attract far more attention. The work was listed among the books available for study in the Paris Faculty of Arts in 1215 and again in 1255,[26] and six commentaries on it have been identified as having been written before the mid-thirteenth century.[27] The *Ethics* faced no official opposition, unlike Aristotle's *Physics* and *De anima* and *Metaphysics*. The moral wisdom of the ancients and their knowledge of virtue had long been accepted as valuable. But Aristotle's *Nicomachean Ethics* presented an opportunity to supplement the tradition of studying ethics as part of the appreciation of literature with a properly philosophical one.

In at least three ways the arrival of the new Aristotle changed the nature of moral philosophy by introducing new themes. One theme was that of the relative merits of practical and of theoretical philosophy. A second theme was the nature of magnanimity. Aristotle and Averroes had explored the difference between magnanimity and pusillanimity. The magnanimous man is one who values virtue above all else. But to Christian thinkers this posed a problem, since God is the greatest of beings and it is the duty of the Christian to value humility.[28] A third theme was the nature of happiness. Aristotle's exploration of the concept of happiness and of human virtue provided a philosophical account of what constitutes or leads to human perfection. The subject of human virtue had always been one which medieval thinkers could approach as part of philosophy; Macrobius (among others) had detailed what was meant by natural virtue. The theological virtues were traditionally faith, hope, and charity, but there was also no hesitancy on the part of Christian thinkers to use to their advantage what Roman writers had worked out about the natural virtues such as prudence, courage, temperance, and justice. What was new, when the first three books of Aristotle's *Ethics* began to be read, was the example he gave of a philosophical enquiry about the good at which all people aim, about the difference between moral and intellectual virtues, and also about the role of deliberate choice. Questions were raised about happiness, whether it consists in the exercise of all the virtues, both moral and intellectual, and whether Aristotle taught that supreme happiness is to be found in the practice of philosophical contemplation. This broadened the scope of philosophical ethics and took it into an area covered by Christian theology. Christian theology defined the perfection to which people should strive as God and withheld the possibility of attaining this perfection during mortal life in this world. Aristotle himself did not maintain that absolute happiness can be attained in this life, but he represented the happiness that is humanly possible as the highest goal to be pursued by human beings, by their own efforts and for its own sake, not God's. The earliest commentaries written on the *Ethics* in the first half of the thirteenth century attempted to understand what Aristotle meant by happiness. Happiness is an activity but Aristotle distinguished different kinds of happiness—social happiness, on the one hand, and the life of contemplation, on the other. Contemplation requires leisure but people have to be educated into virtue and this requires legislators.

Robert Grosseteste

In the thirteenth century the outpouring on a massive scale from the new universities of commentaries, disputation literature (*disputationes*), questions or *quodlibets*, and encyclopaedic *summae* dwarfs the whole output of writing from the schools between the time of Charlemagne and the end of the twelfth century. In addition to secular masters teaching the arts and the higher disciplines of theology, law, and medicine, there were masters who were Mendicant friars—that is, members of religious orders of friars such as those founded by St Francis of Assisi and St Dominic, and later the Order of the Carmelite friars, all dedicated to the ideal of poverty in the interests of following the way of life led by Jesus Christ. The orders entered fully into the mainstream of university education. In the thirteenth, as in later centuries, many of the most formidable thinkers were friar doctors who committed themselves to an extremely heavy task of teaching and writing on a substantial scale, and the best of them were usually given the support, secretarial and other, to achieve their ends. Considerable work was done by such early Franciscan masters as Alexander of Hales and John of La Rochelle, to develop a systematic and comprehensive approach to the teaching of theology, and this entailed a detailed command of philosophical literature including the increasing amount of newly translated material.

In many ways the most considerable and interesting of the scholars in the first half of the thirteenth century who acknowledged and responded to the extension of the range of thought was the Englishman Robert Grosseteste (1168/75–1253). He was not himself a friar, but he taught in the Franciscan house of studies (*studium*) at Oxford. Robert was, among his other activities, a translator of Greek writings, including those of pseudo-Denis as well as the *Ethics* of Aristotle. His translation of the *Ethics*, made *c.*1246–7, was a translation (or perhaps a retranslation) of the whole work—all ten books, including Aristotle's treatment of justice, friendship, and pleasure—and it was accompanied by a Latin translation of a number of Greek commentaries upon it.[29] As a translator Grosseteste had an incalculable influence on later generations. But he was in his own right also a formidable thinker, more perhaps on account of his unique command of the new range of learning than because of his conclusions, but none the less impressive on both counts.[30]

Grosseteste's broad outlook was largely Neoplatonic and Augustinian: he believed in the illumination of the intellect by the divine ideas or the reasons which are in the mind of God. Emanations of divine light create and sustain all things; all knowledge and understanding is provided by the divine light of Truth. In addition to the role of light in knowledge, Grosseteste regarded light as the metaphysical factor in bodies and as the life-giving power in every being. Physical light is therefore only one manifestation of light; other manifestations are divine light and intellectual light, and Grosseteste did not regard these two kinds of light as simply metaphorical—they too were really light. Physical and metaphysical light should therefore be studied together, as should all the natural sciences and philosophy.[31] Grosseteste, who taught at Oxford from about 1225 to 1235, seems to be the single most influential figure in shaping an Oxford interest in the empirical sciences that was to endure for the rest of the Middle Ages.

Another part of Grosseteste's interest in natural philosophy was exhibited in his commentary on Aristotle's *Posterior Analytics*. The *Posterior Analytics* was concerned with the different forms of argument appropriate for mathematics and the sciences, dialectic and rhetoric, and with the nature of the pre-existing knowledge required in order to pursue them, facts in some cases, terms in others. 'Everything that is known', Aristotle had written, 'is known through demonstration' and demonstration is 'a syllogism which makes us know'.[32] Scientific knowledge is demonstrative knowledge, not opinion and not belief. The work had been translated into Latin in the mid-twelfth century, but it had so far made little impression on students of logic. The range of the disciplines covered by Aristotle, together with his concern about how the natural world may be known, are possibly the chief reasons why, among Western logicians in the twelfth and thirteenth centuries, the translation had fallen flat. John of Salisbury had found the work very difficult, and he had pleaded that those most likely to benefit from it—geometricians and astronomers—were more likely to be found living in Arab countries than in Latin ones.[33] However, Grosseteste had a scientific cast of mind, a mind that was at work on scientific lore; he was attracted by Aristotle's work and his own commentary upon it is perhaps the first ever to be written in Western Europe.

It has been well written that Grosseteste was more stimulated by the scientific illustrations which Aristotle had provided in the *Posterior Analytics* than by the forms of argument which Aristotle wished to discuss in their light.[34] These illustrations raised, for Grosseteste, many questions about scientific knowledge which Aristotle had either not seen or had not sufficiently pursued. For example, is the twinkling of the stars due to the straining of the human eye to see objects which are so distant that the eye's vision becomes weak and wavering? Or does the eye become weak and wavering on account of a diminishing angle of vision? Again: does leaf fall in autumn follow a thickening of sap in trees or its drying up? Such questions involved considerations of a physiological and botanical nature. Aristotle, however, had been interested in the more general and fundamental problems of scientific knowledge that they suggested—problems of geometry, for example, in the first case, and problems of cause and effect in the second. Grosseteste had his own firm ideas about scientific knowledge and about its relationship with pre-existing sense impressions. Unlike Aristotle, Grosseteste thought that, *in principle*, sense impressions are not necessary for knowledge:

I say that it is possible to have some knowledge without the help of the senses, for in the divine mind all knowledge, not only of universals but also of all particulars, exists eternally . . . and this would be the case with all human beings, if they were not weighed down under the load of the corrupt body.[35]

But he followed Aristotle in seeing in the senses the essential means *through* which (but not *from* which) fallen man can acquire the primary knowledge needed for scientific demonstration. In the final chapter of the *Posterior Analytics* Aristotle had compared sense impressions to an army of soldiers who are in disarray until someone takes command and instils order. Grosseteste also held that an active power in the soul (which Aristotle had called *nous* or *intellectus*) makes it possible to grasp intuitively the causes of natural events. He was inclined to think that a demonstrative science of nature was possible, even though natural events do not occur always but may occur regularly. Aristotle's favourite example was that of a lunar eclipse— an event that occurs only intermittently but one which, as Grosseteste observed, always occurs when the necessary causes coincide. In addition to Aristotle's views on this, Grosseteste also held that divine illumination makes certainty possible.

Roger Bacon

One of Grosseteste's most famous pupils is the Franciscan friar Roger Bacon (*c.*1214–92/4), also a philosopher and scientist, and a strangely independent figure who alienated much contemporary opinion by his unflattering attacks on other scholars, including the Franciscan friar Richard Rufus and the Dominican friar Albert the Great.[36] Roger Bacon's main work is the *Opus maius* (1267) which, together with his *Opus minus* and *Opus tertium* (1268), sets forth the full range of his academic and scientific interests.[37] He had earlier studied at Oxford from about 1230, though he never became a master there, and he lectured on Aristotle as a master in Paris from 1240 to 1247. He was particularly impressed by Grosseteste's light metaphysic, by the issues arising from visual knowledge and optics, and by the notion of proportion and of measurement applied to forms. Bacon, like other students of Aristotle, understood that knowledge is gained via species, by the process of abstracting concepts from sense experience. Among the five senses, sight is the most interesting: Bacon argued, largely under the influence of Avicenna, that visible objects (e.g. the sun) generate or 'multiply' species of light and colour in the adjacent medium (the air), and these are powers (or 'similitudes' or 'intentions') which act on the senses and on the intellect and on matter. Within a human being, visual impressions are multiplied in the eye and transmitted to the brain. Bacon believed that visible species (such as colour) are required in the eye for vision, and they represent to sight the colours of which they are the species. Bacon contributed therefore to what is known as 'the multiplication of species', a doctrine which sought to explain how the species assist the sense organs, and which enjoyed much support in the thirteenth century, although it also created many difficulties.

Bacon's notion of perspective (*perspectiva*) is the basis of his idea of experimental science which is set forth in the fifth part of the *Opus maius*. For example, he enquires into the causes of the rainbow, and the mutability of its location in relation to an observer's position, as well as the nature of the rainbow's colours. Bacon, like other perspectivists, thought that the rainbow's location and colours are like images in a mirror, being appearances which change according to the perspective of the observer, although the rainbow is not itself created by an observer. The rainbow is an extra-mental object or (as later thinkers would say) an intentional being.[38] Perspective is a notion which embraces psychology, epistemology, and semantics as well as physics.

Roger Bacon was impressed by William of Sherwood, the logician, and himself wrote works of logic, especially his *Summule dialectices* (*c.*1250), which are similar to William's.[39] In this work Bacon launched his attack upon the common view (*sentencia communis*) that terms name objects whether or not these objects exist; he maintained, both here and in later writings, that terms name objects only when they currently exist.[40] In his last years he wrote but did not finish a *Compendium of the Study of Theology* in which he showed himself to be an able semanticist. He again faced the issue whether names directly signify extra-mental objects or whether they signify concepts directly and objects indirectly. Bacon attempted to formulate some rules governing the use of names by distinguishing between different kinds of signs. One was based upon Aristotle's *Prior Analytics*: relations between signs or names are distinct from relations between causes, but signification and causation are compatible. When two signs are regularly associated (e.g. cock crow and the hour of night; dawn and the rising sun; lactation and giving birth; motherhood and love; a red sky in the morning and rain later; or wet ground and rain earlier), an inference—either probable or necessary—may be made. A second rule is that signs may conform to their subjects—for example, signs may present a likeness of a subject through the use of sound or the suggestion of an image; the image is thus linked to the world of objects. Thirdly, relations between signs may be linked to the relationships between causes and effects; for example, smoke is an effect of fire. These three kinds of sign do not exhaust all possible modes, and obviously one can arbitrarily invent names for anything and any idea one wishes, but Bacon calls these signs natural since they are less than artificial and since there are natural relations between them and objects. They signify something outside the mind primarily and a concept or species secondarily. The late Jan Pinborg, who did much to reveal Bacon's contributions to logic and semantics, detected in the second of these formulations one of the main roots of the later terminist analysis of language.[41] On this issue, which was to attract an increasing amount of attention henceforth, both Duns Scotus and William Ockham took a similar position to that of Bacon: words directly and principally signify objects but are subordinate to concepts.[42]

Natural philosophy

An initial phase in the assimilation of the new Aristotle may be said to draw to a close in the 1250s, when the Parisian masters began to lecture also on Aristotle's books on natural philosophy—his *libri naturales*. The field of study was now the whole of philosophy, not just the basic art of dialectic, but also the higher sciences of moral and natural philosophy. Moreover, natural philosophy was a discipline in its own right, a *scientia* with its own subject matter and methodology that were independent of the discipline of theology.

Challenges to this autonomy were made by theologians and, indeed, in the 1260s an organized opposition, sometimes in the name of Augustine, begins to appear. There were invectives against Aristotle in the *Collationes in Hexaemeron* written and preached by Bonaventure, the Franciscan master in Paris, in

1273. Such opposition was resisted by a series of masters of arts in Paris, including Siger of Brabant, Boethius of Dacia, Bernier of Nivelles, and Goswin de la Chapelle. They were less ready to accept that philosophical speculation should be set within the bounds of Christian theology. They argued for the right to pursue philosophical discussions to their own logical and philosophical conclusions. And in their study of Aristotle's natural philosophy they arrived at conclusions concerning the eternity of the world, the eternity of species, the denial of universal providence, and the unicity of the possible intellect that were non-Christian.

The moves by the theologians to suppress Aristotelian natural philosophy in the Faculty of Arts were apparently successful. Condemnations were officially pronounced in Paris in 1277 and for thirty years after 1277 the masters of arts hardly commented on the *libri naturales*, and very few texts containing their teaching survive. The study of the *libri naturales* was, however, taken up again in the early fourteenth century.

Bonaventure

The foremost Franciscan thinker in the 1250s was Bonaventure (c.1217–74). He became a master of arts in Paris around 1243, master of theology there in 1254/5, and minister general of the Franciscan Order in 1257.[43] Like Augustine he was above all concerned with the journey to be made by the human soul towards God. The title of his best-known work is in fact *The Journey of the Mind to God* (*Itinerarium mentis ad deum*).[44] All study and thought, including philosophy and theology, were subordinate to this end. But Bonaventure had a broad and powerful vision of this task and brought philosophy fully within this ambit. In this respect too he owed much to Augustine. He took from him the doctrine of illumination which Augustine had developed from the works of the Platonists before him, and which was now also available from Avicenna and the *Liber de causis*. Of all the forms present in physical bodies, Bonaventure held, the ultimate form is that of light. And the degree to which bodies are lit is their degree of nobility. From Augustine too Bonaventure received the doctrine of seminal tendencies. The problem to be explained was how a substance might be changed into another or how the potentiality of matter to receive one or another form is actually realized. The secondary agent used by God for this purpose was the so-called seminal reason, the seed or tendency within substances enabling them to change.

On cognition Bonaventure opposed the Arabs. The human intellect has both agent (or active) and possible faculties. There is no need to place the agent intellect outside the human mind as a separate entity. The human mind is capable of perceiving intelligible species through the cooperation of its agent and possible faculties. However, the human mind needs divine light to know that what it perceives is true and real, and this divine light reflecting the divine ideas is, according to Bonaventure, the 'rule of truth', for truth is unchanging, although all created beings are changeable. So the mind needs to be illuminated by the divine ideas—that is, by the 'eternal reasons'—in order to attain to the certainty of truth. Knowledge of God is innate and God is more real than other beings. Knowledge of the other beings is obtained by the mind from external sources, but knowledge of God is direct.

As regards matter and form, Bonaventure accepted, like Roger Bacon before him and like many other Franciscans afterwards, the tradition of thought that both are found in all beings other than God. God is simple but everything else, including angels, is composite. Matter, and potentiality, are intrinsic to all such beings, there being a spiritual matter in the soul, just as there is a corporeal matter in beings which also have bodies. This is the doctrine known as universal hylomorphism. Not a little difficulty was found in defining matter, whether it is one in kind and whether it can be considered apart from forms. There is also a difficulty for readers of Bonaventure to know what he precisely thought was the relationship between forms when soul and body are joined together as they are in the creation of a human being. Bonaventure certainly held that the substance or

form of a man is his soul, that all souls have both form and
matter, and that the substance of the body is joined to the soul so
that they are one being. Yet the body retains its own form of
corporeality, albeit one now taken over and absorbed by the
soul.[45]

The Franciscan friars, in order to develop the spiritual and
mystical aspects of Christianity which (among others) Francis
had exemplified, turned to the more eclectic but traditional
sources for Christian philosophy including Augustine, Proclus,
and Plotinus. Franciscans, such as Bonaventure, Peter John
Olivi, William de la Mare (d. *c*.1285), Matthew of Aquasparta
(*c*.1240–1302), and John Peckham (d. 1292), were agreed that all
knowledge was ultimately acquired through a process of direct
divine illumination. God is the source of all goodness and truth.
Man can partake in goodness and truth only in so far as he opens
his soul to the light of God.

The notion of light was important to the Franciscan understanding of creation. 'Let there be light' are God's words in the
book of Genesis. Light was the first form given to prime matter,
and man should contemplate the divine ideas which served as
exemplars for God's creation. The soul arrives at a knowledge of
God—its prime object—by introspection. The notion that the
soul received divine light also focused Franciscan attention on
the nature of the soul. Franciscans did not consider the soul to be
the unique substantial form of the body. The body and its functions are composed of a plurality of forms, and the soul is a
complete substance in its own right, capable of existing independently of the body. But it illuminated the body which it
inhabited. Franciscans were not opposed to the study of Aristotle but they were opposed to the wholesale acceptance of
Aristotelian natural philosophy. They rejected the method of
starting with a knowledge of sensible things in order to infer the
existence of God. They countered the Dominicans with the argument that from the basis of physical bodies one can infer only
physical causes. If one tries to prove the existence of God solely
on the basis of natural philosophy, then the God whose existence is proved can never transcend the physical order. The

Dominicans, by equating God with the Aristotelian prime mover and final cause, ended up by denying the liberty and omnipotence of God to act as he wills.

Conflict between Franciscans and Dominicans began with the disputation between Aquinas and Peckham in 1270 over the unity of the substantial form in man, and after 1277 it became clear that the Orders were split as to what exactly constitutes the correct use of Aristotelian natural philosophy.

Albert the Great

Albert (1193/1206–80), who was known to his contemporaries as Albert the Great on account of his immense and encyclopaedic learning, is of importance above all else for showing the wide scope of human learning in all fields that were now available for study. He was a Dominican friar who, when he arrived in Paris c.1240, was engaged in writing two enormous encyclopaedias, one being an exposition of the whole Aristotelian *corpus* of writing on logic, metaphysics, psychology, ethics, and natural philosophy, and the other being a *summa* of theology known by the title *De creaturis*. Philosophy and science he pursued for their own sake, but above all he valued the authority of Aristotle, and he set out to present Aristotle's thought in its fullest extent to his contemporaries, albeit with a theological interpretation in many respects, and one which often departed from Muslim sources. To do this he prepared editions of Aristotle's works and added a continuous commentary on them.[46] It is often difficult to define Albert's own thought, for he devoted himself so much to elucidating Aristotle's meaning. He showed positive leanings on certain issues such as the nature of the intellect. He was opposed to Averroes' views on a single agent intellect. He was also inclined to support the plurality of forms. Like Aquinas, he rejected the thesis of the 'Jewish philosophers' (Isaac Israeli, Maimonides) concerning the angels as movers of the heavenly bodies.[47] He also rejected Aristotle's teaching on the eternity of the world, and he defended the personal immortality of the human soul. But on other occasions Albert maintained that he did not expound his own views when expounding Aristotle. His writings on Aristotle are later than his writings on theology, and this is unusual; they emerged between 1250 and 1270. Albert recognized that the new materials translated from Muslim and Jewish sources had to be studied and made intelligible to Christians, and he strongly opposed those, especially within the Dominican Order, who thought otherwise. Albert's output is large even by the standards of the thirteenth century, and his commentaries also included works on the Bible and on the *Sentences*.

Albert's contemporaries, in their study of Aristotelian logic, practised the study of discourse in the sense that they focused upon the logic of proposition and argument. Albert also studied Aristotelian logic but, under the influence of Avicenna, he tried to shift the emphasis away from discourse to the study of mental intentions (*intentiones*), making logic a *scientia rationalis* in preference to a *scientia sermocinalis* or science of words. To his other commentaries Albert brought not so much elements from the Arabic and Jewish commentators of Aristotle—he was largely out of sympathy with them—as an unswerving attention to the detail of Aristotle's own thought supplemented by observations of his own that included at times his own empirical observations of the fauna and flora in his native Rhineland. He was, however, completely familiar with the available Arabic and Jewish texts. His commentary on Aristotle's *Metaphysics*, which was written in 1262–3, contains reflections on Aristotle's celebrated doctrine (found in book Lambda) of God as Thought thinking itself. To Albert this suggested that intellect is transcendent and that God is Pure and Prime Intellect. Albert cites Averroes' commentary on the same book of the *Metaphysics*: intelligence is delectable and everyone would like to be able to elucidate the divine intellect.[48] To be able to do so would secure the release of people from sadness and from time. But by human intelligence alone human beings are not able to know fully the goodness which constitutes the primary principle or prime mover. Human beings are limited by corporeality and can see only a shadow of God (*in umbra*).[49] Pure Intellect is, however, the primary principle which acts upon intelligent subjects and moves them to be intellective. The First Principle is active; it works like a builder, putting knowledge into practical effect. The supreme and the unique cause of all is Intellect, which is at work everywhere (*universaliter agens*); God's knowledge is the cause of all being.[50] Although Albert is here expounding the text of Aristotle, he turns to the teaching of Augustine and of Denis for the view that the cause of all is the creative Ideas in the mind of God. Albert writes in a similar way in his commentary on Aristotle's *De anima*.[51] Aristotle had written that an intellect in action is identical with the object that is being thought. Albert takes up this argument with a Neoplatonic accent: God's intellect is absolutely separate from all things, but it is always in action and is never potential. It is in possession of everything that is intelligible but also constitutes all that is intelligible.

Albert shows his agreement with John the Scot who had written that God knows existent realities but not because they exist; rather it is because God knows them that they do exist.[52] One of Albert's favourite axioms is: *opus naturae est opus intelligentiae*—nature acts as intelligence directs.[53] He quotes Averroes on God's knowledge as the cause of being; this knowledge is, however, unlike human knowledge, which is caused by the beings that people know.[54] Albert turns to Augustine also: by his intellective thought (*per suum intelligere*) God causes everything, for his *esse* is his *intelligere*: understanding is his being.[55] In God being and knowledge are identical. God's knowledge is not something different from God's intellect but is identical: the First Principle is One.

Albert wrote the first full commentary in Latin on Aristotle's *Nicomachean Ethics* in Cologne between 1248 and 1252, and then followed this up with a second *c.*1263–7. Albert had the gift of being able to get directly to the point, and the commentaries were frequently cited by later writers. Albert was not obviously troubled by the question of the relationship between the concept of happiness for a Christian and that for an Aristotelian:

Aristotle had written about the happiness achievable by human
actions in this life.[56] Christianity teaches that happiness is finally
to be found with God, and Christianity adds that God is the first
cause of the happiness at which people aim in this life also.
Albert saw no fundamental tension between these perspectives;
they complement each other. But the everlasting happiness discussed by the theologians transcends the happiness that may be
sought through philosophy and the use of human reason. Contemplation of God may be undertaken by a philosopher but for
a theologian such contemplation goes beyond the use of reason.[57] Albert regarded action as superior to theory, and ethics as
a practical science, but this science is a part of philosophy with a
theoretical aspect—which leads to knowledge—as well as an
applied aspect which bears upon actual moral conduct.[58] Moreover, contemplative happiness is superior to social or civil happiness. Albert also saw no contradiction between Aristotle's
praise of magnanimity and the Christian duty of humility. Magnanimity and humility are two kinds of human inclination, one
towards what is beyond self, the other a recognition of human
frailty. To Albert also we owe the first Latin commentary on the
work which accompanies Aristotle's *Ethics*—namely, his *Politics*. Albert only knew a translation that covered books I–II,
chapter 11.[59]

To his successors Albert set an example of a committed
Aristotelian. He was, however, a thinker of such great range that
his Neoplatonism proved to be not much less influential. He
commented on the *Divine Names* of Denis while at Cologne
between 1248 and 1254. Aquinas was one of his hearers, and a
series of German Dominican thinkers, including Ulrich of
Strassburg (d. *c.*1278) and, later, Eckhardt, Dietrich of Freiberg
(d. after 1310) and Berthold of Moosburg, found in Albert a
source of Neoplatonist inspiration and as well put Proclus' *Elements of Theology* at the centre of their Neoplatonism.[60] In the
first chapter of this commentary Albert presents God as the
measure (*mensura*) of being, a simple essence (*simplex essentia*)
in which all other things participate. Their being (*entitas*) is an
image of the being of God who is the First Being and from whom

comes a form which is the likeness (*similitudo*) of God and through which all other existences participate in him. However, there are degrees (*gradus*) of participation in God and degrees of nearness to the First Being or of farness from it. Beings that are closer (*propinquiora*) to God and are more like him are more simple, more powerful, and less composite than those which are less like him and further away; the former have being more truly (*verius esse*). Existence, on the other hand, does not increase or decrease.[61] Undoubtedly it is Albert's exposition of this theme, provided by Denis and by the *Liber de causis* (which drew upon the ideas of Proclus), that led Aquinas into a powerful elaboration in the following years.

Thomas Aquinas

Of all medieval thinkers Thomas Aquinas (*c*.1225–74) is the best known and has been the most studied in the modern world. And if a brief description may be offered of the nature of his achievement, then it should lie in his adaptation of Aristotelian philosophy to the requirements of Christian thought in such a way as to produce an original philosophical system. He brought together the Greek idea of nature and the Christian idea of creature.[62] Born in southern Italy in 1224/5, Aquinas entered the Dominican Order in 1244 and thereby became the pupil of Albert, if not at Paris (as is possibly the case) then at Cologne from 1248. He heard Albert lecture and himself edited the text of some of Albert's lectures. Aquinas studied theology in Paris between 1252 and 1256 and taught it as a master from 1256 to 1259 and then for ten years in Italy before returning to Paris from 1269 until 1272, when he returned to Italy. Like Albert he accepted Aristotle as the supreme philosopher, the supreme exponent of the power of human reason to know the world of nature and to abstract principles from it. However, as a Christian, Aquinas also accepted that there was beyond the world of nature, the created universe, a supernatural world that Aristotle did not know and which reason, human reason, cannot of itself discover in full. God is known partly by reason and partly by virtue of the revelation imparted to the Jews and Christians and contained within the Old and the New Testament. Aquinas sought to explore and to determine the relationship between the two worlds, those of nature and of supernature, and, with the aid of both reason and faith, to study the relationship between nature and grace.

Aquinas was indebted to the earlier masters of philosophy and theology whose writings were available to him. He was indebted in particular to his immediate predecessors who taught in the schools and universities of the thirteenth century—especially Albert, who had built up a routine as well as a momentum of teaching, and a curriculum of questions and topics, and who had also evolved a scholastic method consisting of questions, the marshalling of texts extracted from authorities—Christian and Scriptural as well as pagan, Muslim, and Jewish—the consideration of objections, and the resolution of all the arguments, for and against, in a final determination. He drew selectively and critically upon the writings of the Arabs and Jews. Late in life, around 1272, he revealed, on philological grounds, that the *Liber de causis*, on which he wrote a commentary, was largely excerpted by an Arab philosopher, not from Aristotle, but from Proclus' *Elements of Theology*, a work that had been translated into Latin out of Greek in 1268 by William of Moerbeke.[63] To some extent he accepted the Platonic theory of forms or ideas, though these were found only in the mind of God. His attachment to Aristotle was qualified by Platonism. He was resolutely opposed to Averroes' interpretations of Aristotle's thought about the intellect, and especially his doctrine of the single universal agent intellect. He was a voluminous writer of treatises and commentaries, well supported by a staff of secretaries.[64] Among his principal works are his *Commentary* on the *Sentences* of Peter Lombard (1252–7), his *Summa contra Gentiles* (*c.*1258/ 9–64), in which Aquinas develops rational arguments in favour of religion, and, above all, his *Summa of Theology*, which was composed in stages, I and II between 1266 and 1272, and III in

1272–3, but left unfinished at the time of his early death in 1274, before the age of 50. This *Summa* is a vast exploration of Christian theology in which philosophical issues and philosophical erudition are very much in evidence.

The separation of the scope of rational enquiry from that of revealed truth meant for Aquinas that the human mind could only understand what had been put to it by the evidence of sense experience and that it could understand this reliably. Empirical observation and experience were the basis on which the mind could, according to Aristotelian doctrine, abstract ideas and come (for example) to a knowledge of causes and effects. God could not be known directly, because God is not evident to the senses. But God could be known indirectly from his work, creation, as any cause may be posited from a knowledge of its effects. Aquinas built up a series of arguments to show that all created being must come ultimately from a single cause, a First Cause which is itself uncaused.

It is in respect of the understanding of being that Aquinas is perhaps most original and important in the history of medieval philosophy.[65] He used certain key distinctions such as those between essence and existence, potency and act, indeterminate matter and determinant form. In his *De ente et essentia*—literally, *On Being and Essence*—Aquinas shows, among other debts, one to Avicenna in that essence in itself is not existence. In God alone there is no distinction between essence and existence, no becoming, no potency, because he is pure existence without contingency or finiteness. But every finite being comes into existence through the actuation of its potentiality and through determination by being given a form. Finite beings do not exist of themselves and are not self-caused. Finite beings are the result of causation, and within the universe of created causes there is a chain of being which includes both causes and effects, as is most obvious to us perhaps in the case of biological reproduction and of ecological balance. Aquinas himself did not enter into scientific detail, but he illustrated his view from time to time: among the elements, earth is lowest and fire highest;

among the animals, man is highest; lifeless things form a grade
below animals and plants; heavenly bodies are variously higher
or lower.

Another way of expressing this view of being, one that is
Platonic in its ultimate inspiration, is through the notion of
participation: every finite being participates in other beings
through being both the cause of other being and the effect, and
the different levels of being are (so to say) vertical or hierarch-
ical, from the most purely material and indeterminate at the
bottom level to the most spiritual and incorporeal at the top.
Thus every being reflects its cause and every being, to a graduated extent, reflects its original creator. These key ideas of
Aquinas about God as the measure of being, and of ascent and
descent in a scale of being, are not basically new ones. In all
likelihood Aquinas brought greater clarity than his immediate
predecessors had done to the issue of the relation between potency and actuality: the essence of, say, an angel has less potency
or possibility the higher its position is in the ranks of angels and,
therefore, the closer and the more like it is to God, who is pure
act; and, conversely, the further an angel is removed (*recedit*)
from God, and from likeness (*similitudo*) to God, the less actuality but the more potency it has. Similarly with matter and form:
forms which are closest to God (who is pure act) subsist without
matter; forms which are more distant from God have matter and
therefore have more potency and (paradoxical as this may seem)
less actuality. The grade of perfection is determined by the
degree of retreat (*recessus*) from potentiality and the degree of
access (*accessus*) to pure act. The more access a creature has to
God, the more being it has; and, conversely, the less it has of
being, the more it recedes from him. These themes pervade
many of Aquinas' works. They raise, however, the question of
how to explain the 'infinite distance' that exists between God
and other beings, if God is also in the genus of being as well as
constituting its perfection, its first principle, and its measure, and
if all other beings participate in him. Aquinas' way of dealing
with this problem is to deny that God falls under the genus of
substance as creatures do, and to explain their participation in

his being in terms of similitude, the resemblance that can be described between God and other beings; to distinguish also between pure act, which God is, and potency, which every other being has, even those nearest to him and highest in the scale of simplicity. All created beings receive being, and God is present in all beings as creator and as conservator of their existence. But he is above all other beings and there is a dissimilitude of nature (as well as of grace) between him and creatures. The similitude that exists between God and other beings rests on analogy (*analogia*).[66] It is this perspective, in which God is seen as beginning and end, and all else exits from and finally returns to him, which shapes the plan of Aquinas' great syntheses, the *Summa theologiae* and the *Summa contra Gentiles*.

Aristotle offered no vision of God as the source of a cascade of being created by himself. Aquinas makes this the centre of his own metaphysics. It is a doctrine of exemplarism: every creature reflects its creator as every effect carries a trace of its cause. Yet God is transcendent and beyond finitude. So, when we say that creatures resemble their creator—for example, in showing love, pursuing truth, exhibiting beauty—the terms we use (love, truth, beauty) have different meanings when applied to God, whose love, truth, beauty, and so on are beyond our ability to comprehend. We use these terms analogically of God. If we used them only in the human sense, our conception of God would become anthropomorphic. God is ultimately beyond language and beyond the power of reason to define and to describe. So the language we use in discussion of him is reduced to the level of analogy.

Using Aristotelian natural philosophy, Dominican friars in particular strove to show that a study of the material world enabled the human mind to rise to a knowledge of God as the author of nature. Their philosophy was part of a theological enterprise. Both philosophical and theological truths had to be consistent, since all truth came from God. Aquinas argued that philosophy complemented theology. It was the preamble to theology and its handmaid. Philosophy proves God's existence and demonstrates some of his attributes, although not the nature of the divine trinity, which is a revealed mystery. Dominicans like Aquinas used Aristotle to show that a correct understanding of the natural world led to a true understanding of God.

Aquinas rejected the notion that the soul had an innate knowledge of God because it was illuminated by divine light. For him the soul had a knowledge of external material things which were made present to it in the senses. All natural knowledge originated in man's sense experience or knowledge of physical objects. But man had been given a soul capable of contemplation and reason, and through exercise of these faculties he was expected to come to an understanding of God. Aquinas supported this by maintaining the Aristotelian doctrine that the highest faculty of the soul was its power of abstracting universal truths from individual forms in the passive intellect. This part of the soul was not exercised upon or through matter and must therefore be immortal.[67]

The 'five ways' which Aquinas offers as paths to proving the existence of God through the use of human reason build upon these considerations. The first of these builds on our experience of movement: whatever is moved in this world is moved by something else, which brings potency to act. Aquinas rejects an infinite regress of moved movers in favour of the conclusion that there must exist a first mover that is not moved by anything else and that everyone understands to be God. The second way is based on the observation of causes and their effects; Aquinas again rejects an infinite series of efficient causes in favour of a first uncaused cause which is God. The third way is based on possibility and necessity: things are capable of existing and not existing, of generation and corruption, but there must be a being which is not corruptible but necessary. The fourth way is based on degrees of perfection: everything that we know is more or less perfect or good or true, but these relative differences of degree require a maximum, something that is most perfect or best or truest; therefore there must be a cause of all degrees of perfection which is itself their maximum. The fifth way arises from Aristotle's doctrine that in the natural world all things seek the end to which they are fitted and seek to obtain what is best for them, even things that lack knowledge. Therefore there must be an intelligent and knowing being which orders all things towards their final end.[68]

Aquinas also strove to show that ultimately all things have their being in God. He adopted the Aristotelian theory that all physical bodies may be conceived as a composition of prime matter and a unique substantial form. By prime matter Aquinas, like Albert, meant pure potentiality and not in itself substantial. To this composition Aquinas added a third principle: in the composite of form and matter all entities are endowed with existence and being. The existence of a necessary being explains the existence of all contingent beings.

In his *Metaphysics* book 12, chapter 3, Aristotle discussed the substantial forms of material things and the question of their possible prior and posthumous existence. Aquinas interpreted Aristotle as saying that the intellective soul of man is the substantial form of man and did not exist before man himself but does survive the dissolution of the body because it is incorruptible. But Aquinas insisted, against the opinion of others, that Aristotle's view concerned the substantial form of man, not man's intellect only. To say that only the intellect is incorruptible would make the intellect a substance in its own right and it would not then be the substantial form of man.[69]

There were other views which we may group under the heading of the doctrine of 'the plurality of forms'. There were thinkers who regarded the human soul as a composite of matter and form, and who regarded the body too as a composite of matter and form, so that there was a plurality of forms in man. Forms were multiplied in the embryo and, before the intellective soul enters the body, the principles (forms) of sensation and of growth are already actualizing the body. Other faculties, virtues, and potentialities were erected into forms. Against this Aquinas was resolutely opposed on the ground that the soul is pure form and its matter is the body, and when the human body is born, the intellective soul takes over the supreme role as the one form of human life in which sensation and growth do not feature as separate forms of life apart from the soul. Earlier, in the 1230s,

John Blund had already affirmed that there is only one substantial form in man, the rational soul which makes man what he is. With Aristotle, Aquinas insisted that nothing is a unity unless it has a single form and that a single form is necessary to hold together the various powers of a human being, both intellective and moral. This was a metaphysical point of view, and Aristotle had not explored in any detail the relationship between the soul and the human body. Christian thinkers, on the other hand, had plenty of questions to pursue regarding life after bodily death and the meaning of personal life after the soul has left the body. One such question related to the separation of the soul and the body of Christ for three days following Christ's crucifixion and before his resurrection. Critics of the unity of form complained that, if the rational soul was indeed the only substantial form in man, and if it gave man's body its identity but departed from it upon death, Jesus' body in the tomb could not properly be said to be Jesus' body. Aquinas had to steer a delicate course on this when he was under attack from other masters between 1269 and 1270; his *Quodlibetal Questions* reflect fierce controversy.[70] As he formulated his own position in Lent 1271 and again in the third part of his *Summa theologiae*, Christ in the tomb was both a dead man *and* not unequivocally a man: his soul was not there.

Another central plank of Aquinas' thought about being is the rationality which gives order. The universe is the result of divine reason and the divine mind. So Aquinas develops a theory of law on the basis of his metaphysics: the universe is sustained by eternal law, a divine order or ordering which is susceptible of being expressed rationally and in legal language, as it has been in the divine law revealed, for example, in the Ten Commandments. And just as there is a chain of natural, contingent causes and effects dependent on the First Cause, so too there is a natural law derived from the eternal law which governs nature. Everything is for a purpose. Nothing happens in vain. In the natural law there are perceived universal imperatives for mankind, such as the human instincts of self-preservation and of reproduction.

Aquinas' moral theory is most fully laid out in the second part of his *Summa theologiae*.[71] Like Aristotle, Aquinas discussed ethics within the broadest framework, that of metaphysics in particular, and in the light of the belief that everything in nature attempts to achieve the end which is apt to itself. To man it is possible to attain by reason *theoria* or the vision of truth, and this is the goal which produces happiness. He was quite clear that Aristotle's discussion of happiness dealt with imperfect, created happiness only, because perfect, uncreated happiness and mortality do not go together. Indeed, perfect happiness lies not only beyond this life but also beyond the scope of rational enquiry altogether. Only God can bring complete happiness, and God alone is the object of the wish for complete happiness. Happiness is the end (*finis*) at which human nature aims: this meant, for Aquinas, that happiness is achievable by people in general, because it is of the nature of things that they do achieve their ends. Aquinas does not have an élitist view of the possibility of achieving supreme happiness.

Aquinas was led by his starting-point to a readjustment of the relationship between moral theory and practice: since God is the goal, the happiness he can bring is theoretical (or uncreated). But, by defining happiness as activity (*operatio*), Aristotle provides a key with which to explain the relationship with action: happiness is a mental activity, concerned not with purely human pleasure but with the highest aspiration of knowing and loving God. Happiness is, therefore, an activity of theoretical reason, as Aristotle would also say. But Aquinas in addition defines this activity as one that is enjoyed beyond this life. None the less, Aristotelian ethics was an invaluable component of practical moral science in this life. Imperfect happiness in this world is not utterly unlike perfect happiness; it bears a resemblance to it. Aquinas accepts that, in this life, there are two kinds of happiness, one social and the other contemplative, and the former, which is inferior, should be directed towards the latter. In other words, a well-ordered society is one which also promotes theoretical happiness.

Aquinas's answer to the question whether what makes us

happy exists principally in the understanding or in the emotions
reflects his view that intellect is a nobler (*altior*) faculty
than will.[72] The intellect drives the will in terms of final
cause, because the intellect decides on the final reason for
an action and 'presents the object' to the will.[73] Of course, will
also drives intellect, but only as an efficient, not as a final,
cause.[74] Thus, beatitude, which consists in the vision of God,
is an activity of the intellect. The experience of love, which
arises in the will, is the flowering of this activity, bringing it to
perfection.[75]

The Parisian Faculty of Arts

Thinkers such as Aquinas and Albert were both theologians and
philosophers; not uncommonly they considered questions of
metaphysics and of ethics within a theological context and
alongside theological questions. Such was the case, for example,
in the *Summa theologiae* and *Summa contra gentes* of Aquinas,
works which are classical examples of how a thirteenth-century
theologian might juxtapose arguments arising from both
Judaeo-Christian religious teaching and from Greek, Latin,
and Arab philosophical sources, from both faith and reason.
But there were also philosophers in the Faculties of Arts
who had a responsibility to teach Aristotle but none to teach
theology. There emerged during the thirteenth century a
number of dedicated arts teachers whose commitment to philosophical enquiry brought them sometimes openly to the point of
conflict with other parties committed to teaching Christian
points of view.

There are in Aristotle's writings difficulties of interpretation
on problems that are central to Christian thought. These topics
include the existence and nature of God, the problem of time
and eternity, the individuality and immortality of the human
soul, the nature of free will and also of happiness. Such topics
had been considered by Aristotle's many commentators in the
Hellenistic period and then in the Arab world by both Muslims

and Jews. By mid-century, when many of Averroes' works were available in Latin translation, it was bound to be the case that those studying Aristotle's writings in the Latin West would try to understand Aristotle with the aid of his interpreters and without always feeling obliged, in the name of Christian orthodoxy, to criticize him or to put him to one side or to adjust him by finding a means of reconciling him with Christianity. But even if such teachers (who are often described by historians as integral or radical or heterodox Aristotelians and sometimes as Averroists as well) were purely dispassionate and, as far as they could be, objective in their reading of Aristotle, the guardians of Christian teaching were still liable to feel concerned, if only because of their apparent indifference to implications for Christian thought.

There is also at least the possibility that some of these teachers of arts presented their reasonings as some sort of challenge to received Christian teaching, especially about God and the human soul. At least they could not have failed, however silently, to recognize the discrepancies. But the discrepancies also involved the theologians, who were by no means all united in their approaches to philosophical problems or all in opposition to radical artists. On the question of the eternity of the world, for example, it was possible for philosophers and theologians to agree that, even though the book of Genesis tells us that 'In the beginning God created the heavens and the earth', there was no philosophical reason which disproves the world's eternity. Aristotle in his *Physics* had argued that it was impossible to explain an absolute beginning of motion. But there were reasons why theologians might disagree between themselves over the possibility of an eternal creation, or an eternal beginning, by God, or over the possibility that a cause need not necessarily precede its effect but be simultaneous with it. The strongest disputes of the 1270s and 1280s were not necessarily those between theologians and philosophers, but those between various theologians who held differing philosophical positions. Aquinas himself admitted the possibility of an eternal creation (a possibility which Bonaventure had regarded as a contradiction); in his *De*

aeternitate mundi he held that creation really means original
dependence of being rather than beginning.[76]

Siger of Brabant

Siger (c.1240–81/4) was a prominent member of the Faculty of
Arts in Paris in the 1260s and 1270s and clashed with theologians
such as Aquinas as well as with Bishop Stephen Tempier. He
was a target of some of Aquinas' most determined criticisms,
and acquired a reputation as an Averroist who would not com-
promise Aristotelian teachings for the sake of Christian doctrine. He was accused of heresy in 1276 by Simon du Val,
inquisitor of France, and his murder by an insane clerk in Italy
only served to darken an already shady image. But, just as his
reputation for being a follower of Averroes even more than of
Aristotle has been questioned, so too the nature of the rifts
between him and Aquinas has undergone review. In the course
of expounding Aristotle, Siger advanced arguments in favour of
the eternity of the world, and, in his *Questions* on the third book
of Aristotle's *De anima* (probably written in 1269–70), he argued in favour of Averroes' notion of the oneness of the human
intellect.[77] This single, universal human intellect unites with human beings, not substantially, but in such a way that it thinks
within the human body although it is diversified by association
with the imaginations of individual persons. Siger showed great
interest in psychology. He also showed considerable interest
in Aristotle's ethics, and before 1277 he composed some
Quaestiones morales. However, a lost *Book on Happiness* (*Liber
de felicitate*)—whose teachings were recorded by Augustinus
Niphus (1472–1538) and which contains an apparently pagan
view of happiness—is doubtfully his. He also wrote a commentary on Peter Lombard's *Sentences* which shows a commitment
to theology and makes considerable use of Aquinas' own writings, sometimes summarizing passages from them and sometimes (although not always) without polemical or critical intent.
In all probability the course of Siger's writing represents an

evolution away from radical Aristotelianism towards a position, especially in psychology, which was much like Aquinas's own.[78] In early 1270 Aquinas, in his *Tract on the Unity of the Intellect*,[79] criticized Siger and other members of the Faculty of Arts, although without naming them. Aquinas here attempted to discredit Averroes' interpretation of Aristotle, with the aid, in particular, of the translation by William of Moerbeke of Themistius' paraphrases of the *De anima*, which appeared to prove that there is in each human being an individual agent intellect and an individual potential intellect. Aquinas' position is, basically, that each human being thinks as an individual, and does not simply share thought with a separate intellect; the individual human being understands. The rational soul is the substantial form of the human body. Averroes is a corrupter of Peripatetic—Aristotelian—philosophy; he contradicts philosophical principles. In his *Tractatus de anima intellectiva* written in 1273 or 1274, Siger parts company with Averroes and moves closer to Aristotle, to Aquinas, and to the view that there are individual human intellects because otherwise all human beings would have the same knowledge. He still attacks Aquinas in discussions that are exceedingly difficult to follow in detail. He renewed his criticisms in his questions on the *Liber de causis* shortly before he fled from Paris in 1276.[80] Here he made plain his rejection of Averroes' thesis of the unity of the intellect. Although Siger modified his own position on the oneness of the human intellect under the pressure of attacks, he defended himself by declaring that he tried to interpret the mind of Aristotle rather than to arrive at truth. He also maintained that Aristotle's positions were as far as the human mind could go on the level of human reason. This raised the possibility of a challenge to faith in matters on which faith and reason seemed to conflict—a challenge which Siger himself did not put nor seek to withstand. Until the end of his career disagreement with Aquinas was more evident than agreement, but Dante does have some justification for depicting Aquinas, in the fourth heaven in *Paradiso*, pointing Siger out to Dante, along with Albert from Cologne, as one of the blessed spirits:

> 'That one is the eternal light of Siger
> Who, teaching in the Street of Straw,
> Syllogized unwelcome truths.'[81]

Boethius of Dacia

Boethius of Dacia (*fl.* 1275), Siger's colleague in Paris, wrote a short work *On the Highest Good* (*De summo bono*) which became relatively well known. Its principal theme becomes clearer from some of the other titles attached to it in various copies, such as *The Philosophical Way of Life* or *The Good for Man* (*Vita philosophi*, *De recta vita philosophorum*, or *De bono humano*).[82] It would be untrue to think that Boethius refused to acknowledge that absolute happiness could be found through faith and in a future life. Boethius acknowledges that he writes of the beatitude which is possible for man in this life, as distinct from the beatitude that we expect through faith ('per fidem expectamus') in the life to come, and that he writes of what is the highest good for man, not the highest good absolutely ('non dico summum bonum absolute, sed summum bonum sibi').[83] But in this work Boethius gave all his attention to the study of what Aristotle's conception of purely human happiness had to offer. Somewhat like his namesake in the sixth century, Boethius of Dacia troubled some of his readers by extolling the benefit brought by philosophy without touching on the benefit of Christian belief. He defined the highest happiness that is humanly achievable in terms of the ability of human beings to achieve wisdom by the use of reason and to enjoy the activity of contemplation. He considered that, for a few people, reason is capable of arriving at the highest good through philosophical contemplation of the First Principle. This is the goal that should be chosen, one of seeking wisdom and doing good, of trying to understand and love the uncreated being from which comes all that is good. This is a theoretical as well as a practical task. But only a philosopher can carry it out because only a philosopher can know and understand the different branches of knowledge and—through the study of metaphysics—understand them comprehensively. Whereas Aristotle wrote of two different kinds of happiness, one social and requiring the practice of the moral virtues and the other contemplative and requiring the pursuit of wisdom, and whereas Aristotle had written of happiness as a possibility for people generally, including those who were not philosophers but who lived good lives in society, Boethius went less far: only the philosophical life is the right way of life because only the philosopher understands virtue and vice. Social happiness is not an independent, alternative type of happiness but a by-product of contemplative happiness. Those who do not live the life of a philosopher do not live the right life.[84]

John of Jandun

Another 'radical Aristotelian' in this period was John of Jandun (*c*.1285/9–1328). He too distinguished between Christian faith and what it is possible to hold in philosophy. According to Christianity everything (other than God) has been created. But creation of things out of nothing cannot be demonstrated by reason.[85] It is only by faith, not by reason, that one can hold that the intellective soul is created from nothing and that it is an individual soul for each human being.[86] Within the limits of philosophy Averroes is the best guide to Aristotle's thought and, according to both Averroes and Aristotle, God is not the efficient cause of other beings because he cannot be shown by reason to give his effects their existence. On the other hand, God is their final cause because he conserves and perfects them—that is, he is their end. One of John's writings is the *De substantia orbis*, in which he discusses the Intelligences which move the heavenly bodies—the orbs—and which are themselves moved by God. Those closest to God are more dignified and noble, but John of Jandun avoided a vision according to which beings emanate from God in procession and also return to him.

Dietrich of Freiberg

The Dominican friar Dietrich of Freiberg (*c.*1250–after 1310) also showed several similarities with Siger's thought. For example, Dietrich largely followed Averroes and his *De substantia orbis* in order to criticize Aquinas' view on 'motor angels'—the angels who move the spheres. In his *De animatione caeli* Dietrich considered the question whether the movers of the heavenly bodies—themselves intellectual substances—are united with the latter as their forms; if they are so united in their essence, the heavens can be called animated. Dietrich's solution was that the movers of the heavenly bodies are substances, and are united to the heavenly bodies as their forms, although they are separated from them in being non-material forms. This is close to Siger's position, which was that the moving principle of the heavens is separate in being from them but none the less joined to them in their intrinsic activity (*intrinsecus operans*).[87]

The condemnations of 1270, 1277, and 1284

On 10 December 1270, after strenuous controversies within the University of Paris and involving among others Bonaventure and Aquinas, Stephen Tempier, the bishop of Paris, issued a condemnation of thirteen propositions which were alleged to be supported in the Faculty of Arts.[88] The first of these was the thesis of the oneness of the human intellect against which individual human intelligence was reaffirmed: 'Quod intellectus omnium hominum est unus et idem numero—Quod ista est falsa vel impropria: Homo intelligit.' Other condemned propositions included: the denial of free will and of the immortality or incorruptibility of the soul, the affirmation of the eternity of the world, and the denial of God's knowledge of the universe and of divine providence.

On 7 March 1277, reflecting the concern about erroneous teaching that was felt by Peter of Spain, now Pope John XXI, Stephen Tempier issued a larger and more wide-ranging condemnation of 219 propositions taken, it was said, from teaching in the Faculty of Arts and including the matters previously condemned in 1270.[89] John Peckham said of the matters condemned that the choice was between Aristotle and Augustine— but this is too facile. It has also proved very difficult to link the condemned theses directly to propositions advanced by particular masters who may have been suspect: the condemned propositions are usually not quotations or even close paraphrases of texts that are available to us and which we can use for the purpose of verification. In cosmology this condemnation embraced the thesis that there are several prime movers, the thesis that the prime mover does not move unless acted upon, and the thesis that heavenly bodies are moved by an intrinsic principle, the soul.[90] One of the propositions condemned arose from a proposition (usually attributed to Aristotle but better associated with Avicenna and Ghazali) that only one thing is made by one cause ('ex uno non fit nisi unum').[91] Siger had argued that only one thing can proceed directly from one being;[92] the biblical view of creation was that an entire order of beings was made by a single creator. Albert had reviewed the sources: he cited as the source of the proposition 'ex uno non fit nisi unum' an *Epistola de principio universi esse* which was wrongly attributed to Aristotle but written by Alexander of Aphrodisias and available only in Arabic, not in Latin. Albert argued that the point had been accepted by Al-Farabi, Avicenna, and Averroes, and that the *Epistola* was one of the sources of the *Liber de causis*. In this case, as in others, the condemnation did not bear against Aristotelianism in particular.[93]

The Parisian condemnation of 1277 also bore against the ethical teachings to which Siger and Boethius had probably appeared to contribute, especially the notion that philosophy can lead to the acquisition of perfect happiness. Since perfect happiness was equated with eternal bliss by any theologian, Boethius' view seemed to imply that the sight of the essence of God could be achieved by human intellectual effort alone,[94] if not also in this life, and that the life of philosophy was the highest state of life.[95]

Eleven days after Tempier's condemnation, on 18 March 1277, Robert Kilwardby, formerly a Dominican master in Oxford[96] and now archbishop of Canterbury, in a special congregation of the masters of the University of Oxford, condemned thirty propositions, some in grammar and in logic, others in natural philosophy. These propositions have no obvious connections with those condemned at Paris. In a letter to Peter of Conflans, Kilwardby made it clear that he was not condemning theological heresy, but forbidding masters and bachelors to teach in the schools certain points which were false, inconsistent with philosophical truth, or in conflict with Christian belief. He now pressed the case against unity of form, affirming that the human soul is composite, not simple.[97] It is likely that, in trying to tighten control over teaching in Oxford, Kilwardby took as the norm his own outlooks when a master, and that he was not attacking his fellow Dominican, Thomas Aquinas, in particular. He had in mind positions which had been the source of divisions over the years among various scholars, particularly in Oxford.[98] In logic, Kilwardby condemned the proposition that necessary truth—e.g. 'every man is necessarily an animal'—depends on the existence of the subject, and that there can be no demonstration without existing realities. He had earlier taught that existence in the natural order is not required for a proposition about nature to be true; existence in the conceptual order is sufficient. Roger Bacon had taken the opposite view: the terms of a proposition—e.g. 'Caesar is a man'—must really exist for this statement to be true. Kilwardby likewise condemned the view that every proposition about the future is necessary. Theological considerations may not have been the driving force behind all of Kilwardby's prohibitions; he probably thought that there was too much determinism in the schools at the time and that Oxford needed to be freed from a certain restrictiveness in its approach to knowledge. When he was brought to Rome as a cardinal his successor at Canterbury, John Peckham, a Franciscan friar, renewed Kilwardby's decrees. On 29 October 1284 he solemnly condemned the doctrine of the unity of form as the source of recent heresy.

6

The Thirteenth Century: After 1277

1277: A watershed

The year 1277 brings one period in the history of medieval thought to an end. It also marks the opening of another, although of course the problems that had been tackled by pre-1277 thinkers such as Roger Bacon and Albert, Bonaventure and Aquinas, did not disappear from debate.

One consequence of the condemnations of 1277, or at least part of the aftermath if the condemnations were not the direct cause, was an outbreak of pamphlet warfare between masters in the Franciscan Order of friars and their Dominican counterparts, whom the Franciscans supected of heresy and error. Aquinas was not one of the main targets of the 1277 Parisian condemnation but his teachings were now attacked and defended even more than those of Siger and Boethius. Aristotelians in Paris in the last quarter of the thirteenth century, including those who were Dominican friars, launched a vigorous defence of their approaches to philosophy.

In about 1279, William de la Mare, regent master in the Franciscan *studium* in Paris, wrote his *Correctorium fratris Thomae* in refutation of 108 theses ascribed to Thomas Aquinas. There was prompt response from four Dominican friars—William of Macclesfield, Richard Clapwell, John Quidort, and one of uncertain name; each labelled de la Mare's *Correctorium* the *Corruptorium* and each produced a *Correctorium corruptorii*.[1] The disputes in Paris were also fought out in Oxford. At Cologne things were quieter; the writings of Albert and Aquinas continued to be studied without difficulty by, for example, Dietrich of Freiberg.[2] These disputes were especially fuelled by the disagreements between the orders of friars over knowledge, over the unity or plurality of forms, and over the eternity of the world.

The years from 1277 (the condemnations of Tempier and Kilwardby) to 1284 (Peckham's condemnation) constitute a watershed in the history of medieval thought in so far as the divisions between adherents of positions supported with the authority of Augustine and deriving from the traditions of the Franciscan masters, especially Bonaventure, grouped themselves into a 'school' of thought that was openly split from the speculative conclusions of many in the Dominican Order. Moreover, both 'schools' were committed to the overthrow of out-and-out Aristotelianism, such as was imputed to Siger, and later to John of Jandun and to Marsilius of Padua.

After 1277 use of Aristotelian natural philosophy had to be circumspect. An ascendancy was enjoyed by those who turned to the old Augustinian tradition, notably Henry of Ghent and John Duns Scotus. The lines of disagreement did not precisely follow institutional differences: Dominican friars did not always agree with each other, nor were Dominicans necessarily in conflict with Franciscan masters or with the philosophers in the faculties of arts. There was never a simple line of difference between, say, Aristotelians and anti-Aristotelians. None the less, in 1270 Aquinas and John Peckham, then regent master in the Franciscan school in Paris, had debated the question of the unity of the substantial form and had expressed contrary opinions: others also wrote disputed questions on the issue afterwards. There were no doubt different ways and speeds of reacting to advances of knowledge and changes of opinion: many scholars have observed that Aquinas, who brought about considerable changes very rapidly, had created even within his own order a gulf between new and old ways of thought. Tempier did not condemn any opinion on the unity of form in 1277 in Paris, but in England in that year Robert Kilwardby forbade the Oxford masters to teach publicly the doctrine of the unity of the substantial form. The sixth proposition which he included in his list was 'that the vegetative, sensitive and intellective principles coexist simultaneously during the period of embryo', the seventh 'that, when the intellective principle comes to be, the sensitive and the vegetative principles pass away'. The twelfth forbidden proposition was 'that the vegetative, sensitive, and intellective principles are one simple form', the sixteenth that 'the intellective principle is united to prime matter in such a way that all preceding forms are destroyed'. The thirteenth was 'that a body alive or dead is only a body in an equivocal sense: a dead body is a body from a certain point of view' ('corpus mortuum secundum quod corpus mortuum sit corpus secundum quid').[3] On the other hand, Giles of Rome (c.1243/7–1316), once a supporter of the plurality of forms, and also between 1269 and 1272 a pupil of Aquinas, wrote in 1278 a work entitled *Against the Degrees and Plurality of Forms*; in this he attempted to replace the notion of a form of corporeity in man with a notion of an accident of quantity.[4] He further thought that the meaning of what a form is needed to be clarified, since writers and teachers appeared to him to be using the idea in different ways. Godfrey of Fontaines, another contributor to this debate, preferred the doctrine of the unity of the form in being on philosophical grounds, but for theological reasons he made an exception for human beings.

The 1277 condemnation was arguably a blow to freedom of thought which brought to an end an 'Enlightenment' period in the long history of medieval thought.[5] It inflamed controversy among theologians in Oxford as well as in Paris and put thicker question marks over the study of Arab and Greek thought. But claps of thunder do not necessarily mean a permanent cyclone. There were always thinkers whose interest in Aristotle or Averroes was relatively uncomplicated and trouble-free. To a Spaniard such as Ferrand of Spain, who taught in the Faculty of Arts in Paris towards the end of the thirteenth century, Averroes was a compatriot; they both had much in common, although nothing of that stood in the way of Ferrand's greater attachment to Christian truth.[6] He wrote a commentary on Aristotle's *Metaphysics* after the condemnation of 1277, around the year 1290. When he wanted to justify Averroes in the face of the criticisms

of Aquinas, he did so. Aquinas had criticized Averroes for interpreting Aristotle in a way that removed matter from the definition of man.[7] Not everyone agreed with Aquinas's reproach to
Averroes. Ferrand of Spain produced a list of passages in which
Averroes clearly stated that both form and matter are the essence of a material being.[8] In particular, Ferrand of Spain con-
tended that Aristotle had not regarded the substantial form of
man as being his intellective soul and that trying to force Aristotle's teaching on this into agreement with Christian teaching
on man's creation and immortality results in sophistry. In *Metaphysics* book a, chapter 1 (993[b]), Aristotle compared the human
ability to know with a bat's ability to see the light of day. Following this, Aquinas dwelt upon man's dependence on sense perception for intellectual activity: human knowledge does not go
beyond the limit of abstraction by the mind from sense data and
cannot grasp the essence of immaterial substances.[9] Averroes
had interpreted Aristotle differently, and as indicating only that
man had difficulty in knowing what is immaterial, not that ad-
equate knowledge of such substances is always as impossible as
sight of the sun is to a bat. Nature does nothing in vain, and
whatever has been created has been created in the service of
human knowledge and in order to be known. But Aquinas rejected Averroes' interpretation: immaterial substances do not
exist for the sake of human knowledge nor do they lack meaning
if man cannot know them. After all, although bats cannot see the
sun, the eye of an eagle is well able to do so.[10] But to some, like
Ferrand, Aquinas appeared not only to belittle Averroes' argument but to get into a muddle himself. Knowing substances is
certainly difficult; it did not follow for Aristotle, and should not
follow for Aquinas, that it is impossible. Moreover, it is wrong to
say that immaterial substances are created in vain if they cannot
be known by men; on the other hand, if they can be known by
men, they would exist in vain from this point of view if they are
not known by men.[11] Ferrand was shrewd and versatile: when he
thought that Averroes or Aristotle was wrong or inadequate, or
that Christianity was right, he said so. The 1277 condemnation
has by no means entirely brought to a stop the kind of open-

minded reading of Aristotle practised by Siger or by Boethius of Dacia—or by Aquinas.

Ramon Lull

Evidence of a wish to make a fresh start after the storms of 1277 may be found in the writings of the unusual but very influential Ramon Lull of Mallorca (1232–1316). One should be careful not to trace all developments in the late thirteenth century in terms of a reaction to a crisis: it is better to see a continuing series of initiatives, amid some adjustments of focus, not a radical break with the past. Ramon Lull's *New Logic* (1303) attempted to develop a logic of pure knowing—that is, knowledge of purely intellectual objects which are the necessary objects of the intellect. In this attempt Lull sought to reject and to go beyond Aristotelian logic and psychology which restricted demonstrable knowledge to rational knowledge of sensible things. To do this Lull argued that man must turn away from sense perception and rational knowledge based on contingency without (*ad extra*) and turn within himself (*ad intra*) to find necessary intellectual knowledge.[12] That Lull believed this is possible is because he held that God plays a complementary role in the process of human knowing. Lull draws upon Augustine's comparison of the Trinity with human love: active loving requires a lover, a beloved, and the love which unites them. So too true knowledge requires a knower (God), the person known, and an intimate union between them in knowledge.[13] Another analogy on which Lull relied is that of fire: fire has its own necessary dynamic (*ad intra*) and the objects it burns are contingent (*ad extra*). So too the mind's necessary object is within itself, but the human mind and God are joined together in knowledge.[14] Underlying this is Lull's view of creation: the created universe has been given a dynamic character by God in his likeness—like fire, which, whether it touches wood or heats water, seeks its own intrinsic, substantial perfection in burning. God is united with the created universe, which participates continuously in divine activity.

Important to this representation of the union of God and man
in the activity of knowledge is Lull's thinking about the names
of God—goodness, wisdom, love, truth, and others—which
are not only intrinsic perfections but also perfect activity (*ad
extra*) producing goodness, wisdom, love, and truth in creatures.[15] These are basic principles of Lull's new science, the *Ars
lulliana*.

Henry of Ghent

At the end of the thirteenth century a clear difference of view
had emerged as to how to approach the metaphysics of being. To
some, basing themselves upon Aristotle and Averroes, *essentia*
and *esse* are identical in meaning but perform different functions
in logic. *Essentia* means the same as the act of being, and *essentia*
could also be called *quidditas* ('what it is' or 'whatness'). In
this line of thought we find Siger, Godfrey of Fontaines, and
Dietrich of Freiberg.[16] An alternative approach, based upon
Avicenna and al-Ghazali, was to draw a distinction between
essentia and *esse* that was more than a logical one. *Esse* is an
addition to *essentia*. Aquinas (in his *De ente et essentia*) and
Giles of Rome thought of *esse* as adding actuality to *essentia*,
so that every created thing is seen as a composition of both
essence and being (being here meaning existence or the act of
being).

Henry of Ghent (d. 1293), who was regent master of theology
at Paris from 1276 to 1292, also accepted that *esse* adds
something to *essentia*, but he qualified this by suggesting that
the addition was not actual but implied (*non re sed intentione*).
He made an important contribution to the notion of being
which proved more than helpful to John Duns Scotus a little
later. Henry began by stating that an existing being is an
individual, a single thing, and different from every other
existing being. The implication of this conviction is that all talk
of plurality of forms or of participation in other beings ceases
to matter. Henry allowed that man consists of bodily form

and also of soul, the latter being infused. But he emphasized most that each being is its own thing by reason of its own essence (*esse essentiae*). A univocal concept of being, applicable to existences—both to God and to creatures—is not possible, because God and creatures share no reality which could serve as an objective foundation for such a concept. However, in an analogous sense it is possible to conceive of being which lacks all determination. To conceive of individual beings with the addition of a linguistic sign—e.g. *this* being—adds nothing to the concept of being. *This* being still amounts to indistinct knowledge because *this* does not tell one whether being is animal or vegetable or whatever. By removing *this* we are left with a common term which signifies things which have properties (or *modi essendi*) that allow them to be conceived as this or that being. Henry would say that there are two concepts of being, one perfect (having no determination), the other non-perfect (with determination). But he also said that a common term, such as being, only signifies analogies or common likenesses between individual objects. Being is a homonym, and when we apply the concept of being to God and to creatures, the concept is not the same in each case; it is in fact only an analogously common concept. Henry, thus, distinguished three stages of knowledge of being. The first and most general stage is reached when we form a concept of this being; a less general stage is provided when we convert 'this being' into being; finally, the least general stage is when we recognize analogous being.[17]

On knowledge Henry continued the Augustinian argument that the knowledge gained by means of the senses and by the process of abstraction by the human mind, while being reliably true, is inferior to the higher and purer truth which comes through the divine light displayed to the human mind. Henry of Ghent therefore reaffirmed the Augustinian doctrine of illumination:

man can know pure truth about no thing by acquiring its knowledge through purely natural means, but only by an illumination of the divine light; even when he attains this light in his purely natural condition, man does not attain it by purely natural means, because it freely offers itself to whom it wills.[18]

John Duns Scotus

John Duns Scotus (*c*.1265–1308) was born at Duns near Berwick on Tweed and died at the age of 42 in Cologne, having studied and taught for his Order in the Franciscan convents and in the faculties of theology at Cambridge, Oxford, Paris, and Cologne. His mobility may be one reason for the rapid dissemination of his thought. His works survive, however, in an unfinished state, no doubt due to his frequent moves between places of study and his relatively early death. His followers attempted to bring them to completion but in such a way that a clear picture is still emerging of which texts and manuscripts are definitive. It is a misconception that Scotus produced one commentary on the *Sentences* at Oxford which is the *Ordinatio* or *Opus oxoniense* and a second at Paris which is the *Reportatio parisiensis*. What survives in the form of *reportationes* are reports made of his lectures in diverse ways and forms; the *Ordinatio* is the definitive text.[19]

Scotus's principal achievement was to cut through earlier, rather elaborate theories of being, including Aquinas', in an effort to find a simpler notion. For Aquinas, being admits of variation and degree, from the uncreated being of God to the different grades of created being (inanimate, animal, human, and so on), God being the source of other kinds of being. Scotus replaced this equivocal notion of being with an unequivocal one: being is the same wherever it is to be found, and it is everything and anything that is not nothing. There are no different kinds of being; there is only being, or its opposite which is nothing. There is no distinction between being and existence, because being is what is not nothing. Moreover, being is a concept that transcends the categories and is different from each of them. It is a predicate that can be attached to every subject. Here Scotus claimed support from Avicenna: *ens* and *res*, although confused concepts, are impressed upon the mind even before the categories of substance and accidents.

Scotus was foremost among those in the late thirteenth/early fourteenth century who advocated the study of being as such. In human life, being as being can be studied by the human mind by abstraction from sense data; we have no direct knowledge of being, only an abstract science. Scotus, however, does not start from sense data, but pursues a way of enquiry which transcends physics: he begins with the concept of being as such and distinguishes its modes or determinations such as finite and infinite being.

Scotus holds that infinite and finite beings are part of a single essential order. In this essential order God is prior and more perfect while all else is posterior and imperfect. But all finite being is participation in being, since it has some part in complete and perfect being (*partialitas entitatis*) even though God excels or exceeds all finite being by an infinite proportion. Unlike Aquinas, Scotus does not focus upon the distinction between potentiality and actuality as much as upon what a finite being has that is a positive perfection, and upon what it lacks which is a privation of perfection. A privation—such as the mole's lack of sight—cannot be found in infinite being. However, Scotus does not place as much importance as had many earlier thinkers upon the possible nearness or remoteness of different grades of creatures to or from God, or upon their degrees of perfection or imperfection or privation. His main contribution is a new conception of being. To attempt to know the first principle which causes the world, one should build not upon sensible being (as Aquinas does) but upon being itself, *ens qua ens*. Scotus distinguishes being as it is possible for humans to know, and being as it is in itself. Aquinas had understood *ens qua ens* to be being abstracted from sensible objects by us; and he had ascribed to *ens qua ens*, if only analogously, the characteristics of sensible being. Duns Scotus held that such a metaphysical study of being is restricted by the fact that human knowledge of being is ultimately still only an abstraction from sensible objects. So it is necessary to posit a notion of being so radically undetermined that it applies indifferently to everything which has being. This univocity of being is the true object of metaphysics.

This does not mean that there are no causes or that there is no first cause of being. But to argue back, as the Thomist does, from effect to cause and then ultimately to the first cause of being is, according to Scotus, to stay within the system of the universe. An analysis of sensible effects can never lead beyond their sensible causes. If one argues for the existence of God in this way, one can only arrive at a notion of God who is bound to act as a necessary physical cause. However, a proof of God's being can be attempted by resorting to the distinction between finity and infinity. Finite beings need a single infinite cause, which is God. Scotus's overriding concern is to prove the existence of God as an infinite being, completely free and unlimited in power except by that which contradicts his nature. To prove that infinite being exists, Scotus argues that it is necessary to posit a first necessary being which exists. What is contingent comes from what is necessary, and what is finite comes from what is necessarily infinite. Scotus' analysis of the relationship between infinite and finite being rests not on analogy nor upon a distinction outside the act of being, but upon univocal being. Yet there is a gap between the necessary existence of infinite being and the possible existence of finite being: infinite being exceeds everything else and everything else is contingent upon the former, because contingency is that of which the opposite could happen at one and the same time. The bridge between infinite and finite being is God's will.

Duns Scotus proves the existence of God by (1) proving the possibility of the existence of a Prime Being in the order of things, (2) proving its necessary existence, (3) proving that this Prime Being, which is not limited to being anything, must be infinite, and (4) proving that it must be the highest intelligence and supreme perfection.

Aquinas thought that there is a necessary relation between God and the creation which proceeds from Him. Scotus' view of necessity was innovative. He departs from Aristotle's idea of science and of scientific demonstration and denies, not that there is any design or rationality in the natural world, but that there is any necessity in this. Scotus considered that all finite beings are radically contingent upon the will of an infinite being. Laws of nature are not necessary laws, because the creator freely wills them and can freely alter them. Demonstrative science, therefore, is science of what is possible, not of what is necessary. Although there is regularity in the workings of natural causes and their effects, there is no determinism.

It is part of Scotus' understanding of being that he admits of no real distinction between essence and existence. Like Godfrey of Fontaines and like Siger of Brabant he does not separate existence from essence as if existence were a sort of accident added to essence. The distinction in Scotus' view is a purely formal one or perhaps a purely modal one in which existence is viewed as the intrinsic mode of essence, an aspect of essence which is grasped by intuitive cognition, as when I say to myself 'I exist'. By contrast, essence can only be known abstractively.

In general, Duns Scotus, guided by Avicenna's teaching that the object of understanding is being, whether sensible or not, argued that Aristotle was right as regards the human mind and its powers of cognition, but only as regards the human mind as it is after the fall and before the resurrection. Outside this fallen state, Christian belief is that man is capable of intuition of being, as when he will see God. Within the fallen state, following Aristotle, Scotus accepted that the mind arrives at concepts by abstracting from the evidence presented to the senses; truth can be found without a direct divine illumination. However, whereas Aristotle and Aquinas showed how the mind arrived at generalized essences by means of which individuals could be identified, Scotus argued that the ultimate intelligible object is not the genus and species but the individual. And the mind knows the individual being by a process of intellectual intuition. This intuition is firstly of the 'thisness' of the singular individual being.

This did not lead Scotus to abandon talk of universals or of forms. On the contrary, Scotus allows that the mind uses concepts of form and the universal as a means of understanding and that the network of forms and universals corresponds to the structure of reality. However, species represent indifferently the things that exist (as well as things which do not), whereas intuitive cognition of existing objects (even an illusion) provides certain knowledge of its existence.[20] The abandonment of a theory of cognition *via* species was not, therefore, a turn to scepticism.

Scotus puts at the head of his enquiry into the relationship between the universal and the individual, not so much the question 'what is the nature of the universal?', as the question 'what is it that makes an individual an individual?' He accepted that we can discern common natures but placed his emphasis on the problem of explaining how these common natures are individuated, how, that is, they gain their 'thisness' (*haecceitas*). Scotus denies that it is accidents or matter or existence which individuates. He held it to be axiomatic that only what is distinct and determinate in itself can individuate. Individuating principles do not fall under any of the categories; they have an actuality of their own. For example, human nature is common to all men and therefore is many numerically, but in Socrates it is numerically one. The 'thisness' of Socrates makes human nature in him numerically one and particular to him, yet human nature is also numerically many because it is found in many numerically distinct particulars. Of itself a nature is neither individual nor universal. It cannot exist apart from distinct particulars and is universal only in the intellect where it is not individuated. Yet Scotus is not a nominalist; he teaches that neither common natures nor individuating principles exist only in reason or in concepts.

We have two different explanations of Scotus' distinction between common natures and individuating principles. One version is found in Scotus' *Quaestiones metaphysicae*. Here he invokes an ontology that presents realities as existing in two modes, (a) in reality and (b) as concepts which do not exist in reality. For example, man is a rational, mortal animal. As such, 'man' is neither universal nor particular but indifferent to either: in the intellect 'man' becomes universal, in reality he becomes one. In his *Reportatio* there is another account in which the difficulty is seen of admitting that the intellect alone produces what is common and that the only things that exist are particulars. Such a view makes everything distinct from everything else and turns the universal into a pure fiction. But if nature has a commonness which is outside the mind and which is a distinct entity, such a common nature has to be formally distinct from the individuating entity of *haecceitas*; and when it is grasped by the intellect, it is actualized into the universal. So, when we say 'Socrates is a man', 'man' is a specific nature, common in reality to men.

Scotus distinguishes between abstractive and intuitive knowledge. To know an existing individual, we use intuition; to know a nature or a species, we use abstraction. When the intellect abstracts something, it does so in indifference to the existence of the thing and it makes a pre-judgemental act of knowing what is merely possible or necessary as distinct from what is actual. In this way Scotus qualifies Aristotle's view that the mind generates the universal from a sensible object, and affirms that intuition allows direct knowledge of a sensible object without any mediating species. He broke away from the view that the senses only know singulars and the intellect only universals. And he found intuitive knowledge to be more perfect than abstractive knowledge.

A further example of how Duns Scotus struck out in new directions and strove to break free of some of the restrictions of pre-1277 speculation is his notion of place. In the *Physics* Aristotle had defined place as the containing surface for any body and as necessarily immobile because it served as the fixed point with respect to which all local motion of the contained body could be said to occur. His thirteenth- and fourteenth-century readers used the implications of this to try to understand the ultimate sphere of the universe. There was the problem that the Aristotelians were unwilling to countenance the existence of anything beyond the ultimate sphere which could be said to contain it. But, if the ultimate sphere had no place, how could it be logically demonstrated to be in motion? Before 1277 various solutions were proposed for this problem. It was generally accepted that, for the ultimate sphere to rotate, a fixed centre was required and this was the immobile earth. All local motion required a fixed place of reference in an existing body. Albert the Great argued that the sphere had a place, and this is determined by the earth itself. The circular orbit of the sphere required that its centre be fixed on an immobile mass, i.e. the earth. Aquinas agreed that the immobile earth was the centre for the orbital motion of the sphere.[21]

Duns Scotus, on the other hand, first formulated a theory of place based upon the assumption that a body can have local motion even if no immobile place of reference exists for it. The heavens can rotate with an immobile earth at their centre, because God can move the heavens in any way he wishes, rectilinear, circular, or whatever. Scotus distinguishes two aspects of place: (1) place as a surface or container of a body, (2) place as it refers to the ambient matter contiguous with the body. Place is the act of lodging a body somewhere, as well as the notion of a body being lodged somewhere (*ubi*). An object can occupy a new place at each succeeding moment with respect to its immediate environment, yet may be immobile: a boat at anchor in a flowing river may be said to have a constantly changing *ratio loci* with respect to the water, but it is immobile. In this way Scotus refutes the teaching of Aquinas and others that all motion requires a necessarily immobile place of reference. Instead, all local motion was a product of a series of constantly changing *rationes loci*. Underlying Scotus' view perhaps was the fall-out from the condemnation of 1277 which highlighted what Tempier and others saw as restrictions on the actions of God. The condemnation may have been a factor leading thinkers to consider the possibility that God could move the heavens without positing a completely immobile earth.

A further *impasse* created in 1277 and one which Duns Scotus tried to break through was the problem of infinity created by Aristotle. Aristotle had denied that there could be an actual infinite number of species; infinity is merely a possibility.[22] Aristotle also denied both the actual and potential existence of an infinite magnitude because the universe was limited as to its size and quantity of matter.[23] On the basis of Aristotle, Aquinas had also rejected actual infinity: it would be contradictory to assume that God would create an infinity that was not in the natural course of things: 'just as God cannot make a rational horse, so he cannot create an actual infinity'.[24] The condemnation of 1277 led thinkers to look at this question afresh. On the basis of Aristotle, in order to prove a potential infinity, one had to argue that species potentially exist in all eternity, and also, if this is the case, that there must be potentially an infinite number of souls in heaven. But man was not a species which had existed for all eternity, because God had created Adam in time. And since philosophers now (*post*-1277) should affirm that man began in time, they should argue only for a finite number of souls in heaven. As for the second point, the condemnation undermined the Aristotelian denial of the possibility of an infinite magnitude. Aristotelians had held that there was a limited quantity of matter bound within a limited universe. Now philosophy seemed required to admit that the creative power of God could make any number of worlds and a limitless supply of matter.

Scotus worked out the implications with respect to an actual existence of infinite multitudes and magnitudes. He did so by distinguishing between what the human mind is and is not capable of knowing. Human minds might find it impossible to conceive of anything greater than a potential infinity, but this does not necessarily entail the impossibility of actual infinity. For example, human minds may not be able to conceive of an hour as the sum of potentially indefinitely decreasing parts, but this is not to say than an hour is not composed of an actual infinity of instants.[25]

Scotus also had something very important to say about will and ethics. It is misleading to say that, unlike the Thomists who argued that God ruled by reason and willed what was right and good, and that therefore the good that man does and the law he should follow flows out of the mind of God, Scotus, on the other hand, gave priority to will. For Scotus, God is infinite, necessary, and eternal. He uses will to move out of necessity into contingency, but will and reason in God are identical with each other and with the divine essence, and are only formally distinct. Will is the reason why God wills and why he wills contingently; whatever God wills is rational. What God requires of creation, naturally as well as morally, is what he wills and cannot therefore be demonstrated as necessary. God could require otherwise under his absolute power but wills what he wills in accordance with reason. This is not an arbitrary voluntarism, as has often been thought.

7

The Fourteenth Century

Decline or renewal?

If Roger Bacon is to be believed, rot set in in the thirteenth century:

The third cause of the appearance of the (Mendicant) orders is the fact that for forty years the secular clergy have so neglected the study of theology and philosophy . . . that they have entirely deserted the ways of the wise ancients (*antiqui*) . . . The modern seculars (*moderni saeculares*) have totally abandoned their footsteps.[1]

Bacon wrote this in 1271. He was himself a Franciscan friar, but his likes and dislikes—he admired Grosseteste and William of Sherwood but not Albert the Great—do not correspond to a simple division between supposedly outdated secular clergy and improving friars. Indeed, it is possible that, in contrasting *antiqui* and *moderni*, Bacon had in mind, respectively, Aristotelians and modern critics of Aristotle who rejected his doctrine of universals and the doctrine of the human form.

By many modern historians, however, the fourteenth century has tended to be portrayed as a period when intellectual confidence started to decline following the building-up of great syntheses in the thirteenth century. David Knowles, for example, wrote of 'the breakdown of the medieval synthesis' and, citing Gilson, of a divorce of philosophy from theology 'after a brief honeymoon'.[2] More graphically, Steven Ozment has compared scholars' views of the 'fall' of Western thought in the age of William Ockham with the social catastrophes created by the Black Death, the political disasters of the Hundred Years War, and the religious crisis exacerbated by the great papal schism.[3]

This view reflects an interpretation of later medieval history as being in general laden with doom, with thought in particular being seen as afflicted by tendencies towards doubt and scepticism about the possibilities of knowledge. To arrive at this interpretation it has been customary to explain the confidence of thirteenth-century philosophers in terms of their ability to reconcile pagan philosophy, and particularly Aristotle, with the revealed beliefs of Christianity, a confidence that was checked by the condemnation of many of their tenets by the bishop of Paris in 1277. This year has been picked upon as a symbolical date for the beginning of a general withdrawal of thinkers from natural theology—from a conviction, that is, that revealed beliefs may be reached (or at least given some support) by the use of human reason.

A further indictment of later medieval thought arises from criticisms of medieval scholastic theology that were made largely during the Reformation of the sixteenth century. The debates between Augustine and Pelagius (and their supporters), and the continuations of these debates during the Middle Ages, underlie much of Luther's argument concerning salvation by faith alone. Throughout the Middle Ages the complexities of the relations between divine grace and human action, between predestination and human merit or guilt, had always been recognized and had generated considerable thought as well as some controversy. Peter Abelard, for example, was roundly accused by St Bernard of Clairvaux of being a Pelagian, and condemned too at the ecclesiastical council held at Sens in 1140 for teaching that man responds to God's grace like a patient who is *able* to rise up to swallow the medicine prescribed by his doctor. To follow Augustine was to admit that human merit is the gift of God and the reward for God's work, to admit too that original sin has reduced all mankind to a fallen state, but to be suspected of Pelagian tendencies seemed dangerously to undermine not only the doctrine of original sin (and of its debilitating consequences), but also the consequent need for man's restoration by divine grace. It was always a delicate business to delve into these complex issues and not to offer, in the course of interpretation, a hostage to fortune.

In the fourteenth century considerable sensitivity surrounded arguments which seemed to be Pelagian. Robert Holcot (d. 1349), for example, a Dominican friar and a pupil of William Ockham, gave weight to man's partnership with God under covenant. He took issue with Thomas Bradwardine (1290/5–1349)—a fellow of Merton College, Oxford, until 1335, and briefly archbishop of Canterbury in 1349—who defended God's eternal predestination of the elect by his own will and through the gift of his grace. In his *The Case of God against the Pelagians* (1344), Bradwardine declared that God opens the heart of man to the grace he offers; man is the clay, God the potter (Rom. 9: 21). Bradwardine was himself concerned and frank about discrepant views which he discerned on human choice and divine mercy. In his late twenties Bradwardine described his aversion to the way in which he had been taught philosophy in Oxford:

Idle and a fool . . . I was misled by unorthodox error when I was still pursuing my studies in philosophy. Sometimes I went to listen to the theologians discussing [grace and free will] and the school of Pelagius seemed to me nearest to the truth. In the faculty of philosophy I seldom heard a reference to grace. . . . What I heard day in, day out, was that we are the masters of our own free acts, that ours is the choice to act well or badly, to have virtues or sins.

But, even before he became a student of theology, he underwent a change of view: 'even before I transferred to the faculty of theology . . . I saw from afar how the grace of God precedes all good works.'[4]

Nevertheless, thinkers in the fourteenth century, no more than their predecessors, were not always engaged in demolition, and in so far as they offered criticism of previous philosophical solutions or explanations, or struck out on new paths, there is no need to accuse them on that score alone of starting a decline. On the contrary, criticism can be the sign of continued vitality and vigorous renewal and innovation. The numbers of men who

studied philosophy and wrote on it were certainly higher than in
the previous century, and the informed readership and audience
for philosophical discussion was remarkably large in comparison
with earlier times, not least because so many new universities
were founded in the fourteenth century.

One feature of the fourteenth century which fully deserves to
be highlighted—it is one which could also be illustrated during
the thirteenth century, but not to such an extent—is the remark-
able penetration of philosophy into cultural life in general.
There were many ways in which this penetration occurred. One
example comes from the numerous sermons preached at the
time. From the thirteenth century onwards, and especially in
Mendicant circles, sermons were given a formal structure, with
divisions and distinctions of the kind that were common in academic works such as *Sentence* commentaries and *summae*. Rigorous logical argument, the marshalling of philosophical texts,
citations from the works of recent or contemporary masters,
explicit problem-solving and *quaestiones*—in other words, many
forms of the staple activity of masters and students in universities were also deployed in other contexts. In one sermon,
preached on the text 'It is by the grace of God that I am what I
am' (1 Cor. 15: 10), the Franciscan friar Servasanto da Faenza
chose to explore the nature of being in the presence of people in
Florence in Dante's day. At one point he brought into play his
knowledge of the natural philosophy of Aristotle, the *Consolation of Philosophy* of Boethius, and the *De doctrina christiana* of
Augustine:

Aristotle says in the *Meteors* that all that which does not do that thing
for which it exists, ceases to be what it is. Light was made for shining
and if it should cease to shine, it would certainly not be light. Therefore,
since man was made for the supreme Good, when he recedes from it, he
truly ceases from being. Again, according to Aristotle and to Boethius
himself, and, what is more, to Augustine, being and good are funda-
mentally interchangeable. Therefore, that which falls away from the
good, equally withdraws from being. Therefore, as evil people lose
goodness, they cease to be what they were, since, after they have turned
to evil, they have also lost their human nature.[5]

Another feature of the fourteenth century, not beginning exactly then and not ending within the century either, is the sharpening definition of schools of thought—Dominican friars as followers of Aquinas, Franciscan friars committed to the support of Scotus' teachings, nominalists as disciples of Ockham, and so forth. We must be careful not to harden these lines of division too much. Duns Scotus' teaching on the univocity of being, for example, although accepted by many Franciscans in the fourteenth century, was not accepted by all members of his religious Order and was sharply criticized by some of them—including Richard of Conington, Robert Cowton, Peter Aureol, and Nicholas of Lyra, to mention just a few names.[6] Ockham, too, was repeatedly criticized.

An aspect of the study of Aristotle in the fourteenth century that has attracted the attention of modern scholars is the multiplicity and variety of—so to say—Aristotelianisms which appeared after 1300; at the present time it is still not possible to synthesize available knowledge of the different tendencies.[7] Much interest has centred on the relationship between the Aristotelian interests of humanist as contrasted with scholastic thinkers, on the study of Aristotle in Padua, Bologna, and Venice as distinct from the study of Aristotle in places such as Paris, Oxford, and Cologne, and on the relationship between Aristotle and the birth of modern natural science and of modern ideas of scientific knowledge.

A further preliminary remark about the character of the fourteenth-century intellectual scene concerns the strong influence of English logic, and especially the textbooks written by Oxford masters, in the arts courses of the continental universities. The same may be said of English science. In this century the names of Scotus and Ockham, Burley, Bradwardine, and Heytesbury loom large. They, and especially Ockham, brought about what Gordon Leff has called 'the metamorphosis of scholastic discourse'.[8]

The condemnation of 1277 did not put an end to the type of philosophy represented by Siger and standing quite apart from faith. Averroism continued to flourish in Paris in the early fourteenth century as it had done in the previous century. One example of a leading Averroist of the fourteenth century is Hugh of Utrecht, whose *Questions on the Soul—Quaestiones de anima*—I–II date from *c*.1310–1315 and are found in manuscripts together with the *Quaestiones de anima* III by John of Jandun. Like Siger, Hugh denied that the intellective soul is the *esse* of the human body. *Secundum fidem*—according to faith—the intellective soul is the perfection of the human body to which it gives *esse* and activity, but *secundum philosophiam*—according to philosophy—it gives activity alone. The human soul consists of a vegetative and a sensitive soul as well as of an intellective soul. The first two of these assure the existence of the human body and are its substantial form. But the intellective soul is separate; it is common to the whole human race and it is a substantial form of the body only *per operationem*, by activity.[9]

There are, by way of preliminary observations, two misconceptions which we must try to dispel before approaching the content of fourteenth-century thought. The first concerns the outlook of the mystics and the spiritual writers of the end of the Middle Ages. Some—most famously Thomas à Kempis in his book *The Imitation of Christ* (1418)—turned away from philosophy and retreated into pious longing and affective spirituality. But many other spiritual writers, including Meister Eckhart (1260–1327), Tauler (1300–61), and Ruysbroeck (1293–1381), were influential teachers of philosophy. The second misconception is that Aristotelian philosophy had gained such ground in the thirteenth century that the scholastics of the end of the Middle Ages were all—in one way or another—Aristotelians. Certainly Aristotle continued to provide through his logic the instrument and the vocabulary of philosophical debate, but Platonism in its different varieties was always a powerful current of thought.

The transmitters of Plato's teachings continued to include Denis the pseudo-Areopagite, Avicenna, and Proclus. Proclus' teaching was provided in the *Liber de causis*, which appeared in a Latin translation *c*.1180, and also in works by him which were translated from 1268 onwards. Platonism now represented a view of causality according to which beings constituted a hierarchy above which was an unnameable God. This God is above causation, but through the Word or the One, being is created. This being is intellectual or Intelligence. Dietrich of Freiberg (d. after 1310) was one of a number of German Dominican friars who developed Proclean themes in his own *De intellectu et intelligibili*. He wrote:

According to Augustine's interpretation *Super Genesim ad litteram* (II.6.13), where we read: God said, let there be light, or, let there be the firmament, we should understand: the Word, in Whom it was, engendered it that it might be. From which it appears that this One, Whom Proclus put in first place and above all things, has the fecundity of an intellect.[10]

Eckhart too responded constructively to the pressure of Proclus, though he expressed himself in differing ways through his career.

In the fourteenth century the old division between realists and nominalists has been seen as a continuing and an acute source of conflict. Such a realist—nominalist divide centred upon problems concerning the epistemological status of knowledge and the distinction between intuitive and abstractive cognition.[11] The status of knowledge of the individual and the universal continued also to be debated.[12] The adherents of the new or modern way are usually held to be nominalists, with, as their chief, the English Franciscan friar William Ockham.[13] Realists tend to be linked with Duns Scotus and Aquinas. Nominalists provided a new impetus to the study of logic (both Aristotelian logic and the newer terminist logic of William of Sherwood) and discarded much of the edifice by which earlier metaphysicians were able to support a rational version of theology. As we shall see, Ockham denied the possibility of making distinctions which do not imply separability, so the divine attributes are only the various signs of God who is one, not plural; they are nominal distinctions only. In denying the reality of common natures Ockham denied the existence of the Ideas and of divine Intelligibles. However, as fast as Ockham was establishing his classic positions, critics attempted to demolish them. One such contemporary critic was Walter Chatton, whose *Sentence Commentary* is full of attacks.

Eckhart

The name of Eckhart (*c.*1260–1328) is most often associated with the development of Rhineland mysticism—Henry Suso was one of his pupils in Cologne in the 1320s—and with preaching in the vernacular. But his contributions to logic and semantics and the striking extensions and reinterpretations he gave to some of the conclusions of Aquinas are also an important part of his achievement. Eckhart was born *c.*1260 in Germany. He entered the Dominican order and went perhaps to Paris to the Faculty of Arts before 1277 and before going to Cologne, where possibly he was taught by Albert *c.*1280. In 1293–4 he lectured as a bachelor on the *Sentences* at the Dominican convent of St Jacques in Paris. Between 1294 and 1298 he was prior of the Dominicans in Erfurt. In 1302–3 he held the Dominican chair of theology in Paris. From 1303 to 1311 he was prior of the newly established Dominican province of Saxony. But he was again in Paris from 1311 to 1313 as master of theology before returning to Germany to other work on behalf of his Order. In 1323 or later he taught in Cologne. The archbishop of Cologne, Henry of Virneburg, ordered an investigation of his teaching in 1325–6, and in 1327–8 he was condemned by a commission in the papal court which was now at Avignon. He died in 1328. In the following year on 27 March he was described in a papal bull (*In agro dominico*) as one who wanted to know more than he should and who had planted thistles and thorns in the field of the church.[14]

In 1302–3 he debated his 'Parisian Questions'. The central problem in the first two of these was the relationship between being and intellect in God. Eckhart argues here that God is above being. He denies that God exists, because existence or being is brought into effect by God: 'as soon as we come to existence we come to a creature'.[15] God, however, is thought and Eckhart gave priority to thought over being.

The question whether in God thought and being are identical or whether one of these has priority over the other was by no means new.[16] It had been a frequently discussed *quaestio* in the universities and it had grown out of a realization that, whereas an Aristotelian would give priority to being over thought, a Neoplatonist such as Plotinus saw being as an innerness which is identical with thought itself. In the Middle Ages the question had become linked to the concept of God. Eckhart seems to be out of line in comparison with the mainstream of recent discussion of the question, although this impression should be qualified by recognition that Eriugena had given thought a role in the creation of being, and, very recently, Dietrich of Freiberg, in his *De origine rerum praedicamentalium*, had done something similar. But broadly speaking ontology was seen to be anterior to intellection and masters with an Augustinian inclination (the majority, that is) had sometimes characterized the relationship with the help of the distinction between substance and accidents.

In his first Parisian question Eckhart reverses this order.[17] The question put is whether being and understanding are the same in God (*Utrum in deo sit idem esse et intelligere*). Eckhart's answer is that these terms are not identical and convertible in God nor does God understand because he is: God is because he understands (*quia intelligit, ideo est*).[18] God is understanding or knowing, not being or existence. Eckhart limits *esse* to creatures because something cannot formally be in both a cause and an effect which the cause brings. Moreover, knowing is higher than being because it directs the activity of being; God's knowledge is the cause of beings.

Eckhart understood the author of the *Liber de causis*, when he wrote that 'the first of created beings is being', to mean: 'as soon as we come to being, we come to creature'. God must be something higher than being to be its cause. In the Book of Exodus (3: 14) God docs not say that he is ('I am') but that he will remain something other than being ('I am who I am'). Eckhart identifies this something as understanding. The phrase does not indicate that God is being without qualification, but that he has a hidden purity of being (*puritas essendi*).[19] For Eckhart God is because he knows; 'his understanding is the foundation of his being' (*est ipsum intelligere fundamentum ipsius esse; ipsum esse est ipsum intelligere*). In other words, understanding comes before being (*intelligere est altius quam esse*) and 'by the fact that (God) knows, he is' (*quia intelligit ideo est*). One is reminded of Descartes' *dictum*: I know, therefore I am.

In this way Eckhart projected an Intelligence which extends itself to all and which is transcendent, being restrained by no nature: 'In the beginning was the Word' (John 1: 1)—that is, wisdom and understanding freed of everything else, including being. Wisdom is uncreated and has an infinite character. Étienne Gilson wrote that Eckhart and, after him, Tauler and Ruysbroeck found in Platonism a language and a technique which was well suited to their needs as Christian thinkers; Aristotle's philosophy was less useful to them.[20] In his *Questions* Eckhart preferred not to speak of God as being (or as goodness or truth) but as pure thought and understanding which is prior to being. But in this Eckhart also set himself apart from both Aristotelian and Neoplatonic traditions. He understands being to be something finite and determinate, unlike thought. This break with tradition is not clear-cut because Eckhart does not always use terms in the way his predecessors had done. Moreover, R. Imbach has shown that Eckhart and Aquinas are closer to each other than used to be believed.[21] Aquinas in fact identifies being and understanding in God, but, in arguing that God is pure intellect, Eckhart is in effect stating what God's being is—namely, intellect.

It is not only in the Parisian questions that Eckhart discusses these matters. He does so again in the prologues to his *Opus tripartitum*. This work was begun probably after 1314 and probably was never finished.[22] In the *General Prologue* and in the *Prologue to the Book of Propositions*,[23] Eckhart identifies God and existence and defends the statement *Esse est Deus*. Only

God properly is and is called being, one, true, and good—the four transcendentals. Anything else which is said to be being, one, true, or good does not have this from itself but from God and immediately from God. Other beings, even immaterial and intelligent creatures, cannot be perfectly one, because their being is not identical with their intelligence. Only pure Intellect can be pure Unity; God alone is wholly intellect and one. God is also purely and fully being (*esse est Deus, esse purum et plenum*). When something is said to be this being, this one, this true, or this good, 'this' adds nothing of being, oneness, truth, or goodness to being, oneness, truth, or goodness. Every other being is through His being, just as white things are white through whiteness (*omne quod est per esse est. Esse autem Deus est*). By this reasoning Eckhart seems to deny existence to creatures; if God alone is being, they are nothing. But the argument is in fact designed to place them in being, not to destroy their *esse*. They are nothing *of themselves*. *Esse* inheres in creatures but *esse* is identical with God alone. It is generally agreed by scholars, moreover, that there is no fundamental contradiction between the positions adopted in the *Questions* and in the *Opus tripartitum*. However startling either or both of the conclusions may seem, the differences between them reflect differences in the definition of key terms and in the perspectives from which the issues are approached. Eckhart's starting-point is that there is only one being: substance, as Aristotle said. Everything else (accidents) are *of* being (*entis*). So Eckhart restricts the use of the word *esse* to God alone and assimilates creatures to accidents. This is how he reads Exodus 3: 14: 'I am who I am . . . He who is sent me', and *Job* 14: 4: 'You who alone are.' There is only one being and this is God who is, as the *Book of Causes* (*Liber de causis*) says, the One.[24] Eckhart argues that, if existence were not identical with God, God would owe his existence to something else and would not be the first and uncreated being. He is the existence which cannot not exist, the reality which causes everything else. Eckhart also identifies the trancendentals— unity, truth, and goodness—with God because they are identical with being.[25] As for the existcncc of creatures, Eckhart's position is that their existence is contained within God's. They have this being or that being or this or that transcendental, whereas God is being (or unity or truth or goodness) *tout court*. Creatures are beings by analogy with substance; they have being not *in recto*, but *in obliquo*.[26] Eckhart uses an example found in Aristotle: urine is said to be healthy or unhealthy, although healthiness or unhealthiness is formally only in the animal. It is only by analogy with health itself that we can speak thus of urine.[27] Likewise, when we say, for example, that goodness or truth or being is found in a creature, we employ an analogy because the transcendentals belong to God alone. Although Eckhart was eventually condemned for this teaching, he did not mean to deny what common sense tells us—namely, that there are creatures. But he maintained that their existence is grounded in God. He drew a parallel with the relationship between body and soul: the soul gives the body its existence and life. *Esse* is like an essential form in which creatures participate in order to exist.[28]

Eckhart loved paradox, and took it to excess. He was motivated by a desire to distinguish between God and creatures in a radical way and at the same time to explore their togetherness and union. In his *Commentary* on the Book of Exodus[29] Eckhart wrestled further with these problems in relation to the names we use of God. On the one hand, God is beyond description (*innominabilis*, *incomprehensibilis*, etc.); on the other hand, he contains every perfection we can think of (*omninominabilis*). The choice, of course, is between the positive and the negative ways of contemplating God, between an approach that starts from similarities between the creator and creatures and one that starts from their dissimilarities. Eckhart is very reserved about the scope that there is for making positive affirmations about God. As we have seen, Eckhart (at least in the *Opus tripartitum*) accepts that God is being, one, true, and good; none the less, human beings do not know all that is meant by this. 'Omnipotence is his name' (*Omnipotens nomen eius* (Exod. 15: 3))—but man cannot possibly understand omnipotence. Eckhart prefers to speculate about the perfections of God in a negative sense.

Thus, the oneness of God is a denial of the possibility that God is nothing, the negation of negation (*negatio negationis*).[30]

William Ockham

William Ockham (*c.*1285–?1347) was a Franciscan friar. He takes his name from the village of Ockham in Surrey in England and he began studying at Oxford at a date which is uncertain but at a time when Duns Scotus' thought was of great influence there. Ockham taught as the Franciscan bachelor of the *Sentences* at Oxford from 1317 to 1319, when he began to circulate the *Reportatio* of his lectures. In 1320 he transferred to the Franciscan convent in London, where he turned his Oxford lectures into an *Ordinatio*, took part in disputations, taught logic and physics, and wrote his *Summa logicae*.[31] His lectures on the *Sentences* aroused controversy and his career in England was cut short on being accused of heresy in 1323 by John Luterell, formerly Chancellor of Oxford University. Ockham was summoned in 1324 to the papal court at Avignon to answer charges. He remained there for four years, writing treatises while panels deliberated without reaching a final verdict; Pope Benedict XII (1334–42) did not condemn him. During this period, however, Ockham became involved in the debates over the question of apostolic poverty—the question, that is, whether the Apostles not only espoused poverty but also enjoined it on their followers. The Franciscan Order and Pope John XXII (1316–34) locked themselves into a quarrel over the use and holding of property by Christians, and this led Ockham into polemics over the nature of the church and of papal power. In 1328 Ockham fled Avignon for Munich. He was excommunicated. Under the protection of the Emperor Louis of Bavaria Ockham wrote a number of polemics on the power of the papacy and of the empire. Ockham was a severe critic of the popes of his day. As he wrote:

against the errors of this pseudo-pope 'I have set my face like the hard rock', so that neither lies nor slurs nor persecution of whatever sort . . . nor the multitude, however great, of those who believe or favour or even defend him will ever at any time be able to prevent me from attacking and refuting his errors as long as I have hand, paper, pen and ink.[32]

His most substantial work of political principle is his *Dialogus*, which has seven books. In it, among many matters, in book 1 he defined twenty modes of pertinacity of disbelief in Christian faith. They include denial of parts of the Old and the New Testament, denial of the teaching of the church, and unwillingness to correct oneself once corrected from error.[33] But, to Ockham, the task of defining truth and of defining heresy, was not the job of popes and general councils, rather of masters in the schools. Ockham did not hereby challenge those who had the authority to enunciate and promulgate faith, but, within the church, he thought that academics had the task of concluding enquiry. He died *c.*1347. For the last twenty or so years of his life Ockham engaged in polemics concerning ecclesiastical power; before 1324, however, the year when he went to Avignon, he had written his main works on philosophy and theology, the *Ordinatio* and the *Summa logicae*. These were carefully copied.

Ockham's attitude to Scotus' on univocal being is somewhat guarded, and within the Franciscan Order he was not alone in this reserve. For example, the Parisian master Nicholas of Lyra (1270–1349) distanced himself from Scotus' concept of univocity. Nicholas did not accept that *ens* is a concept distinct from the ten categories. He gave *canis* (dog) as an example: the word may have several meanings, such as a dog of the kind which barks, a dog fish, or a heavenly constellation of stars. But this does not necessitate a separate, distinct concept of dog common to all types of dog. Dog is an equivocal term with no common reality (or *ratio*) corresponding to it. Likewise, the concept of being is not a genus beyond the categories.[34] For Ockham, too, univocal being is not a common nature but a predicated name.

Ockham denies that it is possible to infer infinite being from

finite being or to infer a notion of being from the notion of
another being. Creatures are finite beings and we can observe by
observation that they undergo repeated sense experiences from
which we may empirically conclude that there is some sort of
causality at work. But we cannot perceive this causality or prove
that it is infinite rather than finite, singular rather than plural.

Ockham, like Scotus, did reject a real distinction between
essence and existence. Existence cannot be an accident because
it is not a quality or a quantity; it cannot be a substance because
it does not admit of matter and form. If existence were distinct
from essence, they would unite to produce either essential or
accidental unity. Existence and essence are not actuality and
potency, or matter and form, or accident and substance. Essence
cannot exist without existence as it would be nothing. So essence
and existence are one and the same. *Esse* in Latin is in fact both
a noun and a verb; as a noun *esse* is 'essence', as a verb it is 'to
be' and this signifies the same as does the noun.

Aristotle's doctrine of abstraction permitted the human mind
to know about being beyond the evidence perceived by the
senses. But, as in Peter Abelard's day, in the early twelfth century, so too in the early fourteenth century there was vigorous
debate about such knowledge and about universals. Of particular importance are the positions taken by Duns Scotus with his
theory of common natures and by William Ockham in his teaching about signs.

Scotus' views on common natures gained a number of critics.
Among them, the Franciscan friar Peter Auriol, who lectured on
the *Sentences* in Paris in 1316–18 (d. 1322), rejected both the
need to search for a principle of individuation and Scotus'
teaching about common natures. *Quidditas* does not subsist, but
is the truth of the thing itself. Ockham himself denied the power
of the human mind to abstract from the evidence of sense data
and thereby to arrive at knowledge of essences or common
natures. 'No universal', wrote Ockham, 'exists outside the mind
of the knower.'[35] All that the human mind knows is the individual. Human beings do none the less construct general concepts, but they are purely inside the mind and are purely a sign

that takes the form of a term and serves the function of bringing back into our mind the image we have of individuals. The sign is something fictive (*quoddam fictive*), a mere marker which we attach to our intuition of individuals. Knowledge of universal being is therefore not possible, and therefore metaphysics does not exist. Put simply, Ockham accepted the distinction between sense experience and understanding, but applied to each two different modes of cognition, intuitive in the first case, which is primary, and abstractive in the latter, which follows from the former. In addition, Ockham distinguished apprehension from adjudication—apprehension of anything, but adjudication only of propositions because they require assent or dissent.

William Ockham provided the most thorough refutation of Scotus' positions on common natures and on individuation. Reality is absolutely singular and undivided. A thing cannot be simultaneously singular and universal. If reality included universals, a universal would be a thing, and the individual in which it is realized would be another thing, so that there would be a real distinction between the universal and the individual. The universal does not, therefore, exist outside the mind (*extra animam*). 'Every positive thing existing outside the soul is by that very fact singular.' In simple supposition (*suppositio simplex*)—for example, when we say 'man is a species'—the term 'man' is a notion in our minds only (*in animam tantum*). This notion is not a substance, with a real quality and therefore objective, but simply a thought and a sort of fiction and therefore subjective. Ockham called universals signs. Signs in the mind, or significant general concepts pointing out a plurality, are themselves singular.

Ockham divided signs into two kinds: natural and conventional. A concept is a natural sign because such signs are the same in all human minds whatever language is spoken. All languages have words for familiar concepts (such as dog), but anterior to and independent of any such verbal expression there is a cognition in the soul (*intentio animae*) which, because it is common to all men, is a natural universal. Conventional signs are the verbal expressions of the natural signs and these expressions vary from one language to another. The natural universal, therefore, is more than a word; it is an act of intellect. The early Ockham maintained that concepts have some sort of existence as abstract objects, a cognized rather than a real existence. It is, as we might say, a construct or a fabrication; Ockham's term is *fictum*, which means not fictitious in the sense of being the opposite of fact, but fabricated or made by the mind. Ockham's views on this shifted under pressure from Walter Chatton and he later placed more emphasis on intellection than on the term *fictum*. He came to say that the natural universal is no more a mental *fictum* than, say, smoke is a *fictum* that signifies fire, or groaning a *fictum* that signifies pain, or laughter a *fictum* that signifies joy. Mental notions or signs that are naturally caused in us by their objects are natural products of the intellect. As concepts of the mind they are universal but they always signify something singular.

Ockham turns the universal into an act of understanding; a natural sign is an intellection. Unlike Scotus he does not speak of the universal as a common nature formally distinct from the individual which it encompasses. It is not 'something common' nor is there something extra, such as participation in an essence, that makes Socrates resemble Plato more than, say, a donkey. The resemblance is in themselves, and the universal noun 'man' is its sign. Universals are thus as external to things as words are to their subjects.

Fourteenth-century philosophers were particularly interested in Aristotle's account, in his *Posterior Analytics*, of the requirements for demonstration. Treatises had begun to be written on the subject of knowing and doubting—*De scire et dubitare*.[36] The influence of Robert Grosseteste and of his discussion of the different kinds of *scire* was manifest in some discussions of science and of scientific demonstration. Ockham quoted him: 'The science of principles is not acquired by discursive learning. We only teach and learn something which, when we first apprehend it, is doubtful or appears to be false but which, after it is doubted or controverted, is shown to be true.'[37] Every knowable proposition (*propositio scibilis*) is questionable and doubtful; its truth is established through principles (*per principia*). This is the nature of *scientia* and the task of scientific demonstration. There are, it is true, different kinds of *scientia* and different ways of knowing (*scire*). Knowledge of contingent propositions requires certain conditions to be met, but *scientia* and scientific demonstration in the strict sense are distinct from this, being 'evident knowledge of something true and necessary, and apt to be caused by the premisses used to support it in syllogistic discourse'.[38] In other words, the premisses of such a syllogism must be certain and necessary and also entail the conclusion, but the conclusion, although necessary, needs to be demonstrated to be such.

Ockham's discussions represent only one of very many that were written in and after his own time. The implications of these discussions for the development of theories of science concerning the natural world may be considerable, but are still waiting to be fully unravelled by modern scholars. In Ockham's case, science in the strict sense is about true and necessary propositions, not about the natural or physical world. Others, however, such as John Buridan (*c*.1292–*c*.1359), argued that science embraces the natural world as well as propositions: explanations of natural phenomena and events which regularly occur can also be logically robust and reliable, even though demonstrative science as Ockham understood it is for Buridan a rather marginal and specialized aspect of science. For others, such as Peter Auriol, a major problem was the fact that the senses can, as it were, deceive the intellect. He and others engaged in debate on such problems as the apparent breaking of a stick when partly submerged in water or the movement of trees on land when one sails past in a boat. Illusions notwithstanding, knowledge may none the less be guaranteed by the objectivity of what is known from the evidence of the senses and the activity of the mind. It may, furthermore, be guaranteed by the independent activity of the mind itself. If, as Duns Scotus argued, the laws of nature are not necessary (because God is free to override them), there are no unconditionally necessary truths about the natural world. For Scotus, therefore, demonstrative science seeks to discover what is possible, not what is necessary in nature.

From the first decade of the fourteenth century onwards, interest grew in the distinction between intuitive and abstractive cognition. Intuitive cognition is immediate, direct knowledge of an object, without sensible species being present in the senses and without being aware of anything passing from the object to the senses—that is, without the need for a 'representation' or 'image' of the object. Intuition was studied carefully, partly because it showed the possibility of immediate cognition without the mediation of species. But is intuition the result of intellectual evidence and is abstraction the result of evidence perceived by the senses? Ockham's views attracted considerable attention, although, as so often was the case, his near predecessors had already come to define the particular issues now to be more intensively debated. It appeared to Ockham that sensation involved intuition, since the evidence of singular objects may be perceived even where there is no science, science here meaning science of the general as distinct from the particular. Furthermore, cognition is not caused by the presence of objects but by virtue of its own nature which is the power to know. One can have intuitive cognition of a thing which does not exist. 'Intuitive knowledge is not of itself and necessarily the knowledge of something that exists; it may well be of something that does not exist.'[39] What Ockham meant by evident cognition is easily grasped: concepts can occur in the mind as a result of knowledge gained by experience of matters of fact or when conclusions are drawn demonstratively from necessary premises or when there are self-evident propositions. Intuitive cognition is more difficult to explain: for Ockham it meant assent to a true proposition which may not have an extra-mental reality—e.g. 'the wall is white' may be intuited even though in fact the wall is still to be built.

Ockham does not explain how to distinguish an intuitive cognition from a deception. It is not possible to prove the existence of something from the evidence of intuition of it. Ockham allowed that God could provide an intuition in the same way as an object external to the human mind. But we cannot by the use of intuition prove the existence of God or even of the form or soul within us. This is not necessarily scepticism: Ockham allows for the existence of absolute certainties such as the principle of non-contradiction and of knowing one's own existence, and he distinguishes also ordinary certainties.

A number of Ockham's contemporaries, especially in Paris and including Henry of Ghent, also cast doubt on the need to invoke species, whether intelligible or sensible, or in the medium, in explaining cognition. Knowledge involves a knowing subject and a known object. But Ockham did not think that it requires something in between the two, an intermediary such as a species. The intellect knows something immediately. When an object is white we see something white, not the species whiteness. The object and the intellect are sufficient to explain sensible intuition and the abstract knowledge flowing from it; experience teaches us nothing of the species. What then is a general concept? To understand Ockham's view of this it is necessary to look further at his doctrine of supposition.[40] Supposition is the positing of something for something else. This may take place in a variety of ways which had been distinguished since antiquity. When we say 'each man is an animal', the term 'man' supposits or stands for any individual man—that is, it points out the very thing which it signifies, not something common to all men. This kind of supposition (known as personal supposition because the term stands for individual objects) is also a signification.[41] Another kind of supposition (which is called simple supposition) occurs when we say 'man is a species'. Here 'man' stands for or supposits the notion or concept we have in our minds of 'man', not what the notion signifies—i.e. 'men'. Simple supposition, unlike personal supposition, is, in Ockham's view, not signification. In the statement 'man is a species', the notion of man is a confused one and does not signify individuals—i.e. 'men'. None the less, Ockham maintained that every concept, including the concept 'man', is about a singular, not about a general, object. To reach this conclusion Ockham divided concepts into two kinds, those which are distinct (e.g. my concept of Socrates when I see him in front of me) and those which are confused (e.g. my concept of 'man'). So, when I say 'Socrates is a man' (a personal supposition), I mean in effect 'the Socrates I know distinctly is the Socrates I also know confusedly to be man'. 'Man' here signifies nothing other than my own concept of man; it does not distinctly represent any individual man, but it is still about a singular because in predicating the general of the particular (as previous logicians would have put it) all we are doing is predicating the singular confusedly known of the singular distinctly known.[42]

Does understanding begin with contingent facts, that is with facts which may or may not occur, or does it begin with necessities? Is the order of nature subject to fixed laws which determine its operations or is it an order of liberty willed by its creator or cause? In the fourteenth century questions about necessity and possibility were extensively debated. One reason for the magnitude of the debates may be that difficulties arise if nature is held to be subject to a rational order—that is, to laws which are intrinsically right. If this is so, then the first cause may appear to be constrained by rationality. To preserve the freedom of the first cause from any kind of necessity one could say that the first cause is free to will whatever it chooses, even the contrary of what is in fact willed. Debate focused on the kind of power exercised by God: it cannot be limited if God is omnipotent, so there is an absolute power (*potentia absoluta*) which can, for example, even order men to hate God. On the other hand, it is a limited power (*potentia ordinata*), since it is subject to the principle of contradiction.

In the order of nature a human action is the result either of necessity or of free will; will and necessity cannot coexist or coincide. But can they coincide in God? Can God's will be supremely free and yet supremely reasonable and good? Other questions, relating to events in time, developed from traditional debates over predestination and free will. If God is free to will the contrary of what he wills, what happens is not necessary. If

God is like, say, an air traffic controller overseeing the movements of aircraft at a busy airport, he uses his intellect to consider possibilities which then become true or false following a choice made by him, and this choice is a judgement made by reason which is willed into effect. What happens as a result of this is not necessary; it may have been foreseen and be part of a strategy, but, even if it happens as planned and foreseen, it is still not inevitable. Although God knows for certain what will happen, most fourteenth-century thinkers would agree that he is, none the less, free to know and act otherwise than he knows and acts. When we come to consider statements about events in time and want to know if they are necessary or contingent, true or false, we face a number of questions. To take one famous example, if it is true that 'Antichrist will come', the statement cannot become false. Therefore, there is no contingency if what is said about the future is true, at least in the case of this future event which is immutably and necessarily true.

Many thinkers, including Peter Auriol, William Ockham, and Gregory of Rimini, sought to preserve future contingents and questioned whether a statement about the future can be either true or false. Ockham's view became an influential one: he argued that both the past and the present, unlike the future, are necessary; what has happened and what is happening are facts, although Peter Auriol dissented from this view about the past and Duns Scotus dissented from this view about the present. For Ockham, past and present events are not contingent, because there is no longer the possibility of their occurring otherwise than they have done or are now doing. On this Ockham, along with other thinkers, was indebted to Aristotle's *De interpretatione*, chapter 9, where Aristotle argued that, although it may seem highly implausible, any proposition about the past, the present, *and* the future is either true or false. There is no middle ground between it being true or false. If it is true now (for example) that the air traffic controller has charge of an aeroplane, this is necessarily true, and so it is with propositions about the past: what is true about the past was necessarily true. Aristotle had also been clear about the past in his *Nicomachean Ethics*, book VI, chapter 2, where he had written:

choice is not concerned with anything that has happened already: for example, no one chooses to have sacked Troy . . . what has happened cannot be made not to have happened . . . Hence Agathon is right in saying: 'This only is denied to God, the power to make what has been done undone.'

Ockham too writes that 'it is generally conceded by philosophers and theologians that God cannot make what is past not to be past without its afterwards always being true to say that it was past'.[43] Here Ockham appears to be writing about a logical impossibility.

As regards the future, however, Aristotle's arguments about the possibility that everything that happens happens necessarily has an obvious bearing upon Christian doctrine on predestination and free will. This seemed like a fatalism which is at odds with human free will. Ockham's view was that every proposition about the future is true or false according as it corresponds or fails to correspond with reality. In this way God's foreknowledge is not put at risk. But is human free choice put at risk? Ockham thought not: the future is not necessary in the same way as the past is. The statement 'it is true that Antichrist will come', while it is expressed in the present tense ('it is true now that . . .') is really a statement about the future and therefore is a statement about a future contingent until we bring into consideration the infallibility of God, who is in this case the source of our knowledge and certainty that Antichrist will come. Prophecy which is divinely guaranteed is categorical, not contingent, and can categorically assert that such and such will happen.[44] Otherwise, future events are contingent and are not necessary in the way that present and past things are necessary, although some things in the past and in the present can necessitate a future occurrence.

A particular problem for the freedom of the will was divine predestination—the belief that God wills that some human beings shall, and others shall not, enjoy supreme blessedness in a future life after death. Ockham resorted to a distinction between an antecedent and a consequent disposing divine will: 'the will of God is twofold—the disposing will [*voluntas beneplaciti*] and the revealed will [*voluntas signi*].'[45] God's revealed will is signified through his commandments and counsels; the disposing will is whatever God wishes to come about and this will may be antecedent or consequent. If consequent, it is not capable of being impeded; nothing acts contrary to it. But this does not remove all future contingents, since the consequent disposing will of God is not determined by something present or past. The antecedent disposing will of God, on the other hand, cooperates with human free will: God permits people to use their free will, but antecedently wills them to pursue the objective of supreme blessedness. Some people decline to follow this antecedent will of God: 'although nothing occurs contrary to the [consequent] disposing will of God, something may occur contrary either to the antecedent or to the revealed will of God.'[46] Ockham's position might in part seem to undermine predestination by reducing it to the point where God antecedently wills the salvation of all people and is frustrated by those who act contrary to this will. But Ockham has added that the consequent disposing will of God cannot be so obstructed; in other words, predestination is something that will be actual in the future, not something that was actual in the past.

A related problem is that of God's foreknowledge of future contingencies: if God knows with certainty what people will do in the future, what role is there for human free choice? And, given that people have free will, how can God know with certainty what they will choose to do? Ockham writes:

I ask whether or not the determination of a created will necessarily follows the determination of the divine will. If it does, then the will necessarily acts, just as fire [necessarily heats], and so merit and demerit are done away with. If it does not, then the determination of a created will is required for knowing determinately one or the other part of a [future choice].

In this case, a created will can oppose the determination of the will of God, and God does not have certain knowledge of what a created will may determine.[47] Once more Ockham resorts to the distinction between the antecedent and the consequent disposing will of God. The antecedent will determines that people have a free will and reason, and that they are given commandments and counsels to guide them in the direction of making meritorious choices; it does not ensure that God has infallible foreknowledge of what those choices will be. However, the consequent disposing will of God, while it may lead us to understand the compatibility of predestination and human free will, does not help Ockham to explain the compatibility of divine infallible foreknowledge and human free will. Here Ockham took issue with Scotus, who thought that God's foreknowledge is infallible. Ockham argued that the consequent disposing will of God regarding the truth of a future contingent is itself contingent:

when something is determined contingently, so that it is still possible that it is not determined and it is possible that it was never determined, one cannot have certain and infallible knowledge based on such a determination. . . . God cannot have certain knowledge of future contingents based on such a determination. . . . I maintain that it is impossible to express clearly the way in which God knows future contingents.[48]

Scotus and Ockham led the fourteenth-century attacks on philosophical necessitarianism. Both Scotus and Ockham sought to free God from limitation and from dependence. Thus Ockham suppresses essences, universals, and Ideas and knowledge of causes. God does not need Ideas in order to know. Being God is to know all. God does not need secondary causes to produce effects and men do not know when God dispenses from the use of natural causes. Causality is a univocal notion: it is the same for divine power as it is in physics and as it is in acts of understanding. The classically scholastic way of searching for a philosophical understanding of faith is abandoned. Like Duns Scotus, Ockham developed the theme of the absolute power of

God, God's utter freedom, and man's inability to scrutinize by reason his activity. But it did not follow for Ockham, any more than for Scotus, that Ockham thinks 'of the divine will as expressing simply power':[49] God is also infinite goodness and mercy.

Nominalism in the fourteenth century

Some historians have described the consequences of the nominalist teachings of Ockham as the growth of 'psychologism'. By this is meant the abandonment of the notion that cognition requires species to act as intermediaries between the knowing subject and the object which is known, and the according of primacy to intuitive knowledge (which excluded species) as distinct from abstractive knowledge. Some of the consequences of nominalist thought were summed up by John of Mirecourt, a Cistercian monk who flourished in Paris in 1345 and who distinguished two orders of evidence. The first is the intellectual evidence of the first principle which is the principle of non-contradiction: a thing is that which it is, and the human intellect knows infallibly everything whose evidence is reduced to that of the principle of non-contradiction. The second order of evidence is that of experience, which may be either internal or external. Internal experience also includes infallible knowledge, for man has a direct cognition of his own existence which he cannot doubt without affirming it. External experience consists of intuitive knowledge: no species stand between the object known and the intellect, unless as a *fictum*. The propositions that we formulate about the external world are based on empirical evidence or the evidence of natural causation in the world of natural science.

Is there a link between nominalism and the growth of modern natural or empirical science? The suggestion is often made, for the nominalists did not begin with species. Whatever links there were between nominalism and the rise of science, they are not easy to state, but, in all probability, advances in scientific explanation were not generally made as a direct consequence of nominalist theories of knowledge. In England, in particular, students of Aristotle's *Physics*, when they debated questions about the reality of number or of space or of infinity, tended to show in the late thirteenth and early fourteenth centuries a keen sense of mathematics and perhaps also a general bias towards a realist understanding of such mathematical entities. Perhaps the legacy of Grosseteste's writing, and particularly his theories concerning light, were especially influential on English writers of commentaries on the *Physics*. Nicholas of Autrecourt, who taught in the Sorbonne in Paris between 1320 and 1327, is often quoted in this connection:

As the knowledge of things could be acquired in a short time starting from natural appearances, it is astonishing that certain people study Aristotle and Averroes up to the age of decrepitude, neglect moral problems, and care for the common welfare, for the study of logic . . .

I have maintained in my disputes in the Sorbonne that I have an evident certitude of the objects of the five senses and of my psychological operations.

Nicholas appears to defy the dialectical culture of established scholastics and to unfurl a banner proclaiming the usefulness of the social and natural sciences. But, as is nowadays clear, Autrecourt was himself unaware of Ockham's epistemology, although he was aware of the logical and theological work of Ockham's English critics.[50] Moreover, Katherine Tachau has shown that the fourteenth-century Oxford 'Calculators', who gained a European-wide fame for promoting the arts of measurement, were not notably Ockhamist, and that, furthermore, Ockham's theory of knowledge was largely rejected in England by such scholars as Walter Chatton,[51] Adam Wodeham (who had been taught by Ockham as well as by Chatton), and Robert Holcot.[52] Thirteenth-century outlooks favouring cognition by species and deriving from (among others) Grosseteste and Bacon continued to find favour in the next century, which historians have tended to portray as one in which nominalism prevailed. Ockham, as Professor Tachau has written, did not establish a school of nominalists; at Oxford Chatton insisted on species generated by and multiplied from objects as mediators in cognition processes and as guarantors that concepts need not be formed arbitrarily. Scotus' views continued to be expounded and defended at Oxford—for example, by Henry Harclay and William Alnwick. At Paris Ockham's theological works cannot be found before the early 1340s.

Modern scholars continue to explore the many changes in theology, logic, and natural philosophy that took place, especially in the first half of the fourteenth century, but it is now clear that it is an exaggeration to present the advances made in the study of problems of cognition purely in terms of a swing in favour of nominalist outlooks. An interesting test case is the work of John Buridan.[53] Buridan was certainly a nominalist, but he was also a powerful critic of Ockham, and he rehabilitated the terminology of universals and of essences. He taught that there is a reality which we call 'man' when we speak of Socrates as a man; such a common name or universal both signifies singular things in a universal way and signifies the universal mode under which we conceive singulars. 'Socrates' and 'man' signify a same reality perceived under different aspects. As regards empirical knowledge, Buridan reacts against the tendencies he saw in some nominalist writers to limit knowledge to infallible certainties, such as the principle of non-contradiction. There are different degrees of proof that may be required in the different branches of knowledge. Mathematics demands rigorous demonstration, but ethics cannot require such absolute certitude. A science such as ethics or natural science (*scientiae naturales et morales*) is not invalidated if its conclusions run foul of the principle of non-contradiction. There exists a realm of relative evidence (*evidentia ex suppositione*) which is more extensive than that of absolute evidence (*evidentia simplex*), and the seeker after truth cannot turn his back on empirical knowledge. Demonstrative science which deals in absolute certitudes is a peripheral branch of knowledge. Natural science includes the study of phenomena which do not always behave according to an expected pattern and therefore lacks such certitude. As examples of unexpected interferences in the course of nature, Buridan mentions eclipses in the skies. So Buridan defends the use of common-sense anti-sceptical reasoning.

Buridan wrote widely on logic, metaphysics, natural philosophy, and ethics. He became Rector of the University of Paris in 1328 and again in 1340. Among his pupils in Paris were Nicole Oresme, who became celebrated as a scientist and a mathematician, Albert of Saxony (1316–90), and Marsilius of Inghen (c.1330–96). Albert became the first Rector of the University of Vienna in 1365; Marsilius was Rector of the University of Paris in 1367 and 1371 and later Rector of the University of Heidelberg from 1386 to 1392. Through them both Buridan's thought was widely promoted. It is no longer thought that there was a serious crisis in the University of Paris in 1339 and 1340 caused by a wholesale clearing out of entrenched Ockhamist opinions while Buridan was rector. There was a restriction put upon the study of Ockham's writings in the Faculty of Arts and decreed by statute on 25 September 1339; and in a further statute promulgated on 29 December 1340—the so-called nominalist statute—some propositions were condemned. But these were propositions which Autrecourt had taught, not Ockham. Those against whom the statute was directed were criticized for wishing to be wiser than they should be (*cupientes plus sapere quam oporteat*).[54] Buridan was not rector at the time when either statute was issued, and both statutes should be seen as part of a series issued between 1337 and 1347 which were not much concerned with Ockham but were more concerned to restore the authority of the masters (as distinct from that of the bachelors) in running the university. It is possible that the worries of the masters concerned new methods, especially linguistic methods, being developed by the bachelors. Ockham's theological works had not been much read in Paris until the 1340s, whereas the theological works of some of his English contemporaries, especially Duns Scotus, were rather better known, and also remained so after the 1340s.

Logic

Logic always occupied an important position in medieval thought, but medieval logic had many parts and they evolved from the twelfth century onwards.

There came into being, besides numerous commentaries on ancient logic, which was largely the logic provided by Aristotle, Cicero, Porphyry, and Boethius, a number of specialized studies. One of these focused on fallacies or sophisms. This largely reflects the importance of Aristotle's *De sophisticis elenchis*, which provided a wide range of sophisms, including (to take a famous example) the Coriscus problem (179^{a-b}) which is this: you know Coriscus and Coriscus is the one approaching you, but is it valid to infer that you know the one approaching? Aristotle hereby raised the question of whether one may know and not know the same thing at the same time—for example, you may not know the one approaching if Coriscus is wearing a mask, but you may know Coriscus. Buridan accepted that you *do* know the one approaching because you can see him, even if you do not know who he is, but Ockham did not.[55] In part also the interest in fallacies reflects the importance of the practice of live disputation in the schoolroom in the course of which arguments were proposed and then opposed. A science of opposing came to be recognized as a separate science from that of argument.

Because of the importance attached to the practice of disputation, great attention was paid to methods of coping with the stages reached in argument and with inferences arising from propositions. For example, if someone were to propose that 'good cricket is played at Lord's, therefore you must grant that good cricket is played at Lord's', the question might arise whether the inference that is proposed is what is called an obligation. 'An obligation', wrote Roger Swyneshed, 'is an expression by means of which someone is bound to reply affirmatively or negatively to the *obligatum*.'[56] Were an opponent to 'posit' that 'good cricket is played at Lord's', and were the *positio* to be admitted by a respondent, then hereafter, assuming there is no relevant change in the world of cricket, the respondent would be obliged to reply affirmatively to the *obligatum*: 'good cricket is played at Lord's.' If the opponent withdraws the proposition (by *depositio*), and if the respondent agrees with this *depositio*, then an *obligatio* comes into being whereby the respondent has to reply negatively if the opponent posits afresh that 'good cricket is played at Lord's'. The difficult part comes when the opponent advances further propositions on the basis of the first. To these the respondent may agree, or he may deny them, or he may indicate a doubt. Rules were formulated to govern these situations: if good cricket is played at Lord's, what should the respondent admit if asked to agree that Middlesex has had a disappointing season there? Is this irrelevant (*impertinens*)? A whole literature of *Obligations* came into being in the fourteenth century. The treatise on *Obligationes* written by the Benedictine monk Roger Swineshead (*c.*1330/ 1335) was amongst the most influential. In one short, anonymous treatise *On the Art of Obligation* (*De arte obligatoria*), written in Oxford in the 1330s or 1340s, the link with the practice of disputations is made very clear:

this art (of obligation) trains the respondent so that he pays attention to what is granted and denied, in order not to grant two incompatible things within the same time. For in *Sophistical Refutations* (XV. 174[a]17) Aristotle teaches the arguer to put forward many things so that the respondent who does not remember because of the large number may be refuted as regards his response to the things put forward. It is partly from this that the art has derived its structure, so that as long as we pay attention we may keep ourselves from being tricked. Just as it is important for a liar to have a good memory in order to make claims without asserting contraries, so for someone who is good at responding it is appropriate that he respond formally regarding the things admitted, granted, and denied—and remembered.[57]

The links between rhetoric and logic were not missing even in the medieval logician's classroom.

The rules governing disputation and types of argument were also developed in works which bore such titles as *Insolubles*, *Sophisms*, and *Knowing and Doubting*. Examples of frequently debated problems include paradoxical propositions such as 'I know that I do not know', 'I know that I know nothing', 'I know what I doubt'. Examples of the sort of rules that were formulated for obligations are: 'if a consequence is sound and its antecedent is known, the consequent must also be known', and: 'if a consequence is sound and its consequent is doubtful, the antecedent must also be doubtful or known to be false'. The distinction between valid/invalid consequences on the one hand and true/false consequences on the other was made. Ockham's list of false rules includes such rules as: the premisses are false/known/believed/doubtful/proved, therefore the conclusion is false/known/believed/doubtful/proved. Ockham was making the point that one of the premisses might be known/believed etc. by one person, the other known/believed etc. by another, and the conclusion known/believed etc. by neither.[58] Richard Kilvington, in his *Sophismata* written in the 1320s, put together a collection of puzzles involving words such as know/doubt/believe. His rules of obligations—rules for granting, denying, or doubting—were rules to be observed in disputations in which he dealt logically with mathematical and mechanical concepts such as those of velocity, change, and strength.[59] The application of logical techniques to problems that had a bearing on natural philosophy was, in fact, something of an Oxford tradition in the fourteenth century and those who promoted it were known as the 'Calculators'. One of these, William Heytesbury (born before 1313, d. c.1372), followed Kilvington, and in his treatise on *The Rules for Solving Sophisms* (*Regule solvendi sophismata* (written c.1335)) also showed an interest in the logical analysis of problems in physics.[60]

There were developments, too, in respect of modal logic— that is, the study of sentences concerning possibilities and necessities.[61] Aristotle was the starting-point for the study of modal logic, but by the fourteenth century new ideas of what is meant by possibility were in existence. Traditionally, distinctions had been drawn between possibility in the sense of what is opposite to impossibility, and possibility in the sense of what is not necessary. And traditionally such distinctions were applied to problems such as free will and the providence of God. Duns Scotus, however, developed a notion of logical, as distinct from real, possibility. Real possibility means that something that is possible can actually happen, and whatever is actual is really possible. But, since not everything that is possible can actually happen, Scotus withdrew the notion of possibility from the realm of what may become actual to the realm of logic. Not all logical possibility can be realized in the actual world. For example, if I say of the human free will that a man cannot will something and its opposite at the same time, I would be met by Scotus' objection that, although a man cannot actually will both simultaneously, it is none the less logically possibly for him to will each of two opposite objects at the same time.

A further branch of writing on logic dealt with insolubles. An example of these is the paradox 'I am lying'. Swineshead, Heytesbury, Fland, and Billingham, among others, contributed to it in the fourteenth century. When Thomas Bradwardine surveyed the field in 1321–4, he concluded that 'I am lying' does not say nothing, but he meant only that those words were uttered.

Ivan Boh has clarified the way in which the early 1300s represent an important landmark in the development of logic. Before the early fourteenth century, and indeed since Aristotle, the study of argumentation (the syllogism) was divided into such branches as the demonstrative (scientific knowledge produced on the basis of necessary premises), the topical (broadly speaking: based on probable premises), and the sophistical (fallacious or seemingly probable). The boundaries between these branches were not seen as watertight. Among various logical principles, rules of consequence now gained prominence. Syllogisms contain consequences, but logically prior to these were seen to be other consequences such as those contained in 'if' propositions. The study of topics was sometimes absorbed into the study of consequences. In the fourteenth

century the treatment of consequences was brought together
and consolidated, sometimes in the form of treatises called
Consequentie.[62]

In these developments in the study of logical puzzles, and in
the elaboration of rules for dealing with them, the pioneering
and prolific work of Walter Burley is of decisive importance and
remained influential for more than two centuries. Three of his
early works are, in fact, *Consequentie*, *Obligationes*, and
Insolubilia. His other works include the treatise *On the Purity of
the Art of Logic* (*De puritate artis logicae—tractatus brevior*)—
written in the early 1320s and providing a list of the general rules
for inference and proof[63]—and *Super artem veterem*, which was
completed in 1377. Walter Burley (*c*.1275–*c*.1344) was an almost
exact contemporary of William Ockham (*c*.1285–?1347), and in
the late 1320s, in his *Tractatus longior*, Burley offered criticisms
of Ockham's *Summa logicae* which was itself a comprehensive
and innovative work. Among the pre-eminent logicians of the
later part of the fourteenth century was Ralph Strode (d. 1387),
a fellow in 1359–60 of Merton College, Oxford. His *Logica*,
written in or shortly after 1359, has six parts which were often
copied as separate works (*De arte logica*, *De principiis
logicalibus*, *De suppositionibus*, *Consequentiae*, *Obligationes*,
and *De insolubilibus*). He included a list of rules (twenty-four in
total) governing consequences, a consequence being simply defined as an inference from an antecedent (*illatio consequentis ex
antecedente*—two propositions). The rules that govern these
provide a basis on which to adjudge when consequences are
good or bad, sound or unsound.[64] The fourteenth and fifteenth
centuries are acknowledged to be a period when English logicians were pre-eminent in Europe, and especially in the Italian
universities, where logicians such as Peter of Mantua (d. 1399),
Paul of Venice (d. 1429), Paul's pupil, Paul of Pergula (d.
c.1455), and many others admired and were guided by the writings of Burley, Ockham, and Strode, as well as by those of
Richard Kilvington, Swineshead, and Heytesbury. Paul of Venice, an Augustinian friar, spent at least three years in Oxford
after 1390 before returning to teach in Padua.[65]

Natural philosophy

There was new thinking generated in the fourteenth century on the theory of impetus, especially by Buridan and Oresme, and in relation to the circular movement of the stars and to falling bodies. According to Aristotle, movement was due either to the nature of a being (an internal principle) or to the communication of dynamism by a mover in contact with another being (an external principle). In the latter case, movement progressively weakens once contact between mover and moved ceases to be maintained. In the fifth century John Philoponus had answered Aristotle: a mobile, once propelled, is itself a moving force— having a *vis impressa* (a force impressed in itself)—albeit one that progressively weakens. In the fourteenth century, Buridan and others called this *vis* an impetus. We need to note the influence here of an ancient commentator upon Aristotle— Philoponus—whose work was rediscovered in the twelfth century.[66]

There was a seemingly endless debate over the cause of the movement of the heavenly bodies. Robert Kilwardby in 1271 distinguished three broadly differing views: (1) the heavenly spheres are animated and have souls, (2) the heavenly bodies are animated by Intelligences which are in contact with them (although not as their forms), and (3) the heavenly bodies move naturally and are not animated. Aquinas had come round to the Arab view (in his *Quaestiones disputatae de anima* (1268/9)) that the heavenly spheres were animated. But Kilwardby opted for the third view, that the stars move by their own weight. This opinion was to find more favour in the fourteenth century. For example, a contemporary of William Ockham, Francis de Marchia, who was himself a Franciscan friar and who was with Ockham at Avignon, clearly rejected the animation theory, on the grounds that there are no signs of vegetative or sensitive life in the heavenly bodies, and he applied the notion of impetus (that of a mover acting on a moved being), although with the qualification that, in the case of heavenly bodies, impetus results in a motion which is perpetual.[67]

Materialism

The study of natural philosophy led in several directions in the fertile fourteenth century, one of these being materialism, at least in the case of an Italian philosopher whose writings have now been carefully studied and whom one copyist named the *doctor diabolicus*. This is Blasius of Parma (Biagio Pelacani of Parma, *c.*1347–1416), who taught in Pavia, Bologna, and Padua and whose views were condemned as heretical in 1396 by the bishop of Pavia.[68] Blasius' vision of natural philosophy included the elevation of mathematics to the highest position among the sciences on account of the ability of mathematics to provide the highest degree of certainty. Under the influence of the Arabs, and in accordance with this preference for mathematics, he also gave a determinant place to astronomy and astrology. The other natural sciences he relegated to a lower place because they belong to the realm of contingency and provide scope for no more than conjecture and possible demonstration. In his commentary on Aristotle's *Physics* he denied the possibility of demonstrating (by arguing from effects to their causes) the existence of God as the primary cause. The supernatural world was in fact completely inaccessible by way of natural philosophy.

Blasius also completely abandoned earlier teaching on the soul as the substantial and immortal form of man. He took the view that the human soul is material form and should be studied in the light of mathematics, with particular attention given to considerations of quantity and space. The human intellect, like knowledge itself, grows and dies in accordance with natural processes. Human beings are generated from material putrefaction under the influence or *aspectus* of the stars which impress, according to the time and place at which birth occurs, differing physical, moral, and intellectual characteristics on individuals.[69] To the question 'whether the intellective soul can be separated from the body', Blasius gave a negative answer on the ground that the intellective soul is not independent of the sensitive soul or of the body in its activities; like the body, it is also material and corruptible. The difference between the activity of the sensitive and of the intellectual soul is not a substantial difference but merely a difference of perspective about the way the soul functions when a person, for example, feels the need to rest or to take up an activity. Rather than discern in the human person a plurality of souls—both intellective and sensitive—and thereby fall foul of the principle of economy, Blasius maintains that, although we can distinguish different activities undertaken by the soul, the soul is not distinct from the powers that it has. Blasius deduces from this that the human soul is material and mortal. Furthermore, eternal rewards and punishments are not earned through the practice of virtue or vice; the autonomous value of virtue or vice would be diminished if additional reward or recompense were available.

Blasius paved the way that led to a debate about the immortality of the soul and about the autonomy of ethics. A century later, his ideas were taken up by Pietro Pomponazzi who separated philosophy from religion in his *De immortalitate animae*.[70] Like Blasius, and like Siger and others a century before Blasius, Pomponazzi was prepared to deny philosophically what could, none the less, be accepted by faith and on the authority of the church.

8

The Fifteenth Century

Jean Gerson

Jean Gerson (1363–1429) was a renowned orator and preacher who succeeded Pierre d'Ailly as Chancellor of the University of Paris from 1395 to 1418. From 1415 to 1418 he attended the council of Constance; he died in 1429. This was a period of rising civil strife in France, the period also of the unrest created by the Hundred Years War between France and England. Further confusion was created by the papal schism and by the challenges put to the church by John Wycliffe in England and by John Hus in Bohemia. Gerson championed reform with vigour; a mighty stream of treatises, sermons, letters, and poems poured from his pen over many years.

One of his chief concerns as Chancellor of the University was with the teaching of scholastic philosophy and theology. In April 1400 Gerson issued a *Memorandum* concerning the Faculty of Theology and especially concerning its teaching of 'useless doctrines lacking fruit and solidity'. In the eyes of others the professors of theology had sunk to low depths of esteem. Some were held to be *rudes* (ignorant), others to be *curiosi aut phantastici* (curious and imaginary).[1] By the former Gerson meant the nominalist school, the *nominales* or *terministae*. By the latter he meant the Scotists. For over a quarter of a century Gerson repeatedly attacked the two groups, largely on the ground that their divisions and rivalries besmirched and jeopardized the teaching of theology. In 1402, in a work entitled *Contra curiositatem studentium*, he attacked the Scotists for introducing into the absolute simplicity of God metaphysical forms and quiddities and a thousand other divisions.[2] In 1426, in another work entitled *De modis significandi*, he again attacked the Scotists for rejecting Aristotle's logic; they, in turn, accuse their own critics (the nominalists) of being ignorant terminists who are non-realist in metaphysics (*rudes et terministae nec reales in metaphysica*).[3] A central issue for Gerson was the relationship, which is discussed in distinction VIII of Peter Lombard's *Sentences*, between God's simplicity and his perfections.

Gerson's polemics mislead us if we try, as historians used to do, to define the work of the Parisian theologians around the year 1400 in their light. In fact, Gerson was prolonging his experiences as a student in Paris twenty years before.[4] Before 1389 he himself had written a commentary on the *Sentences*, although this is now lost. However, we have evidence of these earlier struggles between Ockhamists and Scotists in a Commentary on the *Sentences* written by Peter of Candia who was in Paris between 1378 and 1381. He described two ways of wondering (*famosiores et moderniores modi imaginandi*) about the attributes of God. The first or Scotist way was to say that the attributes or the perfections of God are really distinct (*attributa sive perfectiones distinguuntur intrinsece ex natura rei*). The second or Ockhamist way was to deny that the perfections in God are really distinct (*nulle perfectiones sunt in divina essentia ex natura rei ab invicem formaliter vel realiter differentes*). To Peter of Candia the two schools were divided by the use of two different methods of enquiry (*modi investigandi*): the Ockhamists were engaged in logical investigations while the Scotists pursued metaphysical ones.

As a guide to philosophical investigations still taking place Gerson can no longer be trusted. His picture of *formalizantes* (a vague term) and nominalists quarrelling with each other is not a true picture of the opening years of the fifteenth century; rather it existed in his memory of his student years and, indeed, probably represents more nearly the years when Gerson's own teachers had been students themselves—that is, between 1360 and 1380. He prolongs earlier quarrels arising from the writings of Scotus, François de Meyronnes, and John de Ripa. He appears to be the last of the teachers of the fourteenth century to

feel dominated by the Ockhamist–Scotist divide. His anxiety
was primarily for theology. His nostalgia and conservative leanings are manifest in his letter *Jucundum*, written on 29 April
1400, in which he praised the great masters of the *Sentences* who
had taught in the thirteenth and early fourteenth centuries—
Bonaventure, St Thomas, Durand of Saint-Pourcain, and Henry
of Ghent.[5] None the less, although Gerson was, in a sense, living
in the past—an example of a university head who still thought in
the terms in which he himself had been taught—he was so
outspokenly critical of the state of philosophy that many must
have felt the power of his rhetoric and conviction. His strictures
bore upon the application of philosophical procedures to theology. He insisted that theologians adhere to patristic and scholastic tradition and to Aristotle's logic. He blamed the Scotist
formalizantes for inclining both to Platonism and to Augustinian
exemplarism, equating the divine ideas with universals and applying the formal distinction. Jerome of Prague, who was regent
master in arts in Paris in 1405, must have been in Gerson's mind.
Gerson's letter *Contra curiositatem studentium*[6] contains a com-
plaint against Platonizers who place the eternal 'quiddities' outside the mind and God, uncreated by God and indeed neither
creatable nor destroyable by God. He also fought against the
neo-Albertists (as they are now called), who were represented at
the time in Paris by Jean de Maisonneuve[7] and by his disciple
Heimericus de Campo, who wrote commentaries on Aristotle in
Paris before 1422. Gerson also waged battle against the English
for importing logic and metaphysics and even mathematics into
theology.[8] He castigated the followers of Buridan, although they
were no longer active *c*.1400. In short, Gerson impugned the
infertilis varietas of the schools of the time and condemned the
uncontrolled use of the *Sentences* as a place in which to promote
a diversity of views on logic, physics, and metaphysics. But his
attacks were very general. As a theologian and as a man of
letters Gerson was very partisan, ironical, and derisory.

   None the less, he heralds a new outlook: fidelity to tradition
and authority, submitting philosophy to the supreme judgement
of faith, these were to be leading characteristics of much of the

scholastic thought of the fifteenth century. Gerson attacked above all the *formalizantes*. In fact, what crumbled in Paris at this time was the domination of the nominalists and of the followers of Buridan. The latter had maintained that genera and species do not exist outside the mind. Within the Faculty of Arts, Jean de Maisonneuve developed neo-Albertism: Albert himself had found it impossible to decide whether universals exist only in the mind or are also part of the nature of things, but the neo-Albertists after Jean de Maisonneuve (who were fierce opponents of the teachings of Buridan) affirmed that intellectual knowledge was based on the reality of the universal.

Nicholas of Cusa

Nicholas of Cusa (1401–64) stands apart from the mainstream scholastic groups of his time. He shared with critics of the scholastics in the universities a mistrust of Aristotelian dialectic. In particular he rejected the Aristotelian principle of non-contradiction. He also returned to the Platonism found in Calcidius, Macrobius, and Denis, as well as drawing upon the writings of the twelfth-century 'Chartrains' such as Thierry of Chartres and Gilbert of Poitiers. In addition, he made a notable contribution to the controversy about the nature of mystical theology.[9] He was one of the most prestigious ecclesiastical scholars and statesmen of the fifteenth century and a prolific writer with an encyclopaedic range of learning. Through his sermons also, of which around 300 survive, he set forth extensively his unique contributions to philosophical and theological thought.

Why he developed in this way probably defies explanation. But the facts of his career enable us at least to follow the development of his interests. Born at Kues on the Moselle between Trier and Koblenz in 1401, Nicholas spent one year at the University of Heidelberg in 1416 before studying canon law at the University of Padua from 1417 to 1423 when he became *doctor decretorum*. After visiting Rome, he then returned to Germany and in 1425 he entered the University of Cologne to teach canon law but also to study philosophy and theology. However, he also developed an interest in manuscripts containing copies of classical texts during two journeys to Rome in 1427 and 1429/30 in the service of the archbishop of Trier. And in 1432 he was a delegate to the council of Basle, where disputes were pursued over the Hussite heresy in Bohemia and over the issue of sovereignty in the church and the respective claims to this of Pope Eugenius IV and the council. In 1433, still during the council, Nicholas wrote his *Catholic Concordance* (*De concordantia catholica*), a work which commenced as a contribution to the debate on the relationship between pope and council. To this work we shall return, but we need to note that in 1437, after supporting the aims of the council, he changed sides and became loyal to Pope Eugenius IV, having become convinced that the behaviour of the members of the council, as well as the absence of eastern representatives, had invalidated the council's acts as well as frustrated the consent of the church. In 1448 Nicholas became a cardinal and in 1450 bishop of Brixen or Bressanone in the Tyrol. He was heavily involved in conflicts with Sigismund, duke of the Tyrol, and with the violent local nobility as well as with corrupt religious, but none the less continued to write on philosophy and on the reform of the church until his death in Rome in 1464.

Cusa's work, *De concordantia catholica*, has importance as a work of political philosophy. Although he does not acknowledge the fact, he was indebted to the ideas contained in the *Defensor pacis* of Marsilius of Padua (1324), who also argued in favour of the supremacy of the conciliar principle in the government of the church. Cusa draws upon the canon law, the writings of the Fathers and the acts of the earliest councils of the church, and in addition makes practical suggestions for the reform of the empire. He does all this, however, with the support of a philosophical principle which is the notion of consent and of representation. Consent is required for law and government to be legitimate both in the church and in the empire.[10] Cusa invoked the authority of Gratian of Bologna to support the idea (derived from the Roman Stoics and Roman lawyers) that all valid legislation is based on natural law and natural law is based upon reason. Therefore all law is rooted by nature in the reason of man:

since all are by nature free, every governance whether it consists in a written law or is living law in the person of a prince . . . can only come from the agreement and consent of the subjects. For if by nature men are equal in power and equally free, the true properly ordered authority of one common ruler who is their equal in power cannot be naturally established except by the election and consent of the others and law is also established by consent.[11]

Although Cusa stops a long way short of advocating universal suffrage and although his usual idea of consent is probably one of tacit rather than express consent, like Marsilius of Padua he believes in the importance of majorities or of 'the weightier part' (a term taken from Marsilius), whether in church councils, when the pope meets with the bishops, or in imperial councils, when the emperor meets with the princes and the electors.[12] And he believed also in the principle of representation: in a church council, public persons such as patriarchs, cardinals, archbishops, and bishops represent the faithful more fully than does a pope acting on his own, but here too Cusa's idea of representation is implicit rather than explicit. The inclusion of bishops in a council enables such a body to reflect broadly the opinions of the different provinces which constitute the church and which, at least implicitly, have given consent to those who hold office. In this way Cusa is able to maintain that 'all power, whether spiritual or temporal and corporeal, is potentially in the people'.[13] But it comes from God by way of people and councils—that is, by means of elective consent.[14]

Cusa calls this position the 'intermediate' one: power comes from above as well as from below.[15] Finding the intermediate position on, for example, the question of the relationship between pope and council is the way to harmony—to concordance. Cusa's faith in 'catholic concordance' reflects his faith in the rational harmony of the whole universe. He begins *De concordantia catholica* by defining harmony: 'Flowing from the one King of Peace with infinite concordance, a sweet spiritual harmony of agreement emanates in successive degrees to all its members who are subordinated and united to him.'[16] Every concordance is made up of differences, and the less opposition there is between these differences, the greater the concordance and the longer its life. The highest concordance is the ineffable unity in trinity and trinity in unity that is God, and it is on this, with support from the writings of Denis the pseudo-Areopagite, that Cusa rests all his other arguments about concordance among the different grades of created being. As when different iron rings are attached to a magnet which holds them all in order, all gradations of being are held in order by the First Principle. 'These matters are important,' Cusa writes, 'because the investigation of all things in nature and the whole of creation depends on them.'[17]

To study Cusa's own contributions to philosophy, it is essential to start with his thought about the First Principle or God. Cusa was not a typical scholastic using technical terminology and writing *quaestiones* and commentaries in the customary way. Like Anselm of Canterbury he wrote short monographs that are often unparalleled and unique in the whole history of medieval thought. Like Eckhart, Cusa developed a highly dialectical form of speculative mysticism. Cusa also had a gift for imagery.

Cusa developed his ideas about the infinity of God in a number of works. In one of them, *De visione dei* (also known as *De icona*), which was written in 1453, he explored the vision that God has of his creatures as well as the vision that creatures may have of God. God has an eye that is able to see everything at once without turning. We have eyes that see only that to which they are turned and only from a finite angle. The Cause of all things sees all things in their Cause; His eye is an infinite sphere. Cusa drew attention to a celebrated painting by Roger de la Pasture of Christ with an omnivoyant face that appeared to gaze at every viewer at whatever angle.[18] This exemplifies *coincidentia*, the coincidence, which can only be fully effective in God, between seeing and being seen. In another work, *De non aliud*, Cusa wrestles with the problem of showing that God transcends the world yet is immanent in it. Immanent, God is not other than any thing; transcendent, God is Not-Other—without qualification. Nicholas uses an analogy: light is not the same thing as colour, yet in colour light is not other than colour. God can exist without the universe, as light can exist without colour. But just as colour is a modification of light, so too the universe may be represented as a modification of God. Or again: God is not the same thing as the sky which is 'an other', but he is in the sky and 'not other' than it.[19] Cusa's objective is to try to show that God is beyond all the distinctions that creatures can make, such as the distinction between sky and not-sky. Thus, God is not 'other than the sky' and not 'other than not-sky'. God is other than the universe, but in the universe God is 'not-other' than the universe.[20] God transcends these categories since he is 'Not-Other' absolutely.[21] With regard to the trinitarian nature of God, Nicholas turned to Thierry of Chartres and to his idea that the Holy Spirit is the *connexio unitatis et aequalitatis*, the union between Unity (God the Father) and Equality (God the Son).[22] Unity, Equality, and Union clearly indicated God's indistinction from himself, the undifferentiated nature of his being and his 'not-otherness'. He was also attracted to Thierry's representations of God as *forma essendi* and *entitas omnium rerum* (the form of being, the being of all things).

Cusa's works have been described as a series of attempts 'to transcend the usual conceptual confines'.[23] As a result Cusa delivered paradoxes which are liable both to intrigue and to appal his readers. His concern with the problem of God was never purely philosophical; it owed as much to the fifteenth-century debates over the nature of mystical theology. These concerned the roles of love and knowledge in the practice of faith and also the question whether a 'face-to-face' experience of God is possible in this life. Gerson had distinguished clearly between speculative theology and mystical theology, the former being the work of the intellectual power of the rational soul and the latter being the task of its affective power. Mystical theology, therefore, requires love of God, moral virtue and a perfect soul, not formal study; mysticism is, in fact, accessible to any believer whether learned or not.[24] Cusa certainly knew Gerson's work and was influenced by it. His own special contribution was the notion of 'learned ignorance'. His exploration of this theme, as well as of the 'negative way', like his efforts to overcome distinctions, was a lifelong activity.

This activity began in earnest in 1440 when he wrote his *De docta ignorantia* (*On Learned Ignorance*), in which he set out to explore the continuity and the interpenetration of faith and reason.[25] Like Anselm, he could write that 'faith enfolds in itself everything understandable; and understanding is the unfolding of faith'.[26] He discussed divine infinity and cosmic indefiniteness; man, who is the link between the two, is situated on the horizon between time and eternity. Cusa's definition of infinity was: absolute maximum and one. The absolute maximum is everything and all things are in it. Being also one, nothing can be added to, or subtracted from, infinity. The absolute maximum involves everything by implication. So God implicates all things in the sense that all things are in him; he also explicates all things since he is in all things. Thus, the maximum implicates motion, which is the explication of rest, and it implicates time, which is the explication of eternity. Time is an ordered present (the present is now, the past was present, and the future will be present). Finite beings participate in infinity, for otherwise they would not exist. But the infinite overcomes and transcends the finite order which is one of opposites or contraries. Infinity is the perfect coincidence of contraries (*coincidentia oppositorum*). The whole universe is in everything in a contracted way; everything contracts within itself the universe. To posit contradiction and then progressively to overcome it is the way to truth.

For seeking to show that God is all things (*deus est omnia*), and for thus appearing to promote pantheism, Nicholas suffered strong criticism from John Wenck, professor of theology in Heidelberg. Nine years later in 1449 Cusa revised his views in his *Apologia doctae ignorantiae* (*An Apology for Learned Ignorance*). Learned or acquired ignorance is itself a form of knowledge, a science or discipline (*scientia ignorantiae, doctrina ignorantiae*), to be pursued through the *via negativa*, following Eckhart's example. He denied that he received the idea of learned ignorance from Denis and asserted that he received it 'from above' (*desuper*). Again Cusa provoked controversy. In 1453 Vincent of Aggsbach, a Carthusian prior, denied that human reason can grasp mystical theology. If it could, such theology would cease to be mystical. Vincent argued that Cusa had overlooked the fact that the true way to union with God was through pure love, without the accompaniment of thought. Union with God was a pure gift of grace. But Cusa rejected the Carthusian's claim and sought, following the example of Eckhart, to present the 'concordances' between apparently opposite terms such as reason and faith, and nature and grace. He saw continuity, coincidence, and connection between such ideas, unlike his opponents who saw in them differences and contradictions.

Between 1452 and 1456 Cusa, who was by now bishop of Brixen, also corresponded on these matters with the abbot and prior of the Benedictine abbey of Tegernsee.[27] And in 1458 he wrote for the monks of Tegernsee a work entitled *De Beryllo* (*On the Wolf*) in which he presented as the key idea the intimate link between knowing and unknowing. He called this an enigma which is a guide in meditation and a key to unlocking an intellectual treasury. He rejected Aristotle's—the 'miserable' Aristotle's—principle of non-contradiction.[28] Cusa pursued and developed his views on learned ignorance in a number of other works also, such as the dialogue, *Idiota de Sapientia* (*The Wisdom of a Simpleton*), written in 1450, in which he urged, against the contentions of the Orator, that wisdom is not so closely related to learning, and learning not so closely related to the study of authority, that it cannot be attained without education. The simple layman is right who believes that wisdom is available to all who desire it; it does not require a formal education. In *De non aliud* (*On The Not-Other*), Cusa demonstrates how God is known unknowably or through ignorance. To know that God is is not to know what he is; we comprehend God incomprehensively. Cusa describes God as an undifferentiated being (that is, as a being which contains no difference within itself). We know something about him—namely, that we cannot know anything determinate about him. The paradox, when we recognize that God is not a differentiated being, is that we also recognize that we cannot intellectually know what the nature of this being is.[29]

In 1460 Cusa wrote his *Trialogus de Possest* in which he provided a final account of the main lines of his philosophical quest. Once again he upheld the view that a mystical vision of God is attainable by the pursuit of learned ignorance, by following the negative way, and by acceptance of the idea of *coincidentia oppositorum*. He also ranged widely over the fields of mathematics, astronomy, and cosmology.[30] His love of paradox was unabated, as when he explained how invisible things are seen and how God may be seen invisibly: when the intellect understands what the eye reads, it invisibly—that is, mentally—sees the invisible truth which is hidden behind what is written down. Invisible truth is the object of the intellect and cannot be seen in any other way.[31]

In May 1453 the city of Constantinople fell to Turkish forces. This victory of Islam over Christendom highlighted the concerns of many thinkers in the later Middle Ages about religious diversity. Cusa had visited Constantinople in 1437 to discuss, on behalf of the council of Basle, the unification of the eastern Orthodox Christians with their Latin Catholic counterparts in the West, and, while he was there, he discussed the *Koran* with eastern Christians. In September 1453 Cusa wrote a work *On the Peace of Faith* (*De pace fidei*) in which he promoted the idea of 'a single faith' (*una fides*) so that 'henceforth all the different religions might be harmoniously reduced, by the common consent of all men, to one'.[32] For 'there is one religion and worship which is presupposed in all the diversity of rites'.[33] And, 'since truth is one, and since it cannot fail to be grasped by every free intellect, all the diverse religions will be led into one orthodox faith'.[34] Perhaps only Cusa could have written in this way with such characteristic attention given to the power of intelligence, an optimistic confidence in finding harmony and concord, the possibility of common consent, and the oneness of truth.

But the roots of his latest peace initiative lay deep in earlier medieval thought. Nicholas had copied and read the works of Ramon Lull of Mallorca (1232–1316), including Lull's inter-faith dialogues, the *Liber de quinque sapientibus*, and the *Liber Tartari et Christiani*.[35] He also drew, as did many others, upon book VIII, chapter 9 of Augustine's *De civitate dei*, where Augustine proclaimed that all philosophers and all wise men in all nations have thought of God as the creator of all that exists, as the light of all that is knowable, and as the goodness in all that is to be done, the origin of nature, the truth of doctrine, and the happiness in life. And Augustine listed those philosophers from many nations who were witnesses to truth.[36] Similar convictions were shared by Cusa's companion at the council of Basle and in Constantinople, the Spanish cardinal, John of Segovia, archbishop of Caesarea (c.1393–1458), who hoped for the peaceful conversion of the Saracens and who wrote a long letter to Cusa on this subject in 1454.[37]

Humanism

In the fifteenth century the basic activities of university teaching, as established in the thirteenth and fourteenth centuries, were maintained, refined, and elaborated. Logic continued to be studied and taught. Commentaries on Aristotle were written and earlier medieval works were copied, read, and, from the later part of the century, printed. Scotists and Albertists were vigorous and numerous. Aquinas found an influential champion in John Capreolus (c.1380–1444), who ably restated his positions in his *Defensiones*.

However, humanist scholars now brought changes. Lorenzo Valla (1407–57) simplified and modified scholastic logic. He was more interested in non-syllogistic forms of argument and in the logic of plausibility and probability. In other words, he was more concerned with everyday ratiocination, with the sorts of arguments men use to support a case or to persuade and convince a partner in conversation or discussion. The art of rhetoric or of discourse was to be learned from Cicero and Quintilian and also from the *De topicis differentiis* of Boethius. Eventually, under humanist influence, the arts course in many European universities, especially north of the Alps, became a general introduction to classical Greek and Latin language and literature and to the use of elegant Latin for debate and clear thinking. There had always been a tension between the three arts of the trivium—grammar, logic, and rhetoric—and their integration could be achieved in a number of ways, according to the priority attached to each art. Moreover, a humanist education came to be increasingly concerned with ethics and politics, pragmatic subjects in which opinion and persuasive discourse played important roles. This too was not completely novel, since ethics and the teaching of the arts had always gone hand in hand. But in some schools in the fifteenth century, the arts course did cease to be a technical training in the use of the linguistic and dialectical tools valued by clerics to solve problems in philosophy or theology, and did become an education in literature and ethics rather than logic.

Shakespeare was later to reflect some of these shifts in *The Taming of the Shrew*, Act 1, scene 1, which is set in Padua ('nursery of arts'). Lucentio and his man Tranio have arrived from Pisa and Florence:

> LUCENTIO. Here let us breathe, and haply institute
> A course of learning and ingenious studies...
> ... therefore, Tranio, for the time I study,
> Virtue and that part of philosophy
> Will I apply that treats of happiness
> By virtue specially to be achieved...
> TRANIO. ... good master, while we do admire
> This virtue and this moral discipline,
> Let's be no Stoics nor no stocks, I pray,
> Or so devote to Aristotle's checks
> As Ovid be an outcast quite abjur'd.
> Balk logic with acquaintance that you have,
> and practise rhetoric in your common talk;
> Music and poesy use to quicken you;
> The mathematics and the metaphysics,
> Fall to them as you find your stomach serves you.

> No profit grows where there is no pleasure ta'en;
> In brief, sir, study what you most affect.

Even within logic, the introductions to logic written by Peter of Spain and Paul of Venice were displaced in the universities of northern Europe during the sixteenth century by the *De inventione dialectica* of Rudolph Agricola (1445–85) and by the *Dialectica* of Peter Ramus (1515–72).[38] Yet, in many ways 'medieval' thought lived on and indeed flourished in the Renaissance period in the sixteenth century. The writings and commentaries of Robert Grosseteste, Albert the Great, Thomas Aquinas, and William Ockham were at least as widely available as in the previous century, and so were the commentaries written by Averroes on the Aristotelian corpus. Averroes remained a central figure for (among others) Pietro Pomponazzi (1462–1525), who wrote a commentary on Averroes' *De substantia orbis* at Padua in 1508, and for Agostino Nifo (*c*.1470–1538), who (in 1497) wrote a commentary on Averroes' *Incoherence of the Incoherence* (*Destructio destructionum*). Nifo was unquestionably influenced by such medieval philosophers as Albert and Aquinas.

However, the arrival of new translations into Latin of Greek works expanded yet again the range of classical thought available for study and new directions were taken. Whereas in the earlier period only a part of Plato's *Timaeus* might be found, and very rarely also Plato's *Meno* and *Phaedo*, in the later fifteenth century nearly all of Plato's works could be read in Latin, including his *Republic*, *Theaetetus*, and *Symposium*. Although older scholastic traditions showed continuing vitality, the newer knowledge of Plato was keenly studied in the fifteenth century, especially in Italy. There was lively discussion of the relative merits of Plato and Aristotle—witness the work devoted to this by George of Trebizond (1395–*c*.1472) and entitled *Comparatio philosophorum Aristotelis et Platonis* (published in 1458).[39] George's strictures on Plato, including his accusation that Plato held that there were intermediate gods such as snakes and cattle, drew a sharp response from Cardinal Bessarion (*c*.1403–72) in his *In calumniatorem Platonis* (written in Greek in 1459 and revised in Latin in 1469). Bessarion was devoted to Plato but probably no less devoted to Thomas Aquinas, whom he called 'the greatest theologian and the wisest man'. Marsilio Ficino (1433–99), the most celebrated philosopher of the Italian *quattrocento*, was an enthusiastic student not only of Plotinus, Proclus, and Denis, but also of Augustine and Aquinas.[40] His *Theologia platonica* (1469–74)—on the immortality of the soul—was particularly central to his aims.[41]

Moreover, the range of available Greek commentaries on Aristotle expanded hugely after 1490, when the works of Alexander, Themistius, Ammonius, Philoponus, and Simplicius came into the West. New translations and new commentaries were made of Aristotle's works by Italian scholars from the time of Leonardi Bruni in the early fifteenth century. But this still does not mean that earlier scholastic writers or the authorities they discussed ceased to be central in the study of philosophy: Leonardi Bruni's translation of the *Nicomachean Ethics*, for example, was a revision of that of Grosseteste. The spread of printing from the mid-fifteenth century neither overlooked older medieval texts nor displaced the continuing tradition of producing manuscript copies of them. The Arabian commentators on Aristotle, especially Averroes, continued to be relied upon in the Renaissance period, and their works accompanied those of Aristotle in many sixteenth-century editions. The works of thirteenth-century thinkers such as Aquinas and of fourteenth-century thinkers such as Thomas Bradwardine, William Heytesbury, and Paul of Venice went into print, and by doing so became more conveniently accessible to more scholars than before. There was too a deep interest during the Renaissance in Ramon Lull. In many ways it would be better to view the Renaissance period, not as a period in which medieval interests were edged out, but as a time of further renewed enlargement of the range of knowledge that had previously expanded when translations of works out of Greek and Arabic arrived in the twelfth and thirteenth centuries. The corpus of Aristotle's works remained in the sixteenth and seventeenth centuries just as central in university teaching as they were in the thirteenth century and after. In spite of the revival of the study of Greek in the Renaissance, most teaching and writing on philosophy continued to be given in Latin, and in the same universities as before—Paris and Prague, Bologna and Oxford, Salamanca and Louvain, and many others.

Notes

Introduction

1. Ed. A. H. Armstrong (Cambridge, 1967); see Armstrong's introductory ch. 1, esp. p. 9.

2. The sub-title of this volume is: *From the Rediscovery of Aristotle to the Disintegration of Scholasticism* 1100–1600, ed. N. Kretzmann, A. Kenny, and J. Pinborg; associate ed. E. Stump (Cambridge, 1982). See introduction, p. 2: 'it is part of our aim to present the medieval *Aristotelian* tradition and the scholastic innovations that developed in that tradition'.

3. (Cambridge, 1988).

4. G. Verbeke, *The Presence of Stoicism in Medieval Thought* (Washington, 1983), is a pioneering study. For the early part of the period, see M. Colish, *The Stoic Tradition from Antiquity to the Early Middle Ages* (2 vols.; Leiden, 1985). For the twelfth century, see M. Lapidge, 'The Stoic Inheritance', in P. Dronke (ed.), *Twelfth-Century Western Philosophy*, ch. 3.

5. R. W. Southern, *Scholastic Humanism and the Unification of Europe*, i. *Foundations* (Oxford, 1995), pp. vi–vii.

6. On the development of the study of medieval philosophy during the present and the past century, and on the differences in its development in different countries, see *Gli studi di filosofia medievale fra otto e novecento. Contributo a un bilancio storiografico. Atti del convegno internazionale, Roma, 21–23 settembre, 1989*, ed. R. Imbach and A. Maierù (Storia e letteratura, 179; Rome, 1991).

7. *Scholastic Humanism*, i. 17–18.

8. Trans. A. C. H. Downes (New York, 1940).

9. See P. Vignaux, *Philosophie au moyen âge* (Albeuve, 1987).

10. (London, 1955).

11. In 1845 the French Académie des Sciences Morales et Politiques organized a prize for the best work to be written on the history of thirteenth- and fourteenth-century philosophy considered apart from theology as far as it was possible to do so ('autant du moins

que le permettrait le lien intime de ces deux sciences au Moyen Age'). I owe this reference to Alain de Libera, *La Querelle des universaux. De Platon à la fin du moyen âge* (Paris, 1996), 11. The prize was won by Barthélemy Hauréau (1812–86), whose *Histoire de la philosophie scolastique* (Paris, 1872–80) is one of the great monuments in the history of medieval thought.

12. *Logica modernorum: A Contribution to the History of Early Terminist Logic*, ed. L. M. de Rijk (2 vols.; Assen, 1962–7).

13. The *Corpus* is directed by Kurt Flasch and Loris Sturlese and published by Felix Meiner Verlag, Hamburg.

14. *The Cambridge Translations of Medieval Philosophical Texts*, ed. N. Kretzmann and E. Stump (Cambridge, 1988–) are welcome in this regard. As the editors write (i. 1): 'Only a very small percentage of the surviving medieval philosophical literature is available in modern critical editions, and a much smaller percentage is available to readers who do not read medieval Latin.' The opportunities for widening and promoting knowledge in this field are incalculable, partly as a result of the widespread, continuing identification by scholars of manuscript copies of texts, as well as of the continuing willingness of scholars to prepare critical editions with modern language translations.

Chapter 1

1. For Aristotle, see the important collection of essays edited by Richard Sorabji, *Aristotle Transformed: The Ancient Commentators and their Influence* (London, 1990).

2. See esp. H.-I. Marrou, *S. Augustin et la fin de la culture antique* (2nd edn., Paris, 1949), p. xiv. There are excellent studies of Augustine which may serve as introductions to his life and work, among them being: P. Brown, *St Augustine of Hippo: A Biography* (London, 1967), G. Bonner, *St Augustine of Hippo: Life and Controversies* (London, 1963), E. Gilson, *The Christian Philosophy of St Augustine*, trans. L. E. M. Lynch (London, 1961). For information on Augustine's works and on editions of these, see, besides the above, H. Marrou, *Saint Augustine and his Influence through the Ages* (New York, 1957 (in cooperation with J. J. O'Meara)).

3. *De ideis* 2 (Patrologia latina, ed. J.-P. Migne (Paris, 1841–55), vol. 40, col. 30; hereafter cited as PL).

4. Ibid. (*De divinis quaestionibus*, 83, *qu.* 46) (PL 40.31). On some aspects of Augustine's thought on mind, see Janet Coleman, *Ancient and Medieval Memories. Studies in the Reconstruction of the Past* (Cambridge, 1992), 80–111.

5. On ideas of time, see R. A. Markus, *Saeculum: History and Society in the Theology of St Augustine* (Cambridge, 1970), and R. Sorabji, *Time, Creation and the Continuum: Theories in Antiquity and the Early Middle Ages* (London, 1983).

6. See W. H. C. Frend, *The Donatist Church* (Oxford, 1952).

7. Trans. Brown, *St Augustine*, 387–8, from Augustine, *Opus imperfectum* III. 67–71 (PL 45.1278–9).

8. Brown, *St Augustine*, 387.

9. *Confessions*, VI.14. Also IV.6 (with reference to Horace, *Odes* I.3:8): 'How well the poet put it when he called his friend the other half of his soul!' Translations of the *Confessions* include the excellent translation by Henry Chadwick, *Saint Augustine: The Confessions* (Oxford, 1992).

10. *Confessions*, IV.4. See, for orientation, James McEvoy, 'De la *philia* païenne à l'*amicitia* chrétienne: Rupture et continuité', in B. C. Bazán *et al.* (eds.), *Les Philosophies morales et politiques au Moyen Âge—Moral and Political Philosophies in the Middle Ages*, (3 vols.; Ottawa, 1995), i. 136–47.

11. PL 32.591.

12. The *Dialectic* has been translated by B. Darrell Jackson from the edition made by J. Pinborg (Dordrecht, 1975). See also J. Pepin, *Saint Augustin et la dialectique* (Villanova, 1976).

13. M. Grabmann, *Die Geschichte der scholastischen Methode* (Freiburg, 1909; repr. Darmstadt, 1957), i, pt. 3, pp. 148–77: 'Boethius, der letzte Römer—der erste Scholastiker'. See H. Chadwick, *Boethius: The Consolations of Music, Logic, Theology and Philosophy* (Oxford, 1981); M. Gibson (ed.), *Boethius, his Life, Thought and Influence* (Oxford, 1981). For editions of Boethius' writings—the editions in PL 63–4 are the most accessible of the collected editions—Chadwick provides invaluable guidance on pp. 258–9.

14. Boethius' translations of Aristotle's logical works have been edited by L. Minio-Paluello in vols. I, II, III, V, and VI of Aristoteles Latinus (Leiden, 1961–).

15. On them, see Chadwick, *Boethius*, 141–52.

16. Both commentaries have been best edited by S. Brandt in Corpus

Scriptorum Ecclesiasticorum Latinorum, 48 (1906). Porphyry's *Isagoge* has been translated by E. W. Warren (Toronto, 1975).

17. 'Sensible' here (and later in this book) means 'perceptible by the senses', not 'intelligent, reasonable, judicious' (*OED*). 'Sensible' and 'intelligible' ('capable of being apprehended only by the understanding' (*OED*)) are commonly used as opposites in medieval thought.

18. See L. Minio-Paluello, 'The Genuine Text of Boethius' Translation of Aristotle's *Categories*', in *Opuscula: The Latin Aristotle* (Amsterdam, 1972), 1–21.

19. Minio-Paluello, *Opuscula*, 299–309; also Minio-Paluello, introduction to the edition of the text, Aristoteles Latinus, V.1–3.

20. Trans. E. Stump, *Boethius's De Topicis Differentiis* (Ithaca, NY, 1978).

21. For the history of logic in the Middle Ages, see esp. P. Boehner, *Medieval Logic: An Outline of its Development from 1250–c.1400* (Manchester, 1952), I. M. Bocheński, *A History of Formal Logic*, trans. I. Thomas (Notre Dame, Ind., 1961), and William Kneale and Martha Kneale, *The Development of Logic* (Oxford, 1962).

22. 'Aristotelis Platonisque sententias in unam quodammodo revocare concordiam, eosque non ut plerique dissentire in omnibus, sed in plerisque et his in philosophia maximis consentire demonstrem' (*De interpretatione, Editio secunda*, ed. C. Meiser (Teubner Library, 1877–80), 79).

23. H. F. Stewart and E. K. Rand (ed. and trans.), *The Theological Tractates and the Consolation of Philosophy* (London, 1918; rev. edn. by S. J. Tester, 1973). The editions by R. Peiper for the Teubner Library in 1871 still hold the field.

24. For a translation, see n. 23; also V. E. Watts (Penguin Books; Harmondsworth, 1969). Editions include those made by W. Weinberger in Corpus Scriptorum Ecclesiasticorum Latinorum, 67 (1934), and by L. Bieler in Corpus Christianorum, 94 (1957).

25. III, m. 9, ll. 1–12, 22–4, trans. V. E. Watts, p. 97. Chadwick (*Boethius*, 234–5) skilfully summarizes the sources of each idea in the poem, chiefly Plato's *Dialogues* and Proclus' commentary on the *Timaeus*.

26. J. C. Frakes, *The Fate of Fortune in the Middle Ages: The Boethian Tradition* (Studien und Texte zur Geistesgeschichte des Mittelalters, Leiden, 1988).

27. See P. Courcelle, *La Consolation de philosophie dans la tradition littéraire: Antécédents et postérité de Boèce* (Paris, 1967); D. K. Bolton, 'The Study of the Consolation of Philosophy in Anglo-Saxon England', *Archives d'histoire doctrinale et littéraire au moyen âge*, 44, Année 1977 (1978), 33–78.

28. Ed. J. Willis (2 vols.; 2nd edn., Leipzig, 1970); *Macrobius: Commentary on the Dream of Scipio*, trans. with an introduction and notes by W. H. Stahl (New York, 1966).

29. Denis' writings are impressively presented in *Dionysiaca: Recueil donnant l'ensemble des traductions latines des ouvrages attribués au Denys l'Aréopage* (2 vols.; Bruges, 1937). These volumes were prepared by P. Chevallier, monk of Solesmes. The medieval Latin translations are printed together line by line along with the Greek texts (as found in the Paris MS, Bibliothèque Nationale, grec 437), the French translation by C. David, and the thirteenth-century Latin paraphrases of Thomas Gallus. A Latin–Greek Concordance is found in the *Thesaurus Pseudo-Dionysii Areopagitae: Versiones Latinae cum Textu Graeco* published by CETEDOC under the direction of P. Tombeur (Turnhout, 1995). Especially valuable also are the introduction (by R. Roques), edition (by G. Heil), and French translation (by M. de Gandillac) of the *Celestial Hierarchy: Denys l'Aréopagite. La Hiérarchie céleste* (Sources chrétiennes, no. 58bis; 2nd edn., Paris, 1970). For English translations, see C. E. Rolt, *Dionysius the Areopagite: On the Divine Names and The Mystical Theology* (London, 1920), and T. L. Campbell, *The Ecclesiastical Hierarchy* (New York, 1981).

30. These words are the title of A. O. Lovejoy's influential book, *The Great Chain of Being* (Cambridge, Mass., 1936). Surprisingly, Lovejoy scarcely mentions Denis. Lovejoy's work has been reassessed in a volume of essays edited by Simo Knuuttila, *Reforging the Great Chain of Being: Studies of the History of Modal Theories* (Synthese Historical Library; Dordrecht, 1980).

31. The three triads of the nine orders of angels are, according to Denis, seraphim, cherubim, thrones; dominations, virtues, powers, principalities, archangels, angels (*Celestial Hierarchy*, chs. 7–9). Denis, unlike his medieval readers from the twelfth century onwards, does not provide a fully corresponding hierarchy in the church; he presents (*Ecclesiastical Hierarchy*, chs. 5–6) only two triads, one of initiators (bishops, priests, ministers), the other of the initiated (monks, holy people, purified orders).

Chapter 2

1. R. A. B. Mynors's distinguished edition of Cassiodorus' *Institutiones* (Oxford, 1937) includes an important study of the transmission of the work during the Middle Ages; for a translation, see L. W. Jones, *An Introduction to Divine and Human Readings by Cassiodorus Senator* (New York, 1946).

2. *Etymologiarum siue Originum libri XX*, ed. W. M. Lindsay (2 vols.; Oxford, 1911).

3. Aristoteles Latinus, I.1–5, pp. 133–75.

4. Attention began to be given to the text of Aristotle's *Categories* in Boethius' translation in the time of Gerbert of Rheims (d. 1003), who used it in his teaching, and of Notker (d. 1022), who commented on the work. See further John Marenbon, 'Medieval Latin Glosses and Commentaries on Aristotelian Logical Texts, Before c.1150 AD', in *Glosses and Commentaries on Aristotelian Logical Texts: The Syriac, Arabic and Medieval Latin Traditions* (Warburg Institute Surveys and Texts, 23; London, 1993), 77–127.

5. *De nuptiis Philologiae et Mercurii*, ed. A. Dick (Leipzig, 1925; repr. with corrections, Stuttgart, 1970).

6. For a clear summary of Carolingian discussions of theological problems, including those concerning the soul and predestination, see David Ganz in Rosamond McKitterick (ed.), *The New Cambridge Medieval History* (Cambridge, 1995), ii, ch. 28.

7. Augustine, *De quantitate animae*, lib. I, *c.*32, §69 (PL 32.1073).

8. See D. C. Lambot (ed.), *Liber de Anima ad Odonem Bellovacensem* (Namur, 1952).

9. *De divina praedestinatione liber*, ed. G. Madec (Corpus Christianorum, Continuatio Mediaeualis, 50; Turnhout, 1978).

10. *Expositiones in Ierarchiam Coelestem*, ed. J. Barbet (Corpus Christianorum, Continuatio Mediaeualis, 31; Turnhout, 1975).

11. I.27; PL 122.475AB. I. P. Sheldon-Williams (ed. and trans.), *Periphyseon I–III* (Dublin, 1968–81); a new critical edition is in preparation by E. Jeauneau (Toronto). An abridged translation was made by M. L. Uhlfelder and J. A. Potter, *John the Scot, Periphyseon* (Indianapolis, 1976).

12. e.g. *Periphyseon* V.4; PL 122.868C–870C.

13. *Periphyseon* V.4; PL 122.870B.

14. *Periphyseon* IV.4; PL 122.749A.

15. *Periphyseon* IV; PL 122.748D–749A.

16. Ed. E. Jeauneau, *Homélie sur le Prologue de Jean* (Paris, 1969); also Jeauneau (ed.), *Commentaire sur l'Évangile de Jean* (Paris, 1972).

17. *Annotationes in Marcianum*, ed. C. Lutz (Cambridge, Mass., 1939).

18. *Remigii Autissiodorensis Commentum in Martianum Capellam*, ed. C. Lutz (Leiden, 1962–5).

Chapter 3

1. Ed. (with French trans.) A. Cantin, *Pierre Damien, Letttre sur la Toute-Puissance Divine* (Sources chrétiennes, 191; Paris, 1972).

2. Lanfranc, *Liber de corpore et sanguine domini*, PL 150.407–42; *Beringarius Turonensis, Rescriptum contra Lanfrancum*, ed. R. B. C. Huygens (Corpus Christianorum, Continuatio Mediaeualis, 84; Turnhout, 1987).

3. Anselm's *Opera omnia* have been edited by F. S. Schmitt (6 vols.; Edinburgh, 1946–61). Most of Anselm's writings have been translated into English: S. N. Deane, *St Anselm, Basic Writings* (2nd edn., La Sale, Ill., 1962)—*Monologion, Proslogion*, and *Cur Deus Homo*; J. Hopkins and G. Richardson, *Anselm of Canterbury*, (London, 1974)—*Monologion* and *Proslogion*; M. J. Charlesworth, *Proslogion with a Reply on Behalf of the Fool by Gaunilo and the Author's Reply to Gaunilo* (Oxford, 1965); E. R. Fairweather, *A Scholastic Miscellany, Anselm to Ockham* (The Library of Christian Classics, 10; Philadelphia, 1956)—*Cur Deus Homo, Proslogion*; J. Hopkins and G. Richardson, *Truth, Freedom and Evil: Three Philosophical Dialogues* (New York, 1967); D. P. Henry, *The De Grammatico of St Anselm: The Theory of Paronymy* (Notre Dame, Ind., 1964).

4. *Proslogion* I; I.100:18.

5. See Alain de Libera, *La Querelle des universaux. De Platon à la fin du moyen âge* (Paris, 1996).

6. *The Letters of Abelard and Heloise*, trans. B. Radice (Penguin Classics; Harmondsworth, 1974), 60. Another translation of the autobiography, *Historia calamitatum*, is that by J. T. Muckle, *The Story of Abelard's Adversities* (Toronto, 1954). For the Latin text, see J. Monfrin (ed.), *Pierre Abélard: Historia calamitatum* (2nd edn., Paris, 1962).

7. 'Qui autem querit, dubitationem suam exprimit, ut certitudinem quam nondum habet, consequatur' (*Petrus Abaelardus, Dialectica*,

ed. L. M. de Rijk (2nd rev. ed., Assen, 1970), 153). Abelard expressed himself in a similar way when describing his attitude to the study of Christian texts including the Bible and the writings of the Church Fathers: 'The first key of wisdom is assiduous and frequent questioning. . . . Aristotle, the most perceptive of all philosophers, exhorted his students by saying: ". . . Doubting everything will not be useless" (*Categories* 8). For by doubting we come to enquire, and by enquiry we come to the truth. Truth itself has said: "Seek and you shall find; knock and it shall be opened unto you" (Matthew 7: 7)' (*Haec quippe prima sapientiae clavis definitur assidua scilicet seu frequens interrogatio; ad quam quidem toto desiderio arripiendam philosophus ille omnium perspicassimus Aristoteles in praedicamento Ad Aliquid studiosos adhortatur dicens, 'Fortasse autem difficile est de huiusmodi rebus confidenter declarare nisi saepe pertractata sint. Dubitare autem de singulis non erit inutile'. Dubitando quippe ad inquisitionem venimus; inquirendo veritatem percipimus*) (*Peter Abailard. Sic et Non*, ed. B. Boyer and R. McKeon (Chicago, 1976, 1977), Prologue, pp. 103–4).

8. Letter 13, *Peter Abelard. Letters IX–XIV*, ed. E. R. Smits (Groningen, 1983), 271–7; Smits provides a commentary on pp. 172–88.

9. Abelard, *Theologia 'Summi boni'*, II.78, in *Petri Abaelardi Opera theologica*, ed. E. M. Buytaert and C. J. Mews, iii (Corpus Christianorum, Continuatio Mediaeualis, 13; Turnhout, 1987), 141: 'in deo nullum propriam inuentionem uocabulum seruare uidetur, sed omnia que de eo dicuntur, translationibus et parabolicis enigmatibus inuoluta sunt et per similitudinem aliquam uestigantur ex parte aliqua inductam, ut aliquid de illa ineffabili maiestate suspicando potius quam intelligendo degustemus'.

10. *Peter Abelard's Ethics*, ed. and trans. D. E. Luscombe (Oxford Medieval Texts; Oxford, 1971).

11. See P. Delhaye, 'La Place de l'éthique parmi les disciplines scientifiques au XIIe siècle', *Mélanges A. Janssen* (Louvain, 1948), 29–44; 'L'Enseignement de la philosophie morale au XIIe siècle', *Mediaeval Studies*, 11 (1949), 77–99; 'Grammatica et ethica au XIIe siècle', *Recherches de théologie ancienne et médiévale*, 2 (1958), 59–110. Also my own 'Ethics and Politics in the Eleventh and Twelfth Centuries', in B. C. Bazán *et al.* (eds.), *Les Philosophies morales et politiques au Moyen Âge—Moral and Political Philosophies in the Middle Ages* (Ottawa, 1995), i. 74–87.

12. *De differentiis topicis* II (PL 64.1188): 'virtus est habitus mentis bene constitutae'.

13. 'Summum utique bonum aput omnes recte philosophantes non aliud quam Deum dici constat et credi', *Dialogus inter Philosophum, Iudaeum et Christianum*, ed. R. Thomas (Stuttgart, 1970), 127–8. The *Dialogus* has been translated into English by Pierre J. Payer, *Peter Abelard: A Dialogue of a Philosopher with a Jew and a Christian* (Mediaeval Sources in Translation, 20; Toronto, 1979).

14. 'Virtus, inquiunt, est habitus animi optimus; sic e contrario vitium arbitror esse habitum animi pessimum; habitum vero hunc dicimus, quem Aristotiles in *Categoriis* distinxit, cum in habitu et dispositione primam qualitatis speciem comprehendit. Est igitur habitus qualitas rei non naturaliter insita, sed studio ac deliberatione conquisita et difficile mobilis' (Abelard, *Dialogus*, ed. Thomas, 115–16).

15. Ibid. 117–18.

16. Ibid. 124–5.

17. *Policraticus*, ed. C. C. J. Webb (2 vols.; Oxford, 1909), bk. VII, ch. 8; English trans. C. J. Nederman, *John of Salisbury, Policraticus* (Cambridge Texts in the History of Political Thought; Cambridge, 1990). Nederman's translation of the *Policraticus* is of selections of the work, as are the translations made by John Dickinson, *The Statesman's Book* (New York, 1927) and by J. B. Pike, *The Frivolities of Courtiers and the Footprints of Philosophers* (Minneapolis, 1938). But if Dickinson and Pike are used together, an almost complete translation is found. A new edition is being prepared by K. S. B. Keats-Rohan, who has so far published *Ioannis Saresberiensis Policraticus I–IV* (Corpus Christianorum, Continuatio Mediaeualis, 118; Turnhout, 1993).

18. *The Commentaries on Boethius by Gilbert of Poitiers*, ed. N. Haring (Toronto, 1966). See on Gilbert: *Gilbert de Poitiers et ses contemporains: Aux origines de la 'Logica Modernorum': Actes du VIIe Symposium européen de logique et de sémantique médiévales, Poitiers, Centre d'études supérieures de civilisation médiévale, 17–23 juin 1985* (History of Logic, 5; Naples, 1987).

19. R. W. Southern, *Scholastic Humanism and the Unification of Europe*, i. *Foundations* (Oxford, 1995), 58–101.

20. Ibid. 202.

21. Peter Lombard, I *Sent.* d. 8 (Quaracchi, 1916; 3rd edn., Rome,

1971–81). On Peter Lombard, see Marcia L. Colish, *Peter Lombard* (2 vols.; Leiden, 1994).

22. See J. M. Parent, *La Doctrine de la création dans l'école de Chartres* (Publications de l'Institut d'Études Médiévales; Paris, 1938), 124–36.

23. *Guillaume de Conches, Glose super Platonem*, ed. E. Jeauneau (Textes philosophiques du moyen âge, 13; Paris, 1965). For the *Timaeus*, see *Plato Latinus*, ed. R. Klibansky (London, 1940–62), iv. *Timaeus a Calcidio translatus commentarioque instructus*, ed. J. H. Waszink.

24. *De philosophia mundi*, PL 172.39–102 (under the authorship of Honorius Augustodunensis), PL 90 (under the authorship of Bede). A new edition has been made by G. Maurach (Pretoria, 1980).

25. The *Dragmaticon* was edited under the title *Dialogus de Substantiis Physicis* by G. Gratarolus (Strasbourg, 1567; repr. Frankfurt am Main, 1967).

26. *Moralium Dogma Philosophorum*, ed. J. Holmberg (Uppsala, 1929). On the question of authorship, see J. R. Williams, 'The Quest for the Author of the *Moralium Dogma Philosophorum*, 1931–1956', *Speculum*, 32 (1957), 736–47.

Chapter 4

1. *Ethica Nicomachea. Praefatio*, R.-A. Gauthier (Aristoteles Latinus, XXVI.1–3, fasc. 1; 1974), pp. xvi–cli.

2. *Chartularium Universitatis Parisiensis*, ed. H. Denifle and A. Châtelain (4 vols.; Paris, 1889–97), i, no. 20.

3. *Ethica Nicomachea. Praefatio*, Gauthier, pp. cxlii–cxlvii.

4. See *Guillaume de Moerbeke: Recueil d'études à l'occasion du 700ᵉ anniversaire de sa mort (1286)*, ed. J. Brams and W. Vanhamel (Leuven, 1989), also L. Minio-Paluello, 'William of Moerbeke', *Dictionary of Scientific Biography*, ix (New York, 1974), 434–40.

5. *De generatione et corruptione. Translatio vetus*, ed. J. Judycka (Aristoteles Latinus, IX. 1; Leiden, 1986).

6. See C. B. Schmitt and D. Knox, *Pseudo-Aristoteles Latinus: A Guide to Latin Works Falsely Attributed to Aristotle before 1500* (Warburg Institute Surveys and Texts, 12; London, 1985), where ninety-six medieval Latin *spuria* are surveyed.

7. See *Pseudo-Aristotle, 'The Secret of Secrets': Sources and Influences*, ed. W. F. Ryan and C. B. Schmitt (Warburg Institute Surveys and Texts, 9; London, 1983).

8. R.-A. Gauthier, 'Deux témoignages sur la date de la première traduction latine des "Économiques"', *Revue philosophique de Louvain*, 50 (1952), 273–83.

9. As in the Latin West, the study of theology was accompanied often by the study of philosophy; see L. Gardet and M. M. Anawati, *Introduction à la théologie musulmane: Essai de théologie comparée* (2nd edn., Études de philosophie médiévale, 37; Paris, 1970), and R. Caspar, *Traité de théologie musulmane*, i. *Histoire de la pensée religieuse musulmane* (Pontificio Istituto di Studi Arabi e d'Islamologia; Rome, 1987).

10. For al-Ghazali's *Metaphysics*, see the edition by J. T. Muckle, *Algazel's Metaphysics: A Mediaeval Translation* (Toronto, 1933), and for his *Logic*, C. H. Lohr, 'Logica Algazelis: Introduction and Critical Text', *Traditio*, 21 (1965), 223–90. Also see D. Salman, 'Algazel et les latins', *Archives d'histoire doctrinale et littéraire du moyen âge*, 10 (1935–6), 103–27.

11. See C. Baeumker (ed.), *Avencebrolis (Ibn Gabirol), Fons Vitae ex Arabico in Latinum translatus ab Iohanne Hispano et Dominico Gundissalino* (Beiträge zur Geschichte der Philosophie und der Theologie des Mittelalters, vol. 1, pts. 2–4; Münster, 1892–5). H. E. Wedeck has made a partial translation of Ibn Gabirol's *The Fountain of Life* (New York, 1962).

12. Much material on this is provided by A. Hyman and J. J. Walsh, *Philosophy in the Middle Ages: The Christian, Islamic and Jewish Traditions* (New York, 1967).

13. For the Latin translations of Avicenna's works, see *Avicenna Latinus*, ed. S. van Riet (Louvain, 1968–). Among the best studies of Avicenna is J. R. Michot, *La Destinée de l'homme selon Avicenne: Le Retour à Dieu (ma'ad) et l'imagination* (Académie Royale de Belgique, Fonds René Draguet, 5; Louvain, 1986). Part of Avicenna's work has been translated into English by F. Rahman, *Avicenna's Psychology: An English Translation of Kitab al-Najat, Book II, chapter VI* (London, 1952). The *Shifa* has been translated into French by G. Anawati, *Avicenne: La Métaphysique du Shifa* (2 vols.; Paris, 1978, 1985).

14. Averroes' commentaries, printed earlier in *Aristotelis opera cum Averrois commentariis* (Venice, 1562–74), are being critically ed-

ited in the *Corpus Commentariorum Averrois in Aristotelem* published by the Mediaeval Academy of America. Translations of some of Averroes' writings are: *The Incoherence of the Incoherence*, by S. van Bergh (2 vols.; Oxford, 1954); *Averroes on the Harmony of Religions and Philosophy*, by G. F. Hourani (London, 1961); *Averroes on Aristotle's De Generatione et Corruptione, Middle Commentary and Epitome*, by S. Kurland (Cambridge, Mass., 1958). An excellent bibliographical tool has been provided by P. W. Rosemann, 'Averroes: A Catalogue of Editions and Scholarly Writings from 1821 Onwards', *Bulletin de la Société pour l'Étude de la Philosophie Médiévale*, 30 (1988), 153–221. A classic study is by L. Gauthier, *Ibn Rochd (Averroes)* (Paris, 1948). There are important essays by H. A. Wolfson in his *Studies in the History of Philosophy and Religion*, i, ed. I. Twersky and G. H. Williams (Cambridge, Mass., 1973). See now also H. A. Davidson, *Alfarabi, Avicenna and Averroes on Intellect: The Cosmologies, Theories of the Active Intellect, and Theories of Human Intellect* (New York, 1992).

15. An edition of the *Liber de causis* is contained in R. Steele's edition of Roger Bacon's *Quaestiones supra Librum de causis* (*Opera hactenus inedita Rogerii Baconis*, xii (Oxford, 1935)), 161–87. Another edition was made by A. Pattin in *Tijdschrift voor Filosofie*, 28 (1966), 90–203 (and also published separately as a book with separate pagination, *Le Liber de causis*, ed. A. Pattin (Louvain, 1966)). Pattin used over ninety manuscripts for this edition; R. C. Taylor more recently listed 237 manuscript copies in the *Bulletin de la Société pour l'Étude de la Philosophie Médiévale*, 25 (1983), 63–84; here will be found as well a list of commentaries and *quaestiones* concerning the text and written before 1500.

16. C. H. Haskins, *Studies in the History of Medieval Science* (2nd edn., Cambridge, Mass., 1927); M.-T. d'Alverny, 'Translations and Translators', in R. L. Benson and G. Constable (ed.), *Renaissance and Renewal in the Twelfth Century* (Oxford, 1982), 421–62.

17. See C. Burnett (ed.), *Adelard of Bath: An English Scientist and Arabist of the Early Twelfth Century* (London, 1987).

18. Ed. C. Burnett (Leiden, 1982).

19. Aristotle's *De anima* attracted a very large number of commentaries in the Middle Ages; working from published catalogues of manuscripts, over thirty years ago, J. de Raedemaker listed 819 copies of such commentaries and closely related works in *Bulletin*

de la Société pour l'Étude de la Philosophie Médiévale, 5 (1963), 149–83; 6 (1964), 119–34.

20. Themistius, *Commentaire sur le Traité de l'Âme d'Aristote: Traduction de Guillaume de Moerbeke* (Louvain, 1957). See also John Philoponus, *Commentaire sur le De anima d'Aristote*, ed. G. Verbeke (Louvain, 1966).

21. Aquinas, II *Summa contra gentes*, 95: 'Si igitur substantiae separatae non sunt ex materia et forma compositae, ut ex praemissis [cap. 50] patet, non apparet secundum quid in eis genus et differentia specifica accipi possit.'

22. Colette Sirat, *History of Jewish Philosophy in the Middle Ages* (Cambridge, 1985), marks a wonderful advance in knowledge, and I am painfully aware that I have taken undeservedly little advantage of all that it has to offer.

23. Ibid. 247–50, 252–4, 257–9, 273–4, etc.

24. Ibid. 157.

25. S. Liebermann reproduced the 1509 (Constantinople) edition in 1972 (New York).

26. *Moses Maimonides, The Guide of the Perplexed*, trans. S. Pines (Chicago, 1963), I.56, p. 131 (existence); I.68, pp. 165–6, (intellect). See A. Broadie, 'Maimonides and the Way of Negation', in B. Mojsisch and O. Pluta (eds.), *Historia Philosophiae Medii Aevi: Studien zur Geschichte der Philosophie des Mittelalters* (2 vols.; Amsterdam, 1991), i. 105–13.

Chapter 5

1. *Iohannes Blund: Tractatus de anima*, ed. D. A. Callus and R. W. Hunt (London, 1970).

2. A classic, short guide is the work of the late F. Van Steenberghen, *Aristotle in the West*, trans. L. Johnston (Louvain, 1955). In the same year Van Steenberghen published a related short survey, *The Philosophical Movement in the Thirteenth Century* (Nelson, 1955).

3. *Chartularium Universitatis Parisiensis*, ed. H. Denifle and A. Châtelain (4 vols.; Paris, 1889–97), i, no. 246.

4. From the late twelfth century onwards we move into a period when many schools progressed to become universities, and the surviving records for the study of the medieval universities are vast. Fundamental tools of reference include: *Chartularium Universitatis*

Parisiensis, ed. Denifle and Châtelain; P. Glorieux, *Répertoire des Maîtres en Théologie de Paris au XIIIᵉ siècle* (2 vols.; Paris, 1933–4); Glorieux, *La Faculté des Arts et ses Maîtres au XIIIᵉ siècle* (Paris, 1971); A. B. Emden, *A Biographical Register of the University of Oxford to AD 1500* (3 vols.; Oxford, 1957–9); Emden, *A Biographical Register of the University of Cambridge to 1500* (Cambridge, 1963). Recent work on the history of medieval universities includes H. de Ridder-Symoens (ed.), *A History of the University in Europe*, i. *Universities in the Middle Ages* (Cambridge, 1992); *The History of the University of Oxford* (gen. ed. T. H. Aston), i. J. I. Catto and R. Evans (eds.), *The Early Oxford Schools* (Oxford, 1984); Alan B. Cobban, *The Medieval Universities to c.1500* (Berkeley and Los Angeles, 1988); *A History of the University of Cambridge* (gen. ed. C. Brooke), i. D. R. Leader, *The University to 1546* (Cambridge, 1988). See too L. Thorndike, *University Records and Life in the Middle Ages* (New York, 1944; repr. 1971).

5. Alexander's successors in the Franciscan Order in the twentieth century have produced monumental editions of the writings to which he and others contributed: *Summa fratris Alexandri* or *Summa theologica* (written from 1235) (4 vols.; Quaracchi, 1942–8); *Glossa in Quatuor Libros Sententiarum Petri Lombardi* (4 vols.; Quaracchi, 1951–7) (written between 1223 and 1227).

6. For Oxford, see D. A. Callus, 'The Introduction of Aristotelian Learning to Oxford', *Proceedings of the British Academy*, 29 (1944).

7. P. Raedts, *Richard Rufus of Cornwall and the Tradition of Oxford Theology* (Oxford, 1987). Professor Rega Wood of St Bonaventure's, New York, is actively re-examining Rufus' works; see, for example, 'Richard Rufus's "Speculum animae"', in *Miscellanea Mediaevalia: Veröffentlichungen des Thomas-Instituts der Universität zu Köln*, xxiii: J. A. Aertsen (ed.), *Die Bibliotheca Amploniana* (Berlin, 1995), 86–109.

8. The *Opera omnia* of William of Auvergne are available in early printed editions: Paris, 1516; Venice, 1591; Orleans, 1674–5.

9. See S. Ebbeson, *Commentators and Commentaries on Aristotle's Sophistici Elenchi* (3 vols.; Leiden, 1981); also Ebbeson, 'Medieval Latin Glosses and Commentaries on Aristotelian Logical Texts of the Twelfth and Thirteenth Centuries', in *Glosses and Commentaries on Aristotelian Logical Texts: The Syriac, Arabic and Medieval*

Latin Traditions (Warburg Institute Surveys and Texts, 23; London, 1993), 129–77.

10. L. M. de Rijk, *Logica modernorum: A Contribution to the History of Early Terminist Logic* (2 vols. in three parts; Assen, 1962–7). De Rijk acknowledges (i. 19) M. Grabmann's pioneering role in showing that the advances made in medieval logic were not entirely dependent on an influx of new material; whether such a perspective may be discovered for other branches of thought—ethics, for example, or political theory—may be worthy of enquiry. In addition to the texts edited by de Rijk, other texts have been edited in the periodical *Cahiers de l'Institut du Moyen-Âge Grec et Latin*, e.g. in vols. 8–16 (1972–6).

11. *Peter of Spain: Tractatus called afterwards Summulae logicales*, ed. L. M. de Rijk (Assen, 1972).

12. *William of Sherwood's Introduction to Logic*, trans. with an introduction and notes by Norman Kretzmann (Minneapolis, 1966), 13–15. A translation of the *Syncategoremata* was made by J. P. Mullally, *Peter of Spain: Tractatus Syncategorematum and Selected Anonymous Treatises* (Milwaukee, 1964). Kretzmann has also translated *William of Sherwood: Treatise on Syncategorematic Words* (Minneapolis, 1968). A valuable discussion is provided by William Kneale and Martha Kneale, *The Development of Logic* (Oxford, 1962), 231–5, 246–65.

13. *Introduction to Logic*, trans. Kretzmann, 66.

14. Ibid. 111–12.

15. Ibid. 122–4.

16. De Rijk, *Logica modernorum*, i. 14–17; Kretzmann, introduction to *William of Sherwood's Introduction to Logic*, 19.

17. See pp. 87–9.

18. *Liber de philosophia prima* I, c.5.

19. Here I am indebted to various studies by J. A. Aertsen, who has shed considerable light on this important strand of medieval thought. See, e.g., 'The Medieval Doctrine of the Transcendentals: The Current State of Research', *Bulletin de philosophie médiévale*, 33 (1991), 130–47.

20. Ed. N. Wicki (Bern, 1985).

21. II.3, ed. A. de Libera (Hamburg, 1987).

22. On beauty and the transcendentals, see J. A. Aertsen, 'Die Frage nach der Transzendentalität der Schönheit im Mittelalter', in B. Mojsisch and O. Pluta (eds.), *Historia Philosophiae Medii Aevi:*

Studien zur Geschichte der Philosophie des Mittelalter (2 vols.; Amsterdam, 1991), i. 1–22. Beauty is one of the divine names in Denis' treatise, and Aquinas in his Commentary on this work (at *c.*4, *lect.* 22, 590) equates it with good: *pulchrum convertitur cum bono*. But Aertsen warns against seeing beauty in Aquinas' writings as a distinct transcendental; it is not mentioned in *De veritate* I.1. Here Aertsen has in view the study by U. Eco, *Art and Beauty in the Middle Ages* (New Haven, 1986).

23. *De veritate* I.1.

24. See Aristotle, *On the Soul* II.2; also G. E. R. Lloyd, *Aristotle: The Growth and Structure of his Thought* (Cambridge, 1968), ch. 9. Another set of issues concerning thinking and remembering is not considered here but has been very fully, and very interestingly, surveyed by Janet Coleman, *Ancient and Medieval Memories: Studies in the Reconstruction of the Past* (Cambridge, 1992); for Aristotle's *De anima* and *De memoria*, see e.g. ch. 2 and pp. 363–88. See too Mary Carruthers, *The Book of Memory: A Study of Memory in Medieval Culture* (Cambridge Studies in Medieval Literature; Cambridge, 1990).

25. Aristotle, *De anima* II.12.

26. *Chartularium Universitatis Parisiensis*, ed. H. Denifle and A. Châtelain (4 vols.; Paris, 1889–97), i, nos. 20 and 246.

27. Particularly useful for the origins of medieval philosophical ethics are the studies by G. Wieland, chs. 34 and 35 in *The Cambridge History of Later Medieval Philosophy*, ed. N. Kretzmann, A. Kenny, J. Pinborg; ass. ed. E. Stump (Cambridge, 1982), 657–719, and *Ethica-Scientia practica: Die Anfänge der philosophischen Ethik im 13. Jahrhundert* (Beiträge zur Geschichte der Philosophie und Theologie des Mittelalters, NS 21; Aschendorff, 1981).

28. See R.-A. Gauthier, *Magnanimité: L'Idéal de la grandeur dans la philosophie païenne et la théologie chrétienne* (Paris, 1951); and for Roger Bacon and the thirteenth century, see J. Hackett, 'Roger Bacon on Magnanimity and Virtue', in B. C. Bazán *et al.* (eds.), *Les Philosophies morales et politiques au Moyen Âge—Moral and Political Philosophies in the Middle Ages* (3 vols.; Ottawa, 1995), i. 367–77.

29. H. P. F. Mercken (ed.), *The Greek Commentaries on the Nicomachean Ethics in the Latin Translation of Robert Grosseteste, Bishop of Lincoln (+1253)*, i (Corpus Latinum Commentariorum in Aristotelem Graecorum, 6; Leiden, 1973).

30. The basic printed edition of works is by L. Baur, *Die philo-sophischen Werke des Robert Grosseteste* (Beiträge zur Geschichte der Philosophie des Mittelalters, 9; Münster, 1912). R. C. Dales has edited his commentary on Aristotle's *Physics* (Boulder, Colo., 1963), and, with S. Gieben, on the *Hexaemeron* (London, 1982).

31. Grosseteste's *On Light* has been translated by H. Shapiro, *Medieval Philosophy* (New York, 1964), 254–63, and by C. Riedl (Milwaukee, 1942).

32. *Robertus Grosseteste: Commentarius in Posteriorum Analyticorum Libros*, ed. P. Rossi (Florence, 1981), I.2.

33. John of Salisbury, *Metalogicon* IV.6, ed. J. B. Hall and K. Keats-Rohan (Corpus Christianorum, Continuatio Mediaeualis, 98; Turnhout, 1991), 145.

34. R. W. Southern, *Robert Grosseteste: The Growth of an English Mind in Medieval Europe* (Oxford, 1986), 164.

35. On *Posterior Analytics* I.18; trans. Southern, *Grosseteste*, 165.

36. See S. Ebbesen, 'Roger Bacon and the Fools of his Time', *Cahiers de l'Institut du Moyen Âge Grec et Latin*, 3 (1970), 40–4.

37. The standard editions of Bacon's works are those of J. S. Brewer, *Fratris Rogeri Baconis opera quaedam hactenus inedita* (Rolls Series; London, 1859)—*Opus tertium, Opus Minus, Compendium Philosophiae*; of J. H. Bridges, *The Opus Maius of Roger Bacon* (3 vols.; Oxford, 1897–1900); of H. Rashdall, *Fratris Roger Bacon Compendium Studii Theologiae* (Aberdeen, 1911); of F. Delorme and E. Massa, *Rogeri Baconis Moralis Philosophia* (Zurich, 1953); of R. Steele and F. Delorme, *Opera hactenus inedita Rogeri Baconis* (16 fascicles; Oxford, 1905–40). One missing section of the *Opus maius—De signis*—has now been published by K. M. Fredborg, L. Nielsen, and Jan Pinborg, 'An Unedited Part of Roger Bacon's *Opus Maius*', *Traditio*, 34 (1978), 75–136. Translations of some of Bacon's writings have been made by R. B. Burke, *The Opus Majus of Roger Bacon* (2 vols.; New York, 1928; repr. 1962), and by D. C. Lindberg, *Roger Bacon's Philosophy of Nature: A Critical Edition with English Translation, Introduction and Notes of De Multiplicatione Specierum and De Speculis Comburentibus* (Oxford, 1983). Guidance on Bacon's works is available in S. C. Easton, *Roger Bacon and his Search for a Universal Science: A Reconsideration of the Life and Work of Roger Bacon in the Light of his own Stated Purposes* (Oxford, 1952).

38. *Opus maius*, pt. 6, *c*.2–12 (II.172–201).

39. *Opus tertium*, ed. J. S. Brewer, *Fr Rogeri Baconis opera*, i. 13–14; *Compendium studii philosophiae*, ed. Brewer, 428. Roger Bacon's *Summule dialectices* is a textbook in the 'summulist' tradition.

40. 'Quidam dicunt quod terminus appellat de se appellata presencia, preterita et futura, et est communis entibus et non entibus' (*Summule dialectices*, ed. R. Steele, in *Opera hactenus inedita Rogeri Baconis*, fasc. XV (Oxford, 1940), 277). See A. de Libera, 'Roger Bacon et le problème de l'Appellatio Univoca', in H. A. G. Brakhuis, C. H. Kneepkens, and L. M. de Rijk (eds.), *English Logic and Semantics from the End of the Twelfth Century to the Time of Ockham and Burleigh: Acts of the 4th European Symposium on Medieval Logic and Semantics, Leiden–Nijmegen, 23–27 April* 1979 (Artistarium, Supplementa 1; Nijmegen, 1981), 193–234.

41. J. Pinborg, 'Roger Bacon on Signs: A Newly Recovered Part of the *Opus Maius* XI', in Pinborg (ed.), *Medieval Semantics* (London, 1984), 403–12, at 406. See also T. S. Maloney, 'The Semiotics of Roger Bacon', *Mediaeval Studies*, 45 (1983), 120–54.

42. See Pinborg, 'Roger Bacon on Signs'. See too *Roger Bacon. Compendium of the Study of Theology*, ed. and trans. T. S. Maloney (Studien und Texte zur Geistesgeschichte des Mittelalters; Leiden, 1987).

43. Bonaventure's *Opera omnia* were critically edited and published in ten vols. by the Collegium S. Bonaventurae in Quaracchi between 1882 and 1902. Another version of his *Collationes in Hexaemeron* has been edited by F. Delorme (Quaracchi, 1934). J. de Vinck has published a translation, *The Works of Bonaventure* (Paterson, NJ, 1960–70). For introductions in English to his work, see J. G. Bougerol, *Introduction to the Works of St Bonaventure* (Paterson, NJ, 1964) and E. Gilson, *The Philosophy of Saint Bonaventure* (Paterson, NJ, 1965).

44. Ed. with an English trans. by P. Boehner, *St Bonaventure's Itinerarium Mentis in Deum* (New York, 1956). Other works of Bonaventure translated into English include his *De Reductione Artium ad Theologiam*, ed. and trans. E. T. Healy (New York, 1955); *Breviloquium*, trans. E. E. Nemmers (St Louis, 1946); *Disputed Questions on the Mystery of the Trinity*, trans. Z. Hayes (New York, 1979).

45. On the question of Bonaventure's attitude to substantial form, see J. F. Quinn, *The Historical Constitution of St Bonaventure's Philosophy* (Toronto, 1973).

46. New editions of Albert's writings are in progress: *Opera omnia*, ed. B. Geyer *et al.* (Münster i. W., 1951–); these are cited unless it is otherwise noted. The present general editor is W. Fauser. Earlier editions include the Vives edition by A. Borgnet in 38 vols. (1890–9). Translations include Albert's *On the Six Principles*, in H. Shapiro, *Medieval Philosophy* (New York, 1969), 266–93, and his *Book of Minerals* by D. Wyckoff (Oxford, 1967). General studies of Albert are in short supply, but they include A. de Libera, *Albert le grand et la philosophie* (Paris, 1990).

47. Albert, *De causis et processu universitatis* I.4.8, *Opera omnia*, x (Vives edn.; Paris, 1891), 431b.

48. On the *Metaphysics* I, tr. 1, *c*.5 (XVI–1, p. 8).

49. On the *Metaphysics* XI, tr. 2, *c*.11 (XVI–2, pp. 497–8).

50. On the *Metaphysics* XI, tr. 1, *c*.13 (XVI–2, p. 479).

51. On *De anima*, III, tr. 3, *c*.6 (VII–1, pp. 214–15).

52. *Super Dionysium De divinis nominibus*, *c*.4, §223 (XXXVII–1, p. 297).

53. See Weisheipl, in G. Meyer and A. Zimmermann (eds.), *Albertus Magnus* (Mainz, 1980), 441–63.

54. *Super Dionysium De divinis nominibus*, *c*.7 §17 (XXXVII–1, p. 350).

55. Cf. Augustine, *De trinitate* XV, *c*.13, n. 22 (PL 42, 1076).

56. Albert, *Super Ethica* I.10.55, *Opera omnia*, vii (Vives edn.).

57. 'philosophus contemplatur deum, secundum quod habet ipsum ut quandam conclusionem demonstrativam, sed theologia contemplatur ipsum ut supra rationem et intellectum existentem' (Albert, *Super Ethica* X.16 (as cited by Wieland, *Ethica–Scientia practica*, 205–6)).

58. Albert, *Super Ethica*, Prologue 5, *Opera omnia*, vii (Vives edn.).

59. P. Michaud-Quantin, *Politica (libri I–II,11): Translatio prior imperfecta interprete Guillelmo de Moerbeka(?)* (Aristoteles Latinus XXIX.1; Bruges, 1961). The complete translation of all eight books by William of Moerbeke followed shortly after Albert's commentary and in the early 1260s; see R. A. Gauthier's volume in the Editio Leonina (*S. Thomae Aquinatis . . . Opera Omnia. Iussu impensaque Leonis XIII, P.M. edita* (Rome, 1882–)): *Thomae Sententia Libri Politicorum* (Editio Leonina, XLVIII), preface, 44–63.

60. On the German Albertists, see M. Grabmann, *Mittelalterliches Geistesleben* (Munich, 1926) i. 147–221, ii. 324–412. Also

R. Imbach, 'Le (Néo-)platonisme médiéval, Proclus latin, et l'école dominicaine allemande', *Revue de Théologie et Philosophie*, 110 (1978), 427–48. Recent studies by A. de Libera represent a considerable advance in understanding; see his *La Mystique rhenane d'Albert le Grand à Maître Eckhart* (Paris, 1984).

61. On *Divine Names*, esp. chs. 1–5. Cf. Albert, *De causis et processu universitatis*, ii., ed. A. Borgnet, *Opera omnia*, x (Paris, 1891).

62. General guides to Aquinas's thought written or translated into English include: J. A. Aertsen, *Nature and Creature: Thomas Aquinas's Way of Thought*, trans. from the Dutch by H. D. Morton (Studien und Texte zur Geistesgeschichte des Mittelalters; (Leiden, 1987); M.-D. Chenu, *Towards Understanding St Thomas* (Chicago, 1964), trans. from *Introduction à l'étude de S. Thomas d'Aquin* (Montreal, 1950) by A.-M. Landry and D. Hughes; B. Davies, *The Thought of Thomas Aquinas* (Oxford, 1992); F. C. Copleston, *Aquinas* (Penguin Books, 1955); E. Gilson, *The Christian Philosophy of St Thomas Aquinas* (New York, 1956), which includes 'A Catalogue of St Thomas's Works: Bibliographical Notes', by I. T. Eschmann (pp. 381–439); A. Kenny, *Aquinas* (New York, 1980); J. Pieper, *Guide to Thomas Aquinas*, trans. R. and C. Winston (New York, 1962); *St. Thomas Aquinas 1274–1974: Commemorative Studies*, ed. A. A. Maurer (2 vols.; Toronto, 1974). The book by J. A. Weisheipl, *Friar Thomas d'Aquino: His Life, Thought and Works* (rev. edn., Washington, 1983), contains much helpful information. Kenelm Foster's translations and editions in *The Life of Saint Thomas Aquinas: Biographical Documents* (London, 1959) are charming. For the chronology of Aquinas's works, see, in addition to Eschmann and Weisheipl, F. Van Steenberghen, *La Philosophie au XIIIe siècle* (Philosophes médievaux, 9; Louvain 1966), 584 ff.

63. *S. Thomae de Aquino super librum de causis expositio*, ed. H.-D. Saffrey (Freiburg, 1954), 3. In general there was a tendency, during the second half of the thirteenth century, to replace translations of Aristotle's writings, and those of other authors, made out of Arabic by new translations made out of Greek, and also to revise Greek–Latin versions made earlier. William of Moerbeke, the Dominican friar, was active in this as well as in the task of translating out of Greek. Henceforward, the new version (*translatio nova*) was preferred, but was similar to the old (*translatio vetus*), with the result that, over the next 200 years, contamination of one version by

another easily occurred and a mixed text developed (*versio communis*). From the late fifteenth century until the 1930s printed editions reflected this situation, as their editors were unaware of the differences between the old and the new medieval translations. See, for details of editions of Aristotle, A. Mansion in *Bulletin de la Société pour l'Étude de la Philosophie Mediévale*, 3 (1961), 169–76. The task of making critical editions of the medieval Latin translations of Aristotle has been undertaken by the Union Académique Internationale in the series Aristoteles Latinus. In parallel similar undertakings have been made to publish the medieval Latin versions of the works of Greek and Arab thinkers, notably in the series Plato Latinus, Avicenna Latinus, and Averroes Latinus.

64. Critical editions of Aquinas's works are appearing in the Editio Leonina (*S. Thomae Aquinatis . . . Opera Omnia, Iussu impensaque Leonis XIII, P. M. edita* (Rome, 1882–)). For many works the Marietti editions (Turin–Rome) are easy to use, although not prehaps so easy to find. The *Opera omnia* of Aquinas are provided in the Parma edition (25 vols.; Parma, 1852–73; repr. New York, 1948–50) and in the Vives edition (34 vols.; Paris, 1871–9). The Vives edition lacks a general Table of Contents and the later volumes (from 27 onwards) contain a high number of works doubtfully or falsely attributed to Aquinas and usually written by his earliest followers. A useful guide, with an indication of which works are authentic, has been made by C. Viola, 'Table générale et index analytique des œuvres complètes de saint Thomas d'Aquin: Un guide pour l'édition Vives', *Bulletin de philosophie médiévale*, 29 (1987), 178–92. An English translation of the *Summa theologiae*, facing the Latin text, has been produced in sixty volumes by Dominican Fathers in England (London, 1964–76). The *Summa Contra Gentiles* is translated by A. C. Pegis *et al.*, *On the Truth of the Catholic Faith* (5 vols.; New York, 1955–7). A concordance has been published by R. Busa, *Index Thomisticus* (Stuttgart, 1974–80).

65. There are translations of Aquinas's *De ente et essentia* by A. Maurer, *On Being and Essence* (2nd edn., Toronto, 1983) and by J. Bobik, *Aquinas on Being and Essence: A Translation and Interpretation* (Notre Dame, Ind., 1965).

66. Aquinas develops the theme of participation on many occasions including the following: *Scriptum super primum librum Sententiarum* (written *c*.1256), Prol., q.1, a.2 ad 2; d.8, q.4, a.1; d.8, q.5, a.1; d.24, q.1, a.1; *De veritate* (1256–9), q.2, a.3 ad 16 and a.11

ad 4; q.21, a.1; q.23, a.7; *De potentia Dei* (after 1259), q.3, a.5; q.7, a.3; the commentary on Denis' *De divinis nominibus* (before 1268); *De anima* (1269), q.7, and the *Expositio super Librum de causis* (after 1270). I have found very helpful the essay by E. P. Mahoney on 'Metaphysical Foundations of the Hierarchy of Being According to Some Late-Medieval and Renaissance Philosophers', in P. Morewedge (ed.), *Philosophies of Existence Ancient and Medieval* (New York, 1982), 165–257 (with a valuable bibliography at nn. 40 and 43 on pp. 225–7). A classic study is that of L. B. Geiger, *La Participation dans la philosophie de S. Thomas d'Aquin* (2nd edn., Paris, 1953).

67. K. Foster and S. Humphries have translated *Aristotle's De Anima with the Commentary of St Thomas Aquinas* (London, 1951). His *Quaestio disputata de anima*, has been translated by J. P. Rowan, *The Soul* (St Louis, 1949).

68. Aquinas' arguments for the existence of God are deployed in various ways in his works, but it is generally accepted that their presentation in *Summa theologiae* Ia.2.3 is a full one. There is a large literature on the subject, including A. Kenny, *The Five Ways: St Thomas Aquinas's Proofs of God's Existence* (Notre Dame, Ind., 1980).

69. Aquinas, *In 12 libros Metaphysicorum Aristotelis Expositio*, XII, I.3, nn. 2452–3. Aquinas's *Commentary on the Metaphysics of Aristotle* has been translated by J. P. Rowan (2 vols.; Chicago, 1961).

70. *St Thomas Aquinas, Quodlibetal Questions 1 and 2* have been translated by S. Edwards (Toronto, 1983).

71. Aquinas' *Commentary on the Nicomachean Ethics* has been translated by C. I. Litzinger (2 vols.; Chicago, 1964).

72. Aquinas, *Summa theologiae* Ia pars, q.82, a.3–4.

73. Aquinas, *Quaestiones disputatae de veritate* q.22, a.12c.

74. Aquinas, *Summa theologiae* Ia pars, q.82, a.4.

75. Aquinas, *Quodlibetum* VIII, q.9, a.1.

76. See R. Sorabji, *Time, Creation and the Continuum: Theories in Antiquity and the Early Middle Ages* (London, 1983), ch. 13 ('Did the Universe have a Beginning? The Background'); also pp. 220–1.

77. Siger's works have become far better known in the last thirty years. The *Liber de felicitate* uncertainly attributed to him is lost, although its teachings were recorded by Augustinus Niphus (Agostino Nifo, 1472–1538). His arguments on divine unicity are contained in differing redactions of his *Quaestiones in Metaphysicam* (c.1272–4),

ed. W. Dunphy (Philosophes médiévaux, 24; Louvain, 1981), and A. Maurer (Philosophes médiévaux, 25; Louvain, 1983). His *Quaestiones super librum De causis* have been edited by A. Marlasca (Philosophes médiévaux, 12; Louvain, 1972), his *Quaestiones in tertium de anima* (before 1270) by B. Bazán (Philosophes médiévaux, 13; Louvain, 1972), 1–69 (written before 25 Dec. 1270, according to A. Pattin, 'Quelques écrits attribués à Siger de Brabant', *Bulletin de philosophie mediévale*, 29 (1987), 175); in the same volume Bazán has also edited the *Tractatus de anima intellectiva* and *de aeternitate mundi*. The *Quaestiones in libros Aristotelis De anima*, which are edited by F. Van Steenberghen (Philosophes médiévaux, 11, Louvain, 1971), 121–348, were formerly attributed to Siger and show undeniable similarities with Siger's work, but they are now thought to be anonymous although contemporary (and written before the 1270 condemnation). In his fundamental study, *Maître Siger de Brabant* (Louvain, 1977), F. Van Steenberghen also dates to 1270 a work of Siger called *De intellectu* (p. 361 n. 45); however, A. Pattin ('Quelques écrits attribués à Siger de Brabant', 173–7) has cast substantial doubt on the existence of this as a separate work distinct from Siger's *Quaestiones in tertium de anima*. Pattin's correction should be borne in mind by readers of Bruno Nardi's *Sigieri di Brabante nel pensiero del Rinascimento italiano* (Rome, 1945), esp. 17–21. See also *Siger de Brabant: Écrits de logique, de morale et de physique*, ed. B. Bazán (Philosophes médiévaux, 14; Louvain, 1974).

78. See E. P. Mahoney, 'Sense, Imagination, and Intellect in Albert, Thomas, and Siger', in *The Cambridge History of Later Medieval Philosophy*, ch. 30, pp. 602–22; Mahoney, 'Saint Thomas and Siger of Brabant Revisited', *The Review of Metaphysics*, 27 (1974), 531–53.

79. Aquinas wrote against this in *De aeternitate mundi*, a treatise translated by C. Vollert, *On the Eternity of the World* (Milwaukee, 1965). See R. Dales, *Medieval Discussions of the Eternity of the World* (Leiden, 1990). *Thomas Aquinas, On the Unity of the Intellect against the Averroists*, trans. B. H. Zedler (Milwaukee, 1968); '*against the Averroists*' is part of the title in certain manuscripts only.

80. H. Shapiro, in *Medieval Philosophy* (New York, 1964), 415–38, has translated some of Siger's work 'On the Necessity and Contingency of Causes'.

81. *Divina Commedia, Paradiso*, x, ii. 136–8.

82. See N. G. Green-Pedersen, *Boethius von Dacien, Opera*, vi, pt. II. *De aeternitate mundi; De summo bono* (Copenhagen, 1976). In their book *Medieval Philosophy from St Augustine to Nicholas of Cusa* (New York, 1969), 369–75, J. F. Wippel and A. B. Wolter have translated Boethius' *On the Supreme Good or On the Life of the Philosopher.*

83. *De summo bono*, ed. Green-Pedersen, 372, 369.

84. 'haec est vita philosophi, quam quicumque non habuerit non habet rectam vitam' (*De summo bono*, ed. Green-Pedersen, 377).

85. See A. Maurer, 'John of Jandun and the Divine Causality', *Mediaeval Studies*, 17 (1955), 185–207.

86. Questions on the *De anima* III, q.12 (Padua, 1473), cols. 290–1; also q.7, cols. 269–70.

87. To Kurt Flasch and his collaborators we now owe the appearance of critical editions of Dietrich's writings, *Opera omnia* (4 vols.; Hamburg, 1977–).

88. The text is printed in *Chartularium*, ed. Denifle and Châtelain, i, no. 432. See E.-H. Wéber, *La Controverse de 1270 à l'université de Paris et son retentissement sur la pensée de s. Thomas d'Aquin* (Paris, 1970).

89. The condemned propositions are printed in *Chartularium*, ed. Denifle and Châtelain, i, no. 473. The most recent full enquiry into them is that of R. Hissette, *Enquête sur les 219 articles condamnés à Paris le 7 mars 1277* (Louvain, 1977).

90. *Chartularium*, ed. Denifle and Châtelain, i, nos. 66, 67, 92.

91. 'Quod effectus immediatus a primo debet esse unus tantum, et simillissimus primo' (ibid. i, no. 64).

92. Hissette, *Enquête*, 71.

93. A. de Libera, '*Ex uno non fit nisi unum: La Lettre sur le Principe de l'univers* et les condemnations parisiennes de 1277', in Mojsisch and Pluta (eds.), *Historia Philosophiae Medii Aevi*, i. 543–60.

94. 'Omne bonum quod homini possibile est consistit in virtutibus intellectualibus (error est)', *Chartularium*, ed. Denifle and Châtelain, i, no. 36.

95. Ibid. i, no. 40. See Wieland, *Ethica–Scientia practica*, 220.

96. Kilwardby was prominent as both a philosopher and a theologian. His *De ortu scientiarum*—a discussion of the place of the arts in philosophy—has been edited by A. G. Judy (London, 1976).

97. See D. A. Callus, 'The Problem of the Unity of Form and Richard

Knapwell, O. P.', *Mélanges offerts à Étienne Gilson* (Toronto, 1959), 123–60.

98. See O. Lewry, 'The Oxford Condemnations of 1277 in Grammar and Logic', in H. A. G. Braakhuis, C. H. Kneepkens, and L. M. de Rijk (eds.), *English Logic and Semantics from the End of the Twelfth Century to the Time of Ockham and Burleigh: Acts of the 4th European Symposium on Medieval Logic and Semantics, Leiden–Nijmegen, 23–27 April 1979* (Artistarium, Supplementa 1; Nijmegen, 1981), 235–78.

Chapter 6

1. P. Glorieux has edited the *Correctoria* written by William Macclesfield (Paris, 1956) and by Richard Clapwell (Kain, 1927); J.-P. Müller those by John Quidort (Rome, 1941) and by the anonymous friar (Rome, 1954).

2. Dietrich von Freiberg, *Opera omnia*, i. *Schriften zur Intellekttheorie*, ed. B. Mojsisch (Hamburg, 1977).

3. See D. A. Callus, *The Condemnation of St Thomas at Oxford* (The Aquinas Society of London, Aquinas Paper, 5; Blackfriars Publications, 1955), 14.

4. Giles entered the Order of the Hermits of St Augustine and became the Order's first regent master in theology. He taught theology in Paris 1285–91 and was elected General of his Order in 1292. His *Opera omnia* are in the course of being critically edited by F. del Punta *et al.* (Unione Accademica Nazionale; Corpus philosophorum medii aevi, Testi e studi; Florence, 1987–).

5. K. Flasch, *Aufklärung im Mittelalter? Die Verurteilung von 1277. Das Dokument von Bischofs von Paris übersetzt und erklärt* (Excerpta classica, 6; Mainz, 1989).

6. 'Nemo opinari debet, quod in electione opinionum favor patriae ab honore veritatis me retrahat' (cited in A. Zimmermann, 'Remarques et questions relatives à l'œuvre de Ferrand d'Espagne', in H. Santiago-Otero (ed.), *Diálogo filosófico-religioso entre Christianismo, Judaísmo e Islamismo durante la edad media en la Península Iberica* (Brepols, 1994), 213–28, at 212 n. 2; Zimmermann, 'Ein Averroist des späten 13. Jahrhunderts: Ferrandus de Hispania', in *Archiv für Geschichte der Philosophie*, 50 (1968), 152.

7. 'quidam enim dicunt, quod tota essentia speciei est ipsa forma, sicut

quod tota essentia hominis est anima ... volunt quod nullae partes materiae ponantur in definitione indicante speciem, sed solum principia formalia speciei. Et haec opinio videtur Averrois et quorundam sequentium eum. Sed videtur esse contra intentionem Aristotelis' (Aquinas, *In Metaphisicam* VII.1.9, n. 1467).

8. Zimmermann, 'Remarques et questions', 223.

9. 'Unde impossibile est quod anima humana huiusmodi corpori unita apprehendat substantias separatas cognoscendo de eis quod quid est' (*In Metaphisicam* II.1.1, n. 285).

10. Ibid. II.1.1, n. 286.

11. Zimmermann, 'Remarques et questions', 220–1.

12. *Raimundus Lullus, Die neue Logik: Logica nova*, ed. C. Lohr (Hamburg, 1985). I have also found helpful Lohr's essay on 'Ramon Lull and Thirteenth-Century Religious Dialogue', in Santiago-Otero (ed.), *Diálogo filosófico-religioso*, 117–29.

13. Lohr, 'Ramon Lull', 122–3.

14. Lull's main treatment of this theme is found in his *De modo naturali intelligendi*, written in Paris in 1310, *Raimundi Lulli Opera latina*, ed. F. Stegmüller *et al.* (vols. i–v, Palma de Mallorca, 1959–67; vol. vi onwards, Turnhout, 1978–), vi.

15. Lull's thought about the names of God—the *dignitates*—received its final formulation in his *Ars generalis ultima*, written between 1305 and 1308, *Raimundi Lulli Opera latina*, ed. Aloisius Madre, xiv (Corpus Christianorum, Continuatio Mediaeualis, 75; Turnhout, 1986). He aimed to build on the common beliefs of Jews, Muslims, and Christians. On Lull's influence, see J. N. Hillgarth, *Ramon Lull and Lullism in Fourteenth-Century France* (Oxford Warburg Studies; Oxford, 1971).

16. Siger, *Questions sur la Métaphysique*, ed. C. A. Graiff (Louvain, 1948), 11 ff. Godfrey of Fontaines, *Quodlibet*, III, q.1, ed. M. de Wulf-A. Pelzer (Louvain, 1904); cf. John Wippel, 'Godfrey of Fontaines and the Real Distinction between Essence and Existence', in *Traditio*, 20 (1964), 385–410. Dietrich of Freiberg, *Opera omnia*, ii (Hamburg, 1980); cf. A. Maurer in *Mediaeval Studies*, 18 (1956), 173–203.

17. Henry's argument is reported by Duns Scotus, I, d.3, n. 21 (*Opera omnia* 3).

18. Henry of Ghent, *Summa theologiae*, I.2, f. 7, vM, as cited by E. Gilson, *History of Christian Philosophy in the Middle Ages* (London, 1955), 448. Critical editions of Henry's works are in progress,

Henrici de Gandavo Opera omnia, ed. R. Macken *et al.* (Leiden, 1979–). See also S. P. Marone, *Truth and Scientific Knowledge in the Thought of Henry of Ghent* (Speculum Anniversary Monographs, 11; Cambridge, Mass., 1985).

19. Critical editions of Scotus' writings are being published in the *Opera omnia* (Vatican City, 1950–). But for many works—including dubious ones such as the *Theoremata* and *De rerum principio*—the 'Wadding' edition of the *Opera omnia* which was made at Lyons in 1639 and reprinted with additions at Paris in 26 vols. in 1891–5 (the Vives edn.) still holds the field. On Scotus' life see A. G. Little, 'Chronological Notes on the Life of Duns Scotus', *English Historical Review*, 47 (1932), and C. Balic, *John Duns Scotus* (Rome, 1966). For Scotus' thought, see the monumental study by E. Gilson, *Jean Duns Scot* (Paris, 1952); also E. Bettoni, *Duns Scotus*, trans. B. M. Bonansea (Catholic University of America, Washington, 1961).

20. *Opus oxoniense* IV, d.45, q.2 (Vives edn., xx. 305).

21. *Comm. in octo lib. physicorum* 4.7 (Leonine edn., ii. 166–9).

22. Aristotle admitted that there could be a potential infinity in number (1) because the largest number one can think of can always be augmented by one, (2) because any continuous magnitude, since it is not made up of indivisible parts, must therefore be indefinitely divisible, (3) because, owing to the fact that he did not recognize the beginning or end of the universe, Aristotle assumed the possibility of an infinite number of revolutions of the heavenly spheres.

23. See P. Duhem, *Medieval Cosmology: Theories*, ed. and trans. R. Ariew (London, 1985), 405.

24. *Quodlibet* IX a.1.

25. Duhem, *Medieval Cosmology*, 89.

Chapter 7

1. Roger Bacon, *Compendium studii philosophiae*, ed. J. S. Brewer, *Fr Rogeri Baconis opera quaedam hactenus inedita*, i (London, 1859), 428 .

2. David Knowles, *The Evolution of Medieval Thought*, 2nd edn., ed. D. E. Luscombe and C. N. L. Brooke (London, 1988), 263, 273.

3. S. Ozment, *The Age of Reform 1250–1550: An Intellectual and*

Religious History of Later Medieval and Reformation Europe (New Haven, 1980), 8–9 .

4. Bradwardine's *De causa Dei contra Pelagium* was printed in London in 1619. There are two distinguished modern studies of Bradwardine's thought, one by Gordon Leff, *Bradwardine and the Pelagians* (Cambridge, 1957), the other by H. A. Oberman, *Archbishop Thomas Bradwardine: A Fourteenth Century Augustinian: A Study of his Theology in its Historical Context* (Utrecht, 1958).

5. Cited by D. L. D'Avray, 'Philosophy in Preaching: The Case of a Franciscan Based in Thirteenth-Century Florence (Servasanto da Faenza)', in R. G. Newhauser and J. A. Alford (eds.), *Literature and Religion in the Later Middle Ages. Philological Studies in Honor of Siegfried Wenzel* (Medieval and Renaissance Texts and Studies, New York, 1994), 263–73, at 270–1 (I have slightly modified Dr D'Avray's translation).

6. The debates *between* Franciscan philosophers have been richly illuminated by S. D. Dumont and S. F. Brown in a series of studies, including: Dumont, 'The Univocity of the Concept of Being in the Fourteenth Century: John Duns Scotus and William of Alnwick', *Mediaeval Studies*, 49 (1987), 1–75; Dumont, 'The Univocity of the Concept of Being in the Fourteenth Century II: The *De ente* of Peter Thomae', *Mediaeval Studies*, 50 (1988), 186–256; Dumont and Brown, 'Univocity of the Concept of Being in the Fourteenth Century, III: An Early Scotist', *Mediaeval Studies*, 51 (1989), 1–129; Brown, 'Nicholas of Lyra's Critique of Scotus' Univocity', in B. Mojsisch and O. Pluta (eds.), *Historia Philosophiae Medii Aevi: Studien zur Geschichte der Philosophie des Mittelalters* (2 vols.; Amsterdam, 1991), i. 115–27.

7. See C. B. Schmitt, *A Critical Survey and Bibliography of Studies on Renaissance Aristotelianism 1958–1969* (Padua, 1971); *Problemi dell'aristotelismo rinascimentale* (Naples, 1985).

8. G. Leff, *William of Ockham, The Metamorphosis of Scholastic Discourse* (Manchester, 1975).

9. Z. Kuksewicz, 'Hugo d'Utrecht', *Bulletin de la Société pour l'Étude de la Philosophie Médiévale*, 28 (1986), 185–90.

10. E. Gilson, *History of Christian Philosophy in the Middle Ages* (London, 1955), 435.

11. P. Vignaux, *Nominalisme au XIVe siècle* (Paris, 1948), remains a fundamental work. See also G. Cannizzo, *Il sorgere di notitia*

intuitiva all'alba del pensiero moderno, Oxford-Parigi, 1298–1318 (Palermo, 1985).

12. See C. Berube, *La Connaissance de l'individuel au moyen âge* (Montreal, 1964).

13. A modern literary reflection of this view may be found in Umberto Eco's novel *The Name of the Rose* (first published in Italy in 1980; Picador edition in English, Pan Books 1984, here at p. 28), which is full of learned allusion to fourteenth-century thought: Eco has Adso of Melk say of his master William: 'I had heard him speak with great skepticism about universal ideas and with great respect about individual things; and afterward, too, I thought this tendency came to him from his being both a Briton and a Franciscan.'

14. The course of Eckhart's career and writings was put on a reliable basis by J. Koch, 'Kritische Studien zum Leben Meister Eckharts', *Archivum Fratrum Praedicatorum*, 29 (1959), 5–51, 30 (1960), 5–52; repr. in Koch, *Kleine Schriften* (2 vols.; Storia e letteratura; Rome, 1973), 127–8.

15. *Master Eckhart, Parisian Questions and Prologues*, trans. A. A. Maurer (Toronto, 1974), 46.

16. I follow here R. Imbach, *Deus est intelligere. Das Verhältnis von Sein und Denken in seiner Bedeutung für das Gottesverständnis bei Thomas von Aquin und in den Pariser Quaestionen Meister Eckarts* (Studia Friburgensia, NS 53; Freiburg, 1976).

17. In the traditional numbering of the Parisian questions (which I follow here to lessen the risk of confusion), the first of the Parisian questions concerns angels and their understanding, the second concerns God and understanding. But in fact this sequence should be reversed and is so reversed in *Maître Eckhart à Paris. Une critique médiévale de l'ontothéologie. Les Questions parisiennes no. 1 et no. 2 d'Eckhart. Études, textes et traductions*, E. Zum Brunn, Z. Kaluza, A. de Libera, P. Vignaux, E. Wéber (Bibliothèque de l'École des Hautes Études. Section des Sciences Religieuses, 86; Paris, 1984).

18. *Meister Eckhart, Die lateinische Werke*, ed. J. Koch *et al.* (Kohlhammer edn.; Stuttgart, 1938–), v. 40. This edition is usually referred to as *LW*. The Kohlhammer edition of the German writings of Eckhart—*DW*—is by J. Quint *et al.*, *Meister Eckhart, Deutsche Predigten und Traktate* (Stuttgart, 1938–).

19. *LW* v. 45.

20. Gilson, *History of Christian Philosophy in the Middle Ages*, 144.

21. Imbach, *Deus est intelligere.*
22. The first part, *Opus propositionum*, was to contain over 1,000 propositions; its prologue survives. The second part, *Opus quaestionum*, does not survive; the questions were to have been arranged in the order of Aquinas's *Summa.* Several sections of the last part, *Opus expositionum*, survive along with its prologue; this contains Scriptural commentaries and sermons.
23. Trans. A. Maurer, *Meister Eckhart, Parisian Questions and Prologues.*
24. *Prologue to the Book of Propositions*, trans. Maurer, *Parisian Questions and Prologues*, 94–5. Cf. *Liber de causis*, ed. O. Bardenhewer (Fribourg, 1882), 174.
25. Maurer, *Parisian Questions and Prologues*, 95–6.
26. On this view of the 'onto-analogical status' of creatures, and on its originality and background in thirteenth-century logic and semantics, see A. de Libera, *Le Problème de l'être chez Maître Eckhart: Logique et métaphysique de l'analogie* (Cahiers de la Revue de théologie et de philosophie, 4; Geneva, 1980). De Libera draws attention especially to Eckhart's development of a logic which is capable of expressing the metaphysical meaning of analogy.
27. *In Eccli.* n. 52, *LW* ii. 280–1.
28. Maurer, *Parisian Questions and Prologues*, 98–9.
29. *LW* ii.
30. *In Sap.* n. 148, *LW* ii. 486. See F. Tobin, *Meister Eckhart: Thought and Language* (Philadelphia, 1986), ch. 3.
31. Critical editions of Ockham's works are available in *Guillelmi de Ockham opera philosophica et theologica,* ed. G. Gál *et al.* (St Bonaventure, NY, 1967–85). Important studies of Ockham's philosophy and theology include Marilyn McCord Adams, *William Ockham* (2 vols.; Notre Dame, Ind., 1987), G. Leff, *William of Ockham: The Metamorphosis of Scholastic Discourse* (Manchester, 1975); S. McGrade, *The Political Thought of William of Ockham* (Cambridge, 1974), and J. Miethke, *Ockhams Weg zur Sozialphilosophie* (Berlin, 1969).
32. *Epistola ad fratres minores*, ed. H. S. Offler, *Guillelmi de Ockham Opera politica* (4 vols.; Manchester, 1940–), iii. 6–17, at 15. English trans. in *William of Ockham: A Letter to the Friars Minor and Other Writings*, ed. A. S. McGrade and J. Kilcullen, trans. J. Kilcullen (Cambridge, 1995), 13.

33. 1 *Dialogus* iv. 5, in Melchior Goldast, *Monarchia Sancti Romani Imperii* (3 vols.; Frankfurt, 1614), ii. 448.

34. S. F. Brown, 'Nicholas of Lyra's Critique of Scotus' Univocity', in Mojsisch and Pluta (eds.), *Historia Philosophiae Medii Aevi*, i. 115–27.

35. *In I Sent.* d. 2 q. 8.

36. See E. Serene, 'Demonstrative Science' in *The Cambridge History of Later Medieval Philosophy*, ed. N. Kretzmann, A. Kenny, J. Pinborg; ass. ed. E. Stump (Cambridge, 1982), ch. 24, pp. 496–517.

37. *Ordinatio, lib.* I, Prologue, Q. 2 in *Opera theologica* I, ed. G. Gál and S. F. Brown (St Bonaventure, NY, 1967), 77.

38. Ibid. Q. 2, a. 2 pp. 87–8.

39. Ibid. Q. 1, a. 1, p. 36, and cf. p. 38.

40. Ockham, *Summa Logicae, Pars Prima*, ed. P. Boehner (St Bonaventure, NY, 1957), *cap.* 33, 64, 68, 69.

41. Walter Burley disputed with Ockham over this; see *Walter Burleigh: De puritate artis logicae*, ed. P. Boehner (St Bonaventure, NY, 1955), 3, 7. Also P. V. Spade, 'Some Epistemological Implications of the Burley–Ockham Dispute', *Franciscan Studies*, 35 (1975), 212–22.

42. P. D. Henry, 'Suppositio and Significatio in English Logic', H. A. G. Braakhuis, C. H. Kneepkens and L. M. de Rijk (eds.), *English Logic and Semantics from the End of the Twelfth Century to the Time of Ockham and Burleigh: Acts of the 4th European Symposium on Medieval Logic and Semantics, Leiden–Nijmegen, 23–27 April 1979* (Artistarium, Supplementa 1; Nijmegen, 1981), 361–87. L. M. de Rijk has recently drawn attention to the limits Ockham put upon knowledge even of the singular: the only necessary being is God; not only is the universal not part of the nature of things (although it is part of the way the human mind seeks knowledge), but the nature of individual being is contingent and we cannot know what it is. Even the existence of the individual can only be inferred from its sensible qualities ('Ockham's Horror of the Universal: An Assessment of his View of Individuality', in *Quodlibetaria. Miscellanea Studiorum in honorem Prof. J. M. da Cruz Pontes*... (Mediaevalia, Textos e Estudos, 7–8; Porto, 1995, 473–97).

43. *William Ockham: Predestination, God's Foreknowledge, and Future Contingents*, trans. with an Introduction, Notes, and Appendices by

M. McCord Adams and N. Kretzmann (Century Philosophy Sourcebooks; New York, 1969), 85. The Latin text of Ockham's *Tractatus de praedestinatione et de praescientia Dei et de futuris contingentibus* has been edited by P. Boehner (St Bonaventure, NY, 1945).

44. For Ockham's discussion of modes of necessity and contingency, impossibility and possibility, see *Summa logicae* III. 3, cc.10–11, *Opera philosophica*, i, ed. P. Boehner, G. Gál, and S. F. Brown (1974). Also cf. T. Rudavsky (ed.), *Divine Omniscience and Omnipotence in Medieval Philosophy* (Dordrecht, 1985).

45. *Ockham: Predestination*, 17 (from *Ordinatio*, Distinction 46, Question I, B).

46. *Ockham: Predestination*, 19 (from *Ordinatio*, d. 46, q. I, D).

47. *Ockham: Predestination*, 49 (from *Tractatus de praedestinatione*, Question 1, Assumption 6).

48. *Ockham: Predestination*, 49–50 (from *Tractatus de praedestinatione*, Question 1, Assumption 6).

49. F. C. Copleston, *A History of Medieval Philosophy* (London, 1972), 253.

50. K. Tachau, *Vision and Certitude in the Age of Ockham: Optics, Epistemology and the Foundations of Semantics, 1250–1345* (Studien und Texte zur Geistesgeschichte des Mittelalters, 22; Leiden, 1988), pp. xv, 353.

51. See also A. Maurer, 'Ockham's Razor and Chatton's Anti-Razor', *Mediaeval Studies*, 46 (1984), 463–73.

52. Tachau, *Vision and Certitude*.

53. For Buridan's life, see E. Faral 'Jean Buridan', *Histoire littéraire de la France*, 38 (Paris, 1949), 462–605.

54. See R. Paque, *Das Pariser Nominalistenstatut: Zur Entstehung des Realitätsbegriff der neuzeitlichen Naturwissenschaft* (Quellen und Studien zur Geschichte der Philosophie, ed. P. Wilpert; Berlin, 1970); texts of these two statutes are edited here on pp. 306–9 (1339) and 8–13 (1340). But also see for interpretation of these and other statutes, Tachau, *Vision and Certitude*, 336–40.

55. See A. Willing, 'Buridan and Ockham: The Logic of Knowing', *Franciscan Studies*, 45 (1985), 47–56.

56. P. V. Spade, 'Roger Swyneshed's *Obligationes*: Edition and Comments', *Archives d'histoire doctrinale et littéraire au moyen âge*, 44,

année 1977 (1978), 243–85 at 251: 'Obligatio est oratio mediante qua quis affirmative vel negative tenetur respondere ad obligatum.'

57. N. Kretzmann and E. Stump, 'The Anonymous *De arte obligatoria* in Merton College MS. 306', in E. P. Bos (ed.), *Medieval Semantics and Metaphysics: Studies Dedicated to L. M. de Rijk* (Artistarium, Supplementa 2; Nijmegen, 1985), 239–80, at 251.

58. Ockham, *Summa Logicae* III–1, c.30, *Opera philosophica*, i. 436–7.

59. *The Sophismata of Richard Kilvington*, ed. N. Kretzmann and B. E. Kretzmann (Auctores Britannici Medii Aevi, 12; Oxford, 1990). For an English translation, see N. Kretzmann and B. E. Kretzmann, *The Sophismata of Richard Kilvington. Introduction, Translation, and Commentary* (Cambridge, 1990).

60. See the translations made by N. Kretzmann and E. Stump in *Cambridge Translations of Medieval Philosophical Texts I: Logic and the Philosophy of Language* (Cambridge, 1988), ch. 14, pp. 413–72.

61. S. Knuuttila, *Modalities in Medieval Philosophy* (London, 1993).

62. I. Boh, *Epistemic Logic in the Later Middle Ages* (London, 1993), 35.

63. See P. Boehner, *Medieval Logic: An Outline of its Development from 1250 to c.1400* (Manchester, 1952), 84–9. Burley's treatise *De consequentiis* has been published by N. J. Green-Pedersen in *Franciscan Studies*, 40 (1980), 102–66.

64. See Boh, *Epistemic Logic*, 89–100.

65. See the wide-ranging papers presented in A. Maierù (ed.), *English Logic in Italy in the 14th and 15th Centuries* (History of Logic, 1; Naples, 1982), and in P. O. Lewry (ed.), *The Rise of British Logic* (Toronto, 1985). cf. William and Martha Kneale, *The Development of Logic* (Oxford, 1962), 244–6.

66. See R. Sorabji, 'John Philoponus', in Sorabji (ed.), *Philoponus and the Rejection of Aristotelian Science* (London, 1987), 11.

67. N. Schneider, *Die Kosmologie des Franciscus de Marchia* (Studien und Texte zur Geistesgeschichte des Mittelalters, 28; Leiden, 1991).

68. I have profited from the work (and the Italian translation) of Valeria Sorge, *Biagio Pelacani da Parma: Quaestiones de anima. Alle origini del libertinismo* (Naples, 1995), who herself has used earlier work by, in particular, G. Federici Vescovini (listed on pp. 56–7), including Vescovini's edition of the *Quaestiones de anima* (Accademia Toscana di scienze e lettere 'La colombaria', Studi 30; Florence, 1974).

69. To be born under Saturn, without any *aspectus* of the planets which

provide good fortune—Mercury and Jupiter—will result in stupidity; to be born under Mars points to a murderous character; the conjunction of Mercury and Jupiter will ensure wisdom (*Quaestiones de anima* II, q. 7, Sorge, *Biagio Pelacani da Parma* 143). The stars also cause the rise and fall of civilizations.

70. *Petrus Pomponatius, Tractatus de immortalitate animae*, ed. G. Morra (Bologna, 1954). There has been a considerable amount of study devoted to Pomponazzi, who provides a clear indication of the continuity between medieval and Renaissance philosophy. Of especial importance are B. Nardi, *Studi su Pietro Pomponazzi* (Florence, 1965), and E. Gilson, 'Autour de Pomponazzi', *Archives d'histoire doctrinale et littéraire au moyen âge*, 63 (1961), 163–279.

Chapter 8

1. *Œuvres complètes*, ed. P. Glorieux (10 vols.; Paris, 1960–73), ii, no. 3, p. 27.
2. Ibid. iii, no. 99, p. 242.
3. Ibid. ix, no. 466, p. 629.
4. Z. Kaluza, *Les Querelles doctrinales à Paris: Nominalistes et réalistes aux confins des XIVᵉ et XVᵉ siècles* (Quodlibet, 2; Bergamo, 1988).
5. *Œuvres complètes*, ii, no. 5, pp. 33–4. Cf. Letter 26 (1400), ibid. 98.
6. Ibid. iii, no. 99, p. 246.
7. Other forms of his name are John *de Nova Domo* or *de Nieuwenhuyze.*
8. *De duplici logica* (1400/1), *Œuvres complètes*, iii, no. 91, p. 62.
9. The fundamental studies of Cusa's life and thought are by E. Vansteenberghe, *Le Cardinal Nicolas de Cues* (Paris, 1920; repr. Frankfurt, 1963), and by E. Meuthen, *Nikolaus von Kues 1401–1464* (6th edn., Munster, 1982). For his writings the principal editions are those issued by the Heidelberg Academy, *Nicolai de Cusa opera omnia* (Leipzig–Hamburg, 1932–). Important for the study of Cusa's philosophy is K. Flasch, *Die Metaphysik des Einen bei Nikolaus von Kues* (Leiden, 1966).
10. *De concordantia catholica*, bk. II, 8–15, trans. Paul E. Sigmund, *Nicholas of Cusa, The Catholic Concordance* (Cambridge Texts in the History of Political Thought, Cambridge, 1991), 76–105. The Latin text is in *Opera omnia*, xiv (ed. G. Kallen, 1959–68). Two

studies of Cusa's political ideas are M. Watanabe, *The Political Ideas of Nicholas of Cusa* (Geneva, 1963), and P. E. Sigmund, *Nicholas of Cusa and Medieval Political Thought* (Cambridge, Mass., 1963).

11. *De concordantia catholica* II. 14, trans. Sigmund, 98.

12. Of monarchy Cusa writes: 'although there are many good reasons for a hereditary monarchy, if the best man is always to rule the commonwealth by the will of all for the public good, the best method is to have a new election, by all or a majority or at least by those nobles who represent everyone with their consent' (*De concordantia catholica* III, Preface, trans. Sigmund, 211, see also pp. 206, 208–9).

13. *De concordantia catholica* II. 19, trans. Sigmund, 128. Note that Cusa continues this sentence by writing: 'although in order for the power to rule to be activated there must necessarily be the concurrence of that formative radiance from above to establish it in being since it is true that all power is from above—I speak of properly ordered power—just as from the potential of the earth, the lowest of the elements, various vegetable and sensible beings are produced through the mediating influence of heaven'.

14. *De concordantia catholica* II. 34, trans. Sigmund, 194.

15. Ibid.

16. *De concordantia catholica* I. 1, trans. Sigmund, 5.

17. *De concordantia catholica* I. 2, trans. Sigmund, 9.

18. *De visione dei* VIII. 32, *Nicholas of Cusa's Dialectical Mysticism: Text, translation and interpretive study of 'De visione dei'*, ed. J. Hopkins (Minneapolis, 1985), 153.

19. *Nicholas of Cusa, On God as Not-Other: A Translation and an Appraisal of 'De li non aliud'*, ed. J. Hopkins (2nd edn.; Minneapolis, 1983), 7. The Latin text is also provided in this volume in the edition by L. Baur and P. Wilpert, *Directio Speculantis seu De Non Aliud*, *Opera omnia*, xiii (1944).

20. *De non aliud*, ed. Hopkins, 15.

21. Ibid. 14.

22. Thierry of Chartres, *Lectiones in Boethii librum de Trinitate* v. 16–17, ed. N. M. Häring, *Commentaries on Boethius by Thierry of Chartres and his School* (Pontifical Institute of Mediaeval Studies, Studies and Texts, 20; Toronto, 1971), 218.

23. *De non aliud*, ed. Hopkins, 5.

24. *De mystica theologia: Tractatus Primus Speculativus*, ed. A. Combes, *Ioannis Carlerii de Gerson de Mystica Theologia* (Lucani, 1958), 29–30th Consideration, pp. 73–4, 77.

25. *Nicholas of Cusa on Learned Ignorance*, Eng. trans. and appraisal by Jasper Hopkins (Minneapolis, 1981).

26. *De docta ignorantia* III. 11.

27. *Nicolas de Cues, Lettres aux moines de Tegernsee sur la docte ignorance (1452–1456), Du jeu de la boule (1463)*, French trans. by M. de Gandillac (Paris, 1985).

28. For further disparagement of Aristotle, see *De non aliud*, ed. Hopkins, 116–17.

29. Ibid. 6.

30. An edition, translation, and commentary on the *Trialogus de Possest* is provided by J. Hopkins in his *A Concise Introduction to the Philosophy of Nicholas of Cusa* (2nd edn.; Minnesota, 1980).

31. *De Possest* 2.

32. *De pace fidei* XIX, 68; III. 9; *Nicolai de Cusa Opera omnia*, vii, ed. R. Klibansky and H. Bascour (Hamburg, 1970), 63, 10; trans. J. Hopkins, *Nicholas of Cusa's 'De pace fidei' and 'cribatio alkorani'* (Minneapolis, 1990), 71, 37. In the *Cribatio Alkorani—The Sifting* (or *Sieving*) *of the Koran*—Cusa confronts the monotheism of Islam with arguments for belief in the divine Trinity ('*manuductiones ad trinitatem*').

33. *De pace fidei* VI. 16, p. 15; trans. Hopkins, 40.

34. *De pace fidei* III. 8, p. 10; trans. Hopkins, 37.

35. *De pace fidei* ed. Klibansky and Bascour, introduction, pp. xxxvi–xxxvii.

36. Ibid. p. xxxvi.

37. Ibid. pp. xlv–lii.

38. Lisa Jardine, 'Humanistic Logic', in Charles B. Schmitt *et al.* (eds.), *The Cambridge History of Renaissance Philosophy* (Cambridge, 1988), 173–98.

39. See J. Monfasani, *George of Trebizond: A Biography and a Study of his Rhetoric and Logic* (Leiden, 1976).

40. See P. O. Kristeller, *The Philosophy of Marsilio Ficino*, trans. V. Conant (New York, 1943).

41. *Theologia platonica*, in *Opera omnia* (2 vols.; Basle, 1576; repr. Turin, 1959); *Théologie platonicienne de l'immortalité des âmes*, trans. and ed. R. Marcel (3 vols.; Paris, 1964–70).

Select Bibliography

This is primarily a list of the works cited in the text, including works by or on medieval thinkers whose names are presented in alphabetical order.

GENERAL

Aertsen, J. A., 'The Medieval Doctrine of the Transcendentals: The Current State of Research', *Bulletin de philosophie médiévale*, 33 (1991), 130–47.

Aristoteles Latinus, Corpus philosophorum medii aevi, ed. L. Minio-Paluello *et al.* (Leiden, 1939–).

Aristotle in Britain during the Middle Ages, ed. J. Marenbon, Société internationale pour l'Étude de la philosophie médiévale; rencontres de philosophie médiévale, 5 (Turnhout, 1996).

Armstrong, A. H. (ed.), *The Cambridge History of Later Greek and Early Medieval Philosophy* (Cambridge, 1967).

Aston, T. H. (Gen. Ed.), *The History of the University of Oxford*, i: J. I. Catto and R. Evans (eds.), *The Early Oxford Schools* (Oxford, 1984).

Bazán, B. C., *et al.*, (eds.), *Les Philosophies morales et politiques au Moyen Age—Moral and Political Philosophies in the Middle Ages*, 3 vols. (Ottawa, 1995).

Benson, R. L., and Constable, G., with Lanham, C. D., *Renaissance and Renewal in the Twelfth Century* (Oxford, 1982).

Bocheski, I. M., *A History of Formal Logic*, trans. I. Thomas (Notre Dame, Ind., 1961).

Boehner, P., *Medieval Logic: An Outline of its Development from 1250 to c.1400* (Manchester, 1952).

Brooke, C. (Gen. Ed.), *A History of the University of Cambridge*, i: D. R. Leader, *The University to 1546* (Cambridge, 1988).

Burnett, C. (ed.), *Glosses and Commentaries on Aristotelian Logical Texts: The Syriac, Arabic and Medieval Latin Traditions*, Warburg Institute Surveys and Texts, 23 (London, 1993).

Burns, J. H. (ed.), *The Cambridge History of Medieval Political Thought c.350–c.1450* (Cambridge, 1988).

Callus, D. A., 'The Introduction of Aristotelian Learning to Oxford', *Proceedings of the British Academy*, 29 (1943), 229–81.

—— *The Condemnation of St. Thomas at Oxford*, Aquinas Society of London, Aquinas Paper (Blackfriars Publications, 1955).

Carruthers, Mary, *The Book of Memory: A Study of Memory in Medieval Culture* (Cambridge, 1990).

Chartularium Universitatis Parisiensis, 4 vols., ed. H. Denifle and A. Châtelain (Paris, 1889–97).

Cobban, Alan B., *The Medieval Universities to c.1500* (Los Angeles, 1988).

Coleman, Janet, *Ancient and Medieval Memories: Studies in the Reconstruction of the Past* (Cambridge, 1992).

Colish, M., *The Stoic Tradition from Antiquity to the Early Middle Ages*, 2 vols. (Leiden, 1985).

Copleston, F. C., *A History of Medieval Philosophy* (London, 1972).

Dales, R., *Medieval Discussions of the Eternity of the World* (Leiden, 1990).

Delhaye, P., 'La place de l'éthique parmi les disciplines scientifiques au XIIᵉ siècle', *Mélanges A. Janssen* (Louvain-Gembloux, 1948), 29–44.

—— 'L'Enseignement de la philosophie morale au XIIᵉ siècle', *Mediaeval Studies*, 2 (1949), 77–99.

—— 'Grammatica et ethica au XIIᵉ siècle', *Recherches de théologie ancienne et médiévale*, 25 (1958), 59–110.

Diálogo filosófico-religioso entre christianismo, judaísmo e islamismo durante la edad media en la península iberica, ed. H. Santiago-Otero, Société Internationale pour l'Étude de la Philosophie Médiévale, rencontres de philosophie médiévale, 3 (Turnhout, 1994).

Dronke, P. (ed.), *A History of Twelfth-Century Western Philosophy* (Cambridge, 1988).

Ebbeson, S., *Commentators and Commentaries on Aristotle's Sophistici Elenchi*, 3 vols. (Leiden, 1981).

Eco, U., *Art and Beauty in the Middle Ages* (New Haven, 1986).

Emden, A. B., *A Biographical Register of the University of Oxford to AD 1500*, 3 vols. (Oxford, 1957–9).

—— *A Biographical Register of the University of Cambridge to 1500* (Cambridge, 1963).

English Logic and Semantics from the End of the Twelfth Century to the Time of Ockham and Burleigh: Acts of the 4th European Symposium on Medieval Logic and Semantics, Leiden-Nijmegen, 23–27 April 1979, Artistarium Supplementa (Nijmegen, 1981).

Gauthier, R.-A., *Ethica Nicomachea*, in *Aristoteles Latinus*, xxvi. 1–3 (Leiden, 1972–4).

——*Magnanimité: l'idéal de la grandeur dans la philosophie païenne et la théologie chrétienne* (Paris, 1951).

——'Deux témoignages sur la date de la première traduction latine des "Economiques"', *Revue philosophique de Louvain*, 50 (1952), 273–83.

Glorieux, P., *Répertoire des Maîtres en Théologie de Paris au XIIIe siècle*, 2 vols. (Paris, 1933–4).

——*La Faculté des Arts et ses Maîtres au XIIIe siècle* (Paris, 1971).

Grabmann, M., *Die Geschichte der scholastischen Methode*, 2 vols. (Freiburg, 1909; repr. Darmstadt, 1957).

——*Mittelalterliches Geistesleben* (Munich, 1926).

Haskins, C. H., *Studies in the History of Medieval Science*, 2nd edn. (Cambridge, Mass., 1927).

Hauréau, Barthélemy, *Histoire de la philosophie scolastique*, 2 vols. (Paris, 1872–80).

Imbach, R., and Maierù, A. (eds.), *Gli studi di filosofia medievale fra otto e novecento: Contributo a un bilancio storiografico. Atti del convegno internazionale, Roma, 21–23 settembre, 1989*, Storia e letteratura, 179 (Rome, 1991).

Kneale, William, and Kneale, Martha, *The Development of Logic* (Oxford, 1962).

Knowles, D., *The Evolution of Medieval Thought*, 2nd edn. ed. D. E. Luscombe and C. N. L. Brooke (London, 1988).

Knuuttila, Simo (ed.), *Reforging the Great Chain of Being: Studies of the History of Modal Theories* (Dordrecht, 1980).

Kretzmann, N., Kenny, A., and Pinborg, J. (eds.), and Stump, E. (associate editor), *The Cambridge History of Later Medieval Philosophy: From the Rediscovery of Aristotle to the Disintegration of Scholasticism 1100–1600* (Cambridge, 1982).

Kretzmann, N., and Stump, E. (eds.), *The Cambridge Translations of Medieval Philosophical Texts* (Cambridge, 1988–).

Libera, A. de, *La Philosophie médiévale* (Paris, 1993).

——*La Querelle des universaux: De Platon à la fin du Moyen Age* (Paris, 1996).

Lloyd, G. E. R., *Aristotle: The Growth and Structure of his Thought* (Cambridge, 1968).

Lovejoy, A. O., *The Great Chain of Being* (Cambridge, Mass., 1936).

Mansion, A., 'Texte latin d'Aristote utilisé à la fin du moyen âge: Éditions et références', *Bulletin de la Société pour l'Étude de la Philosophie Médiévale*, 3 (1961), 169–76.

Markus, R. A., *Saeculum: History and Society in the Theology of St Augustine* (Cambridge, 1970).

Migne, J.-P., *Patrologia latina* (Paris, 1841–55).

Minio-Paluello, L., *Opuscula: The Latin Aristotle* (Amsterdam, 1972).

Mojsisch, B., and Pluta, O. (eds.), *Historia Philosophiae Medii Aevi: Studien zur Geschichte der Philosophie des Mittelalters*, 2 vols. (Amsterdam and Philadelphia, 1991).

Morewedge, P. (ed.), *Philosophies of Existence Ancient and Medieval* (New York, 1982).

Parent, J. M., *La Doctrine de la création dans l'école de Chartres*, Publications de l'Institut d'Études Médiévales (Paris and Ottawa, 1938).

Pinborg, J., *Medieval Semantics* (London, 1984).

Plato Latinus, ed. R. Klibansky (London, 1940–).

Plato, Timaeus a Calcidio translatus commentarioque instructus, ed. J. H. Waszink, in *Plato Latinus*, iv, 2nd edn. (London, 1975).

Pseudo-Aristotle, 'The Secret of Secrets': Sources and Influences, ed. W. F. Ryan and C. B. Schmitt, Warburg Institute Surveys and Texts, 9 (London, 1983).

Ridder-Symoens, H. de (ed.), *A History of the University in Europe*, i: *Universities in the Middle Ages* (Cambridge, 1992).

Rijk, L. M. de (ed.), *Logica modernorum: A Contribution to the History of Early Terminist Logic* (Assen, 1962–7).

Schmitt, C. B., and Knox, D., *Pseudo-Aristoteles Latinus: A Guide to Latin Works Falsely Attributed to Aristotle Before 1500*, Warburg Institute Surveys and Texts, 12 (London, 1985).

Sorabji, R., *Time, Creation and the Continuum: Theories in Antiquity and the Early Middle Ages* (London, 1983).

Southern, R. W., *Scholastic Humanism and the Unification of Europe*, i: *Foundations* (Oxford, 1995).

Steenberghen, F. van, *Aristotle in the West: The Origins of Latin Aristotelianism*, trans. L. Johnston (Louvain, 1955).

——*The Philosophical Movement in the Thirteenth Century* (Edinburgh, 1955).

226 *Select Bibliography*

Steenberghen, F. van, *La Philosophie au XIIIe siècle*, Philosophes médiévaux, 9 (Louvain, 1966).

Steenberghen, F. van, *Introduction à l'étude de la philosophie médiévale*, Philosophes médiévaux, 18 (Louvain, 1974).

Thorndike, L., *University Records and Life in the Middle Ages* (New York, 1944; repr. 1971).

Verbeke, G., *The Presence of Stoicism in Medieval Thought* (Washington, DC, 1983).

Vignaux, P., *Philosophie au Moyen Age* (Albeuve, 1987).

Wieland, G., *Ethica—Scientia practica: Die Anfänge der philosophischen Ethik im 13. Jahrhundert*, Beiträge zur Geschichte der Philosophie und Theologie des Mittelalters, Neue Folge, 21 (Münster i.W., 1981).

PETER ABELARD

Petri Abaelardi Opera theologica, i–iii, ed. E. M. Buytaert and C. J. Mews, Corpus Christianorum, Continuatio mediaevalis, 11–13 (Turnhout, 1969, 1969, 1987).

Petrus Abaelardus. Dialectica, ed. L. M. de Rijk (Assen, 1970).

Dialogus inter Philosophum, Iudaeum et Christianum, ed. R. Thomas (Stuttgart and Bad Cannstatt, 1970).

Peter Abelard: A Dialogue of a Philosopher with a Jew and a Christian, trans. Pierre J. Payer, Mediaeval Sources in Translation, 20 (Toronto, 1979).

Peter Abelard's Ethics, ed. and trans. D. E. Luscombe, Oxford Medieval Texts (Oxford, 1971).

The Letters of Abelard and Heloise, trans. B. Radice, Penguin Classics (Harmondsworth, 1974).

The Story of Abelard's Adversities, trans. J. T. Muckle (Toronto, 1954).

Pierre Abélard: Historia calamitatum, ed. J. Monfrin (Paris, 1962).

Peter Abelard: Letters IX–XIV, ed. E. R. Smits (Groningen, 1983).

Peter Abailard: Sic et Non, ed. B. Boyer and R. McKeon (Chicago 1976–7).

ADELARD OF BATH

Burnett, C. (ed.), *Adelard of Bath: An English Scientist and Arabist of the Early Twelfth Century* (London, 1987).

ALBERT THE GREAT

Opera omnia, ed. A. Borgnet, 38 vols. (Paris, 1890–9).

Opera omnia, ed. B. Geyer, *et al.* (Munster i.W., 1951–).

Book of Minerals, trans. D. Wyckoff (Oxford, 1967).

Imbach, R., 'Le (No-)platonisme médiéval, Proclus latin, et l'école dominicaine allemande', *Revue de Théologie et Philosophie*, 110 (1978), 427–48.

Libera, A. de, *Albert le grand et la philosophie* (Paris, 1990).

——*La Mystique rhénane d'Albert le Grand à Maitre Eckhart* (Paris, 1984).

Meyer, G., and Zimmermann, A. (eds.), *Albertus Magnus doctor universalis, 1280–1980* (Mainz, 1980).

Shapiro, H. (trans.), *Albert's 'On the Six Principles' in Medieval Philosophy* (New York, 1969).

Weisheipl, J. A. (ed.), *Albertus Magnus and the Sciences* (Toronto, 1980).

Zimmermann, A. (ed.), *Albert der Grösse: Seine Zeit, sein Werk, seine Wirkung* (Berlin, 1980).

ALEXANDER OF HALES

Summa fratris Alexandri or *Summa theologica*, 4 vols. (Quaracchi, 1924–48), with Indexes (1979).

Glossa in Quatuor Libros Sententiarum Petri Lombardi, 4 vols. (Quaracchi, 1951–7).

ANONYMOUS, **Liber de causis**

Liber de causis, ed. R. Steele, in Roger Bacon's *Quaestiones super Librum de causis. Opera hactenus inedita Rogerii Baconis*, 12 (Oxford, 1935), 161–87; also ed. A. Pattin in *Tijdschrift voor Filosofie*, 28 (1966), 90–203, and, published separately as a book, *Le Liber de causis* (Louvain, 1966).

ANSELM OF CANTERBURY

Opera omnia, ed. F. S. Schmitt, 6 vols. (Edinburgh, 1946–61).

Charlesworth, M. J., *Proslogion with a Reply on Behalf of the Fool by Gaunilo and the Author's Reply to Gaunilo* (Oxford, 1965).

Deane, S. N. (trans.), *St. Anselm: Basic Writings, Monologion, Proslogion, Cur Deus Homo*, 2nd edn. (La Salle, Ill., 1962).

Fairweather, E. R., *A Scholastic Miscellany, Anselm to Ockham*, The Library of Christian Classics, 10, *Cur Deus Homo, Proslogion* (Philadelphia, 1956).

Henry, D. P., *The De Grammatico of St. Anselm: The Theory of Paronymy* (Notre Dame, Ind., 1964).

Hopkins, J., and Richardson, G., *Anselm of Canterbury*, i: *Monologion, Proslogion* (London, 1974).

———— *Truth, Freedom and Evil, Three Philosophical Dialogues* (New York, 1967).

Southern, R. W., *Saint Anselm: A Portrait in a Landscape* (Cambridge, 1990).

Anselm: Aosta, Bec and Canterbury. Papers in Commemoration of the Nine-Hundredth Anniversary of Anselm's Enthronement as Archbishop, 25 September 1093, ed. D. E. Luscombe and G. R. Evans (Sheffield, 1996).

THOMAS AQUINAS

Opera omnia, L. Vives ed., 34 vols. (1874–89).

Opera omnia, ed. Leonine Commision (Vatican City, 1882–).

S. Thomae de Aquino super librum de causis expositio, ed. H.-D. Saffrey (Freiburg, 1954).

Pegis, A. C., *et al.* (trans.), *Summa Contra Gentiles*, in *On the Truth of the Catholic Faith* (New York, 1955–7).

Maurer, A. (trans.), *De ente et essentia*, in *On Being and Essence* (Toronto, 1983).

Bobik, J., *Aquinas on Being and Essence: A Translation and Interpretation* (Notre Dame, Ind., 1965).

Foster, K., and Humphries, S. (trans.), *Aristotle's De Anima with the Commentary of St. Thomas Aquinas* (London and New Haven, 1951).

Rowan, J. P. (trans.), *Quaestio disputata de anima* in *The Soul* (St Louis, Mo., 1949).

———— (trans.), *Commentary on the Metaphysics of Aristotle* (Chicago, 1961).

Edwards, S. (trans.), *St. Thomas Aquinas: Quodlibetal Questions 1 and 2* (Toronto, 1983).

Litzinger, C. I. (trans.), *Commentary on the Nicomachean Ethics* (Chicago, 1964).

Vollert, C. (trans.), *Aquinas' 'De Aeternitate Mundi', 'On The Eternity of the World'* (Milwaukee, 1965).

Aertsen, J. A., *Nature and Creature: Thomas Aquinas's Way of Thought*, trans. H. D. Morton, Studien und Texte zur Geistesgeschichte des Mittelalters (Leiden, 1987).

Busa, R., *Index Thomisticus* (Stuttgart and Bad Cannstatt, 1974–80).

Chenu, M.-D., *Towards Understanding St. Thomas*, trans. A. M. Landry and D. Hughes (Chicago, 1964).

Copleston, F. C., *Aquinas* (Harmondsworth, 1955).

Foster, Kenelm (trans.), *The Life of Saint Thomas Aquinas: Biographical Documents* (London, 1959).

Geiger, L. B., *La Participation dans la philosophie de S. Thomas d'Aquin* (Paris, 1953).

Gilson, É., *The Christian Philosophy of St. Thomas Aquinas* (New York, 1956).

Kenny, A., *Aquinas* (New York, 1980).

——*The Five Ways: St. Thomas Aquinas's Proofs of God's Existence* (Notre Dame, Ind., 1980).

Maurer, A. A. (ed.), *St. Thomas Aquinas 1274–1974: Commemorative Studies* (Toronto, 1974).

Pieper, J., *Guide to Thomas Aquinas*, trans. R. and C. Winston (New York, 1962).

Viola, C., 'Table générale et index analytique des œuvres complètes de saint Thomas d'Aquin: Un guide pour l'édition Vives', *Bulletin de philosophie médiévale*, 29 (1987), 178–92.

Weisheipl, J. A., *Friar Thomas d'Aquinas: His Life, Thought and Works*, rev. edn. (Washington, DC, 1983).

AUGUSTINE OF HIPPO

The Confessions, trans. H. Chadwick (Oxford, 1992).

Dialectic, trans. B. D. Jackson from the edn. by J. Pinborg, Synthese Historical Library, 16 (Dordrecht, 1975).

Bonner, G., *St. Augustine of Hippo: Life and Controversies* (London, 1963).

Brown, P., *St. Augustine of Hippo: A Biography* (London, 1967).

Frend, W. H. C., *The Donatist Church* (Oxford, 1952).

Gilson, E., *The Christian Philosophy of St. Augustine* trans. L. E. M. Lynch (London, 1961).

Marrou, H.-I., *S. Augustin et la fin de la culture antique*, 2nd edn. (Paris, 1949).

——(in cooperation with J. J. O'Meara) *Saint Augustine and His Influence through the Ages* (New York and London, 1957).

Pepin, J., *Saint Augustin et la dialectique* (Villanova, Pa., 1976).

ROGER BACON

Fratris Rogeri Baconis opera quaedam hactenus inedita, ed. J. S. Brewer, Rolls Series (London, 1859).

The Opus Maius of Roger Bacon, ed. J. H. Bridges (Oxford, 1897–1900).

230   *Select Bibliography*

Fredborg, K. M., Nielsen, L., and Pinborg, J., 'An unedited part of Roger Bacon's *Opus Maius: De signis*', *Traditio*, 34 (1978), 75–136.

Burke, R. B. (trans.), *The Opus Majus of Roger Bacon* (New York, 1928; repr. 1962).

Compendium Studii Theologiae, ed. H. Rashdall (Aberdeen, 1911).

Maloney, T. S. (ed. and trans.), *Roger Bacon: Compendium of the Study of Theology*, Studien und Texte zur Geistesgeschichte des Mittelalters (Leiden, 1988).

Moralis Philosophia, ed. F. Delorme and E. Massa (Zurich, 1953).

Lindberg, D., *Roger Bacon's Philosophy of Nature: A Critical Edition with English Translation, Introduction and Notes of De Multiplicatione Specierum and De Speculis Comburentibus* (Oxford, 1983).

Summule dialectices in *Opera hactenus inedita Rogeri Baconis*, ed. R. Steele (Oxford, 1940).

Easton, S. C., *Roger Bacon and His Search for a Universal Science: A Reconsideration of the Life and Work of Roger Bacon in the Light of his own Stated Purposes* (Oxford, 1952).

Ebbesen, S., 'Roger Bacon and the Fools of his Time', *Cahiers de l'Institut du Moyen Age Grec et Latin*, 3 (1970) 40–4.

Libera, A. de, 'Roger Bacon et le problème de appellatio univoca', in *English Logic and Semantics from the End of the Twelfth Century to the Time of Ockham and Burleigh: Acts of the 4th European Symposium on Medieval Logic and Semantics, Leiden-Nijmegen, 23–27 April 1979*, ed. H. A. G. Braakhuis *et al.*, Artistarium Supplementa (Nijmegen, 1981), 193–234.

Maloney, T. S., 'The Semiotics of Roger Bacon', *Mediaeval Studies*, 45 (1983), 120–54.

BERENGAR OF TOURS

Beringarius Turonensis, Rescriptum contra Lanfrancum, ed. R. B. C. Huygens, Corpus Christianorum, continuatio mediaevalis, 84 (Turnhout, 1987).

BIAGIO PELACANI

Federici Vescovini, G., *Quaestiones de anima*, Accademia Toscana di scienze e lettere 'La colombaria', Studi, 30 (Florence, 1974).

Sorge, V. (trans.), *Biagio Pelacani da Parma: Quaestiones de anima. Alle origini del libertinismo* (Naples, 1995).

JOHN BLUND

Iohannes Blund Tractatus de anima, ed. D. A. Callus, and R. W. Hunt, Auctores Britannici Medii Aevi, 2 (London, 1970).

BOETHIUS

Opera, Patrologia latina, 63–4.

In Isagogen Porphyrii Commenta, ed. S. Brandt, Corpus Scriptorum Ecclesiasticorum Latinorum, 48 (Vienna, 1906).

Boethius's De Topicis Differentiis, trans. E. Stump (Ithaca, NY, 1978).

The Theological Tractates and the Consolation of Philosophy, ed. and trans. H. F. Stewart and E. K. Rand (London, 1918; revised edn. by S. J. Tester, 1973).

Consolation of Philosophy, ed. W. Weinberger. Corpus Scriptorum Ecclesiasticorum Latinorum, 67 (Vienna, 1934); also ed. L. Bieler in Corpus Christianorum, Series Latina, 94 (Turnhout, 1957).

Consolation of Philosophy, trans. V. E. Watts. Penguin Books (Harmondsworth, 1969).

Bolton, D. K., 'The Study of the Consolation of Philosophy in Anglo-Saxon England', *Archives d'histoire doctrinale et littéraire au moyen âge*, 44, Année 1977 (1978), 33–78.

Chadwick, H., *Boethius: The Consolations of Music, Logic, Theology, and Philosophy* (Oxford, 1981).

Courcelle, P., *La Consolation de Philosophie dans la tradition littéraire: Antécédents et posterité de Boèce* (Paris, 1967).

Frakes, J. C., *The Fate of Fortune in the Middle Ages: The Boethian Tradition*, Studien und Texte zur Geistesgeschichte des Mittelalters (Leiden, 1988).

Gibson, M. (ed.), *Boethius: His Life, Thought and Influence* (Oxford, 1981).

BOETHIUS OF DACIA

Green-Pedersen, N. G. (ed.), *Boethius von Dacien: Opera*, vi/2: *De aeternitate mundi; De summo bono* (Copenhagen, 1976).

Wippel, J. F., and Wolter, A. B. (trans.), *Boethius's 'On the Supreme Good or On the Life of the Philosopher'*, in *Medieval Philosophy from St. Augustine to Nicholas of Cusa* (New York, 1969).

BONAVENTURE

Opera omnia, 10 vols. (Quaracchi, 1882–1902).

Collationes in Hexaemeron, ed. F. Delorme (Quaracchi, 1934).

The Works of Bonaventure, trans. J. de Vinck (Paterson, NJ, 1960–70).

Breviloquium, trans. E. E. Nemmers (St Louis, Mo., and London, 1946).

Disputed Questions on the Mystery of the Trinity, trans. Z. Hayes (New York, 1979).

St. Bonaventure's Itinerarium Mentis in Deum, trans. P. Boehner (New York, 1956).

De Reductione Artium ad Theologiam, ed. and trans. E. T. Healy (New York, 1955).

Bougerol, J. G., *Introduction to the Works of St. Bonaventure* (Paterson, NJ, 1964).

Gilson, E., *The Philosophy of Saint Bonaventure* (Paterson, NJ, 1965; original French edn., 1945).

——*La Philosophie de saint Bonaventure*, 3rd edn. (Paris, 1953).

Quinn, J. F., *The Historical Constitution of St. Bonaventure's Philosophy* (Toronto, 1973).

THOMAS BRADWARDINE

De causa Dei contra Pelagium (London, 1619).

Leff, G., *Bradwardine and the Pelagians* (Cambridge, 1957).

Oberman, H. A., *Archbishop Thomas Bradwardine: A Fourteenth Century Augustinian: A Study of his Theology in its Historical Context* (Utrecht, 1958).

JOHN BURIDAN

Faral, E., 'Jean Buridan', *Histoire littéraire de la France*, 38 (Paris, 1949), 462–605.

Pinborg, J. (ed.), *The Logic of Buridan* (Copenhagen, 1976).

Willing, A., 'Buridan and Ockham: The Logic of Knowing', *Franciscan Studies*, 45 (1985), 47–56.

CASSIODORUS

Institutiones, ed. R. A. B. Mynors (Oxford, 1937).

An Introduction to Divine and Human Readings by Cassiodorus Senator, trans. L. W. Jones (New York, 1946).

PETER DAMIAN

Pierre Damien: Lettre sur la Toute-Puissance Divine, ed. with French trans. by A. Cantin (Paris, 1972).

DENIS THE PSEUDO-AREOPAGITE

Dionysiaca: Recueil donnant l'ensemble des traductions latines des ouvrages attribués au Denys l'Aréopage, ed. P. Chevallier (Bruges, 1937).

Denys l'Aréopagite: La hiérarchie céleste, R. Roques, G. Heil, and M. de Gandillac, 2nd edn. (Paris, 1970).

Dionysius the Areopagite: On the Divine Names and the Mystical Theology, trans. C. E. Rolt (London, 1920).

The Ecclesiastical Hierarchy, trans. T. L. Campbell (New York and London, 1981).

Thesaurus Pseudo-Dionysii Areopagitae: Versiones Latinae cum Textu Graeco, CETEDOC, dir. P. Tombeur (Turnhout, 1995).

DIETRICH OF FREIBERG

Opera omnia, ed. K. Flasch *et al.* (Hamburg, 1977–).

JOHN DUNS SCOTUS

Opera omnia (Vatican City, 1950–).

Opera omnia, ed. L. Wadding (Lyons, 1639, repr. Paris, 1891–5).

Balic, C., *John Duns Scotus: Some Reflections on the Occasion of the Seventh Centenary of His Birth* (Rome, 1966).

Bettoni, E., *Duns Scotus*, trans. B. M. Bonansea (Washington, DC, 1961).

Gilson, É., *Jean Duns Scot: Introduction à ses positions fondamentales* (Paris, 1952).

Little, A. G. 'Chronological Notes on the Life of Duns Scotus', *English Historical Review*, 47 (1932), 568–82.

ECKHAMRT

Koch, J., *et al.* (eds.), *Meister Eckhart: Die lateinische Werke*, Kohlhammer edition (Stuttgart, 1938–).

Quint, J., *et al.*, *Meister Eckart: Deutsche Predigten und Traktate* (Stuttgart, 1938–).

Maurer, A. A. (trans.), *Master Eckhart, Parisian Questions and Prologues* (Toronto, 1974).

Zum Brunn, E., Kaluza, Z., Libera, A. de, Vignaux, P., and Wéber, E., *Maître Eckhart à Paris: Une critique médiévale de l'ontothéologie. Les questions parisiennes no. 1 et no. 2 d'Eckhart. Études, textes et traductions*, Bibliothèque de l'École des Hautes Études, Section des Sciences Religieuses (Paris, 1984).

Imbach, R., *Deus est intelligere: Das Verhältnis von Sein und Denken in seiner Bedeutung für das Gottesverständnis bei Thomas von Aquin und in den Pariser Quaestionen Meister Eckarts*, Studia Friburgensia (Freiburg, 1976).

Koch, J., 'Kritische Studien zum Leben Meister Eckharts', *Archivum Fratrum Praedicatorum* (1959, 1960); repr. in Koch, *Kleine Schriften*, Storia e letteratura (Rome, 1973).

Libera, A. de, *Le Problème de l'être chez Maître Eckhart: Logique et métaphysique de l'analogie*, Cahiers de la Revue de théologie et de philosophie (Geneva, 1980).

FERRAND OF SPAIN

Zimmermann, A., 'Ein Averroist des späten 13. Jahrhunderts: Ferrandus de Hispania', *Archiv für Geschichte der Philosophie*, 50 (1968), 145–64.

JOHN GERSON

Combes, A. (ed.), *Ioannis Carlerii de Gerson de Mystica Theologia* (Lugano, 1958).

Glorieux, P. (ed.), *Œuvres complètes*, 10 vols. (Paris, 1960–).

GILBERT OF POITIERS

The Commentaries on Boethius by Gilbert of Poitiers, ed. N. Haring (Toronto, 1966).

Gilbert de Poitiers et ses contemporains: Aux origines de la 'Logica Modernorum', ed. J. Jolivet and A. de Libera (Naples, 1987).

GILES OF ROME

Opera omnia, ed. F. del Punta *et al.*, Unione accademica nazionale, Corpus Philosophorum Medii Aevi, Testi e Studi (Florence, 1987–).

ROBERT GROSSETESTE

Baur, L. (ed.), *Die philosophischen Werke des Robert Grosseteste* (Münster, 1912).

The Greek Commentaries on the Nicomachean Ethics of Aristotle in the Latin Translation of Robert Grosseteste, Bishop of Lincoln (†1253), i– , ed. H. P. F. Mercken, Corpus Latinum Commentariorum in Aristotelem Graecorum, vi (Leiden, 1973–).

Commentarius in VIII libros Physicorum Aristotelis, ed. R. C. Dales (Boulder, Colo., 1963).

Hexaemeron, ed. R. C. Dales and S. Gieben, Auctores Britannici Medii Aevi, 6 (London, 1982).

De decem mandatis, ed. R. C. Dales and E. B. King, Auctores Britannici Medii Aevi, 10 (Oxford, 1987).

Shapiro, H. (trans.), *Grosseteste 'On Light'* (New York, 1964).

Riedl, C. (trans.), *Grosseteste 'On Light'* (Milwaukee, 1942).

Robertus Grosseteste: Commentarius in Posteriorum Analyticorum Libros, ed. P. Rossi (Florence, 1981).

McEvoy, J., *The Philosophy of Robert Grosseteste* (Oxford, 1982).

——(ed.), *Robert Grosseteste: New Perspectives on his Thought and Scholarship*, Instrumenta Patristica, 27 (Steenbrugge, 1995).

Southern, R. W., *Robert Grosseteste: The Growth of an English Mind in Medieval Europe* (Oxford, 1986).

HENRY OF GHENT

Henrici de Gandavo Opera omnia, ed. R. Macken *et al.* (Leiden, 1979–).

Marone, S. P., *Truth and Scientific Knowledge in the Thought of Henry of Ghent*, Speculum Anniversary Monographs (Cambridge, Mass., 1985).

ISIDORE OF SEVILLE

Etymologiarum siue Originum libri XX, ed. W. M. Lindsay (Oxford, 1911).

JEWISH THINKERS

Sirat, Colette, *History of Jewish Philosophy in the Middle Ages* (Cambridge and Paris, 1985).

Maimonides, *Mishneh Torah*, 1509 (Constantinople) edn. repr. by S. Liebermann (New York, 1972).

Moses Maimonides: The Guide of the Perplexed, trans. S. Pines (Chicago and London, 1963).

JOHN OF JANDUN

Maurer, A., 'John of Jandun and the Divine Causality', *Mediaeval Studies*, 17 (1955), 185–207.

JOHN OF SALISBURY

Metalogicon, ed. J. B. Hall and K. Keats-Rohan, Corpus Christianorum, Continuatio mediaevalis, 98 (Turnhout, 1991).

Policraticus, ed. C. C. J. Webb, 2 vols. (Oxford, 1909).

John of Salisbury, Policraticus (selections only), trans. C. J. Nederman, Cambridge Texts in the History of Political Thought (Cambridge, 1990); also (almost completely) trans. John Dickinson, *The Statesman's Book* (New York, 1927), and J. P. Pike, *The Frivolities of Courtiers and the Footprints of Philosophers* (Minneapolis, 1938).

Ioannis Saresberiensis Policraticus I–IV, ed. K. S. B. Keats-Rohan, Corpus Christianorum, Continuatio mediaevalis, 118 (Turnhout, 1993).

The World of John of Salisbury, ed. M. Wilks, Studies in Church History, Subsidia, 3, (Oxford, 1984).

JOHN THE SCOT (ERIUGENA)

De divina praedestinatione liber, ed. G. Madec, Corpus Christianorum, Continuatio mediaevalis, 50 (Turnhout, 1978).

Expositiones in Ierarchiam Coelestem, ed. J. Barbet, Corpus Christianorum, Continuatio mediaevalis, 31 (Turnhout, 1975).

Periphyseon I–III, ed. and trans. I. P. Sheldon-Williams, Scriptores latini Hiberniae (Dublin, 1968–81).

John the Scot, Periphyseon, trans. M. L. Uhlfelder and J. A. Potter (Indianapolis, 1976).

Homélie sur le Prologue de Jean, ed. E. Jeauneau, Sources chrétiennes, 151 (Paris, 1969).

Commentaire sur l'Évangile de Jean, ed. E. Jeauneau, Sources chrétiennes, 180 (Paris, 1972).

Annotationes in Marcianum, ed. C. Lutz (Cambridge, Mass., 1939).

Jeauneau, E., *Études érigéniennes* (Paris, 1987).

RICHARD KILVINGTON

Kretzmann, N., and Kretzmann, B. E. (eds.), *The Sophismata of Richard Kilvington*, Auctores Britannici Medii Aevi, 12 (Oxford, 1990).

—— —— (trans.), *The Sophismata of Richard Kilvington: Introduction, Translation and Commentary* (Cambridge, 1990).

ROBERT KILWARDBY

De ortu scientiarum, ed. A. G. Judy, Auctores Britannici Medii Aevi, 4 (London, 1976).

LANFRANC

Liber de corpore et sanguine domini, Patrologia latina, 150, 407–42.

RAMON LULL

Raimundi Lulli Opera latina, ed. F. Stegmüller *et al.* (Palma de Mallorca, 1959–67), Corpus Christianorum, Continuatio mediaevalis, 7– (Turnhout, 1978–).

Lohr, C. (ed.), *Raimundus Lullus: Die neue Logik. Logica nova* (Hamburg, 1985).

Hillgarth, J. N., *Ramon Lull and Lullism in Fourteenth-Century France*, Warburg Studies (Oxford, 1971).

MACROBIUS

Commentary on the Dream of Scipio, ed. J. Willis, 2nd edn. (Leipzig, 1970); trans. W. H. Stahl (New York, 1966).

MARSILIO FICINO

Theologia platonica in *Opera omnia* (Basle, 1576; repr. Turin, 1959).

Marcel, R. (ed. and trans.), *Théologie platonicienne de l'immortalité des âmes* (Paris, 1964–70).

Kristeller, P. O., *The Philosophy of Marsilio Ficino*, trans. V. Conant (New York, 1943).

MARTIANUS CAPELLA

De nuptiis Philologiae et Mercurii, ed. A. Dick (Leipzig, 1925; repr. Stuttgart, 1970).

MUSLIM THINKERS

Caspar, R., *Traité de théologie musulmane*, i: *Histoire de la pensée religieuse musulmane*, Pontificio Istituto di Studi Arabi e d'Islamologia (Rome, 1987).

Gardet, L., and Anawati, M. M., *Introduction à la théologie musulmane: Essai de théologie comparée*, Études de philosophie médiévale, 37 (Paris, 1970).

Hyman, A., and Walsh, J. J., *Philosophy in the Middle Ages: The Christian, Islamic and Jewish Traditions* (New York, 1967).

Algazel's Metaphysics: A Mediaeval Translation, ed. J. T. Muckle (Toronto, 1933).

Lohr, C. H., 'Logica Algazelis: Introduction and Critical Text', *Traditio*, 21 (1965), 223–90.

Salman, D., 'Algazel et les latins', *Archives d'historie doctrinale et littéraire du moyen âge*, 10 (1935–6), 103–27.

Baeumker, C. (ed.), *Avencebrolis (Ibn Gabirol): Fons Vitae ex Arabico in Latinum translatus ab Iohanne Hispano et Dominico Gundissalino*, Beiträge zur Geschichte der Philosophie und der Theologie des Mittelalters, 1 (Münster, 1892–5).

Ibn Gabirol, *The Fountain of Life*, trans. H. E. Wedeck (New York, 1962).

Avicenna Latinus, ed. S. van Riet (Louvain and Leiden 1968–).

Avicenna's Psychology: An English Translation of Kitab al-Najat, Book II, chapter VI, trans. F. Rahman (London, 1952).

Avicenne: La Métaphysique du Shifa, French tr., G. Anawati, 2 vols. (Paris, 1978, 1985).

Michot, J. R., *La Destinée de l'homme selon Avicenne: Le retour à Dieu (ma'ad) et l'imagination*, Académie royale de Belgique, Fonds René Draguet, 5 (Louvain, 1986).

Aristotelis opera cum Averrois commentariis (Venice, 1562–74).

Corpus Commentariorum Averrois in Aristotelem, The Mediaeval Academy of America (Leiden, 1949–).

Averroes, *The Incoherence of the Incoherence*, trans. S. van Bergh (Oxford, 1954).

Averroes on the Harmony of Religions and Philosophy, trans. G. F. Hourani (London, 1961).

Averroes on Aristotle's De Generatione et Corruptione: Middle Commentary and Epitome, trans. S. Kurland (Cambridge, Mass., 1958).

Rosemann, P. W., 'Averroes: A Catalogue of Editions and Scholarly Writings from 1821 onwards', *Bulletin de la Société pour l'Étude de la Philosophie Médiévale*, 30 (1988), 153–221.

Gauthier, L., *Ibn Rochd (Averroes)* (Paris, 1948).

Wolfson, H. A., *Studies in the History of Philosophy and Religion*, i, ed. I. Twersky and G. H. Williams (Cambridge, Mass., 1973).

Davidson, H. A., *Alfarabi, Avicenna and Averroes on Intellect: Their Cosmologies, Theories of the Active Intellect, and Theories of Human Intellect* (New York and Oxford, 1992).

NICHOLAS OF CUSA

Nicolai de Cusa opera omnia (Leipzig, 1932–).

Nicolas de Cues: Lettres aux moines de Tegernsee sur la docte ignorance (1452–1456). Du jeu de la boule (1463), French tr. M. de Gandillac (Paris, 1985).

Hopkins, J. (ed., trans., and comm.), *Trialogus de Possest: A Concise Introduction to the Philosophy of Nicholas of Cusa* (Minneapolis, 1980).

——(English trans. and appraisal), *Nicholas of Cusa on Learned Ignorance* (Minneapolis, 1981).

——text, trans. and interpretative study of 'De visione dei' in *Nicholas of Cusa's Dialectical Mysticism* (Minneapolis, 1985).

——trans. and appraisal of 'De li non aliud' in *Nicholas of Cusa, On God as Not-Other* (Minneapolis, 1983).

——(trans.), *Nicholas of Cusa's 'De pace fidei' and 'cribatio alkorani'* (Minneapolis, 1990).

Sigmund, Paul E., *Nicholas of Cusa: The Catholic Concordance*, Cambridge Texts in the History of Political Thought (Cambridge, 1991).

Flasch, K., *Die Metaphysik des Einen bei Nikolaus von Kues* (Leiden, 1966).

Meuthen, E., *Nikolaus von Kues 1401–1464* (Münster, 1982).

Sigmund, P. E., *Nicholas of Cusa and Medieval Political Thought* (Cambridge, Mass., 1963).

Vansteenberghe, E., *Le Cardinal Nicolas de Cues* (Paris, 1920; repr. Frankfurt, 1963).

Watanabe, M., *The Political Ideas of Nicholas of Cusa* (Geneva, 1963).

PETER LOMBARD

Sententiae (Quaracchi, 1916; third edn., Grottaferrata (Rome), 1971–81).

Colish, Marcia L., *Peter Lombard*, 2 vols. (Leiden, 1994).

PETER OF SPAIN

Peter of Spain: Tractatus called afterwards Summulae logicales, ed. L. M. de Rijk (Assen, 1972).

Peter of Spain: Tractatus Syncategorematum and Selected Anonymous Treatises, trans. J. P. Mullally (Milwaukee, 1964).

JOHN PHILOPONUS

Commentaire sur le De anima d'Aristote, ed. G. Verbeke (Louvain and Paris, 1966).

Sorabji, R. (ed.), *Philoponus and the Rejection of Aristotelian Science* (Ithaca, NY, 1987).

PIETRO POMPONAZZI

Petrus Pomponatius: Tractatus de immortalitate animae, ed. G. Morra (Bologna, 1954).

Nardi, B., *Studi su Pietro Pomponazzi* (Florence, 1965).

Gilson, E., 'Autour de Pomponazzi: Problématique de l'immortalité de l'âme en Italie au début du XVIᵉ siècle', *Archives d'histoire doctrinale et littéraire du moyen âge*, 28 (1961), 163–279.

PORPHYRY

Isagoge, trans. E. W. Warren (Toronto, 1975).

RATRAMNUS OF CORBIE

Liber de Anima ad Odonem Bellovacensem, ed. D. C. Lambot (Namur, 1952).

REMIGIUS OF AUXERRE

Remigii Autissiodorensis Commentum in Martianum Capellam, ed. C. Lutz (Leiden, 1962–5).

RICHARD RUFUS

Aertsen, J. A., 'Richard Rufus's "Speculum animae"', in *Die Bibliotheca Amploniana*, Miscellanea Mediaevalia, Veröffentli-chungen des Thomas-Instituts der Universität zu Köln (Berlin and New York, 1995), 86–109.

Raedts, P., *Richard Rufus of Cornwall and the Tradition of Oxford Theology* (Oxford, 1987).

SIGER OF BRABANT

Quaestiones in Metaphysicam (c.1272–4), ed. W. Dunphy, Philosophes médiévaux, 24 (Louvain, 1981).

Quaestiones in Metaphysicam, ed. A. Maurer, Philosophes médiévaux, 25 (Louvain, 1983).

Quaestiones super librum De causis, ed. A. Marlasca, Philosophes médiévaux, 12 (Louvain, 1972).

Quaestiones in tertium de anima, ed. B. Bazán, Philosophes médiévaux, 13 (Louvain, 1972).

Quaestiones in libros Aristotelis De anima, ed. F. van Steenberghen, in M. Giele *et al.*, *Trois commentaires anonymes sur le traité de l'âme d'Aristote*, Philosophes médiévaux, 11 (Louvain, 1971).

Siger de Brabant: Écrits de logique, de morale et de physique, ed. B. Bazán, Philosophes médiévaux, 14 (Louvain, 1974).

Nardi, Bruno, *Sigieri di Brabante nel pensiero del Rinascimento italiano* (Rome, 1945).

Pattin, A., 'Quelques écrits attribués à Siger de Brabant, *Bulletin de philosophie médiévale*, 29 (1987), 173–7.

Steenberghen, F. van, *Maître Siger de Brabant* (Louvain, 1977).

ROGER SWINESHEAD

Spade, P. V., 'Roger Swyneshed's *Obligationes*: Edition and Comments', *Archives d'histoire doctrinale et littéraire au moyen âge*, 44, Année 1977 (1978), 243–85.

THEMISTIUS

Commentaire sur le Traité de l'Âme d'Aristote. Traduction de Guillaume de Moerbeke, ed. G. Verbeke. Corpus Latinum Commentariorum in Aristotelem Graecorum (Louvain, 1957; repr. Leiden, 1973).

WILLIAM OF AUVERGNE

Opera omnia (Paris 1516, Venice 1591, Orleans 1674–5).

WILLIAM OF CONCHES

Guillaume de Conches: Glose super Platonem, ed. E. Jeauneau, Textes philosophiques du moyen âge, 13 (Paris, 1965).

De philosophia mundi, Patrologia latina, 172, 39–102 (under the name of Honorius Augustodunensis); ibid. 90 (under the name of Bede); new edn. by G. Maurach (Pretoria, 1980).

Dragmaticon or *Dialogus de Substantiis Physicis*, ed. G. Gratarolus (Strasburg 1567, repr. Frankfurt-on-Main, 1967).

Moralium Dogma Philosophorum, ed. J. Holmberg (Uppsala, 1929). (The authorship is uncertain.)

Williams, J. R., 'The Quest for the Author of the *Moralium Dogma Philosophorum*, 1931–1956', *Speculum*, 32 (1957), 736–47.

WILLIAM OF MOERBEKE

Michaud-Quantin, P., *Politica (libri I–II, 11): Translatio prior imperfecta interprete Guillelmo de Moerbeka(?). Aristoteles latinus* (Bruges and Paris, 1961).

Minio-Paluello, L., 'William of Moerbeke', *Dictionary of Scientific Biography*, ix (New York, 1974).

Guillaume de Moerbeke: Recueil d'études à l'occasion du 700ᵉ anniversaire de sa mort (1286), ed. J. Brams and W. Vanhamel (Leuven, 1989).

WILLIAM OF OCKHAM

Guillelmi de Ockham opera philosophica et theologica, ed. G. Gál *et al.* (St Bonaventure, NY, 1967–85).
Guillelmi de Ockham Opera politica, 4 vols., ed. H. S. Offler *et al.* (Manchester, Oxford 1940–97).
Goldast, Melchior, *Monarchia Sancti Romani Imperii* (Frankfurt, 1614).
Tractatus de praedestinatione et de praescientia Dei et de futuris contingentibus, ed. P. Boehner. Franciscan Institute Publications (New York, 1945).
Adams, M. McCord, and Kretzmann, N. (trans.), *William Ockham. Predestination, God's Foreknowledge and Future Contingents*, Century Philosophy Sourcebooks (New York, 1969).
William of Ockham. A Letter to the Friars Minor and Other Writings, ed. and trans. A. S. McGrade and J. Kilcullen (Cambridge, 1995).

Adams, Marilyn McCord, *William Ockham* (Notre Dame, Ind., 1987).
Leff, G., *William of Ockham: The Metamorphosis of Scholastic Discourse* (Manchester, 1975).
McGrade, A. S., *The Political Thought of William of Ockham* (Cambridge, 1974).
Maurer, A., 'Ockham's Razor and Chatton's Anti-Razor', *Mediaeval Studies*, 46 (1984), 463–75.
Miethke, J., *Ockhams Weg zur Sozialphilosophie* (Berlin, 1969).
Tachau, K., *Vision and Certitude in the Age of Ockham: Optics. Epistemology and the Foundations of Semantics, 1250–1345*, Studien und Texte zur Geistesgeschichte des Mittelalters (Leiden, 1988).

WILLIAM OF SHERWOOD

William of Sherwood's Introduction to Logic, trans. with an introduction and notes by N. Kretzmann (Minneapolis, 1966).
William of Sherwood: Treatise on Syncategorematic Words, trans. N. Kretzmann (Minneapolis, 1968).

Index